Notre Dame's John Zahm

REVEREND JOHN A. ZAHM, C.S.C.

Notre Dame's
JOHN ZAHM

*American Catholic Apologist
and Educator*

BY

RALPH E. WEBER

UNIVERSITY OF NOTRE DAME PRESS
1961

Nihil obstat:

Thomas T. McAvoy, C.S.C.
Censor Deputatus

Imprimatur:

✠ Leo A. Pursley, D.D., LL.D.
Bishop of Fort Wayne–South Bend
September 21, 1960

The Nihil obstat and Imprimatur are official declarations that a book is free of doctrinal or moral error. No implication is contained therein that those who have granted the Nihil obstat and Imprimatur agree with the contents, opinions or statements expressed.

For
ROSEMARIE

Preface

This is the story of a leading American Catholic priest who dedicated himself to an active and productive intellectual life during the last quarter of the nineteenth century and the first quarter of the twentieth. Earlier, Christianity had been attacked in its own domain of scripture, theology, and philosophy; however, during the nineteenth century, especially the latter half, certain men, philosophizing under the banners of natural and social science, sought to explain away religious dogma and practice by purely scientific formulae. Some American Catholic authors, confused and troubled by onslaughts which denied God and man's supernatural soul, prepared inadequate answers to the well-written expositions of Renan or Haeckel or Huxley, or the equally devastating approaches of Andrew D. White and Robert Ingersoll. These uninformed Christian apologists failed to distinguish between science and theology, revealed truth and pious opinion; consequently they only compounded the confusion. Other apologists arose with an awareness that knowledge was the sole weapon recognized in the modern conflict of intellects and, consequently, only an informed faith provided sufficient protection against the language and literature of the nineteenth century. Father Zahm became the most notable American Catholic apologist within this competent group as he defined a liberal interpretation of evolution by emphasizing the possibilities of theistic evolution, a theory of development which specified that God began and controlled creation although employing secondary agents in subsequent processes of development. More than any other American Catholic, he translated Darwin's theory into terms understandable and at least partially acceptable to his American and European Catholic audiences.

Too, this story is a chapter in the history of the University of Notre Dame and the Congregation of Holy Cross, for he was both their son and inspirer. Like other American Catholic universities, Notre Dame was also a boarding school for elementary and high school students: oftentimes its professors were inadequately trained for university responsibilities. These were pioneering years in Catholic higher education and all too often, the active pursuit of knowledge was deterred by insufficient libraries, inadequate scholarships, and woefully deficient plant facilities. As Professor of Chemistry and Physics, Zahm inaugurated an intensive program to improve the University's facilities and educational offerings, especially in the study of science. Adopting the latest technical advances, he made Notre Dame the first college campus to be lighted by electricity. From the Philadelphia Exposition of 1876, he purchased some of the best machines for the study of physics. Comprehensive museum collections together with the finest acoustical apparatus became part of the University's holdings. Finally, Science Hall, built in 1884, crowned his personal campaign for better science facilities. But perhaps his enthusiasm, which spread through the school, was the greatest contribution he made to Notre Dame during the first years after his ordination. His popular lectures on a wide variety of topics, especially on chemistry and physics, together with those on his travels to distant lands; the thousands of books he gathered for the library, all brought learning into popularity at Notre Dame.

As Vice-President of Notre Dame (1885-1892), he continued the construction of a true university, one which could compare favorably with a Padua, or a Heidelberg, or a Bonn or a Cornell. As Provincial of the Holy Cross Congregation in the United States (1898-1906), he established on a permanent basis the Congregation's theological school, Holy Cross College, in Washington, D. C., in order that his seminarians might become well educated and capable teachers. This decision was a crucial one for the future development of Notre Dame and the Congregation. During these years he brought Notre Dame and the Congregation into the mainstream of American education.

As American as Theodore Roosevelt and Archbishop Ireland, Zahm worked in the advance battalion of those men within the American clergy who sought to explain and defend the separation of Church and State as the best arrangement for the Church in the United States. As an "Americanist," and perhaps too enthusiastically, he praised wholeheartedly the ideals of an American clergy, devoted to God and the United States.

Finally, Father Zahm understood that his era was different from the Age of Faith. He realized that when commercial spirit, overpowering intellectual pride, love of luxury and ease were joined in politics with atheism, communism, and socialism, the result was a "forgetfulness of God."

> Men seeking after facts and forgetting principles, framing theories, & giving them the force of dogmas, eulogizing the powers of nature & forgetting the Creator, banishing the supernatural & endeavoring to explain everything by the operation of natural causes . . . & reducing all things to mere brute matter & natural forces" [1]

resulted in neglect of God. His life and writings sought to counteract these modern influences for his ultimate frame of reference was the Eternal Truth.

In presenting the life and writings of Father Zahm, I have been motivated by scientific rather than partisan purposes. I have examined all the major sources bearing on his life. Zahm apparently destroyed most of the letters he received, especially prior to 1896 and after 1906. Fortunately, what remains of his correspondence and papers have been preserved in the Archives of the University of Notre Dame and the Provincial Archives in South Bend, Indiana. His correspondence with Archbishop John Ireland, Archbishop John Keane, Bishop Denis O'Connell, Reverend Gilbert Français, C.S.C., Reverend James A. Burns, C.S.C., Theodore Roosevelt and the very valuable letters to his

[1] His sermon, "Forgetfulness of God," written at Juniata Mills, Pennsylvania. PA.

brother, Albert F. Zahm, proved most enlightening. Interviews with his surviving associates and relatives provided a better understanding of his personality and objectives. The unpublished accounts of the University of Notre Dame and the Congregation of Holy Cross, found in the Provincial Archives, reveal his role and influence within the Congregation—this is particularly true of the Collection of Reverend James A. Burns, C.S.C. Catholic magazines such as the *Catholic World, American Catholic Quarterly Review, Ave Maria, Catholic University Bulletin, Donahoe's Magazine,* and the *American Ecclesiastical Review* were valuable sources for his writings and those of his contemporaries. The Notre Dame *Scholastic* was an excellent source of information. The *Review* between 1896-1902, edited by Arthur Preuss, represented the ultra-conservative position regarding the relationship between Catholicism and the theory of evolution. The *Catholic Citizen* of Milwaukee gave the liberal position on this controversial issue as well as Father Zahm's role in the Western Catholic Summer School movement. Also, the New York *Daily Tribune* reported Zahm's ideas on evolution during the eighteen-nineties. Individual issues of certain other newspapers, some of which were found in Zahm's Collection, added to the total picture of this priest's life. Reverend Thomas T. McAvoy's *The Great Crisis in American Catholic History (1895-1900), The Life of Archbishop John Ireland* by Reverend James H. Moynihan and Reverend Patrick Ahern's *Life of John J. Keane* helped me to evaluate Zahm's position with respect to certain liberal questions affecting American Catholicism. Quotations from these various sources have been liberally used to recapture the thought and spirit of Father Zahm and his times.

I am indebted to many friends, scholars and colleagues. Reverend Thomas T. McAvoy, C.S.C., formerly Head of the Department of History at the University of Notre Dame, suggested this study and made many valuable suggestions while patiently and kindly guiding me along the narrow path of scholarship. His unselfish sharing of many important documents and his knowledge of this period set the highest example of scholarly cooperation. Dr. Aaron I. Abell of the University of Notre Dame, encouraged me at each stage of the study. Reverend Bernard Mullahy, C.S.C., kindly gave me permission to use the Provincial Archives of the Congregation of Holy Cross. Dr. Albert Zahm gave of his time and knowledge unselfishly and indicated important ideas in the life of his brother. Another brother, Pius Zahm, and a nephew, Albert Moore, also gave me important information, as did other relatives. Father Zahm's friends and associates at the University of Notre Dame, especially Reverend Thomas Crumley, C.S.C., Reverend Matthew Schumacher, C.S.C., and Reverend Joseph Maguire, C.S.C., along with Reverend Eugene Burke, C.S.C., Reverend William McNamara, C.S.C., and Brother Peter Hozinski, C.S.C., all shared their recollections of his life, character and work. Reverend James H. Moynihan gave me the letters between Zahm and Archbishop Ireland. Reverend Henry J. Browne, Archivist at the Catholic University of America, sent me the correspondence between Archbishop Keane, Bishop O'Connell and Zahm. Sister Joanne of Arc at St. Mary's College aided me in my search for information relative to Zahm's sisters who were members of the Holy Cross Sisters. Mr. Humphrey Desmond of Milwaukee permitted me to use the back copies of his father's newspaper, the *Catholic Citizen*. Reverend Anthony Deye shared his knowledge and copies of Bishop Maes' letters involving Zahm, which are located in the Covington Archives.

I am indebted to the staffs at the library of the University of Notre Dame, the Public Library and St. Francis Seminary Library in Milwaukee, Marquette University Library, the Library of Congress, and the Newberry Library for their cooperation. Especial thanks are due Reverend James Gibbons, C.S.C., for his assistance in the Provincial Archives of the Congregation of Holy Cross, and to Reverend E. J. Drummond, S.J., at Marquette University, for making available the time necessary to prepare this manuscript. I am grateful to Reverend William McNamara, C.S.C., Dr. Marshall Smelser, Dr. Bernard Norling, and Dr. Vincent De Santis, all of the University of Notre Dame, for their reading of the manuscript and their excellent suggestions; to my parents, to Reverend John C. Desmond, and to Reverend Walter Reger, O.S.B., for their inspiration. To my wife, Rosemarie, whose patience, sacrifice, and encouragement made the completion of this study possible, I am deeply grateful. Finally, a note of gratitude to Mrs. Neil F. Hoyt and Miss Margaret Porubsky who gave valuable assistance in the preparation of this manuscript.

The following publishers graciously granted permission to quote excerpts from works published by their firms: Alfred A. Knopf, Inc., New York (*The American Leonardo* by Carleton Mabee); Appleton-Century-Crofts, Inc., New York (*Great Inspirers, Along The Andes and Down The Amazon,* and *Woman in Science,* all by Father John Zahm); Harvard University Press, Cambridge, Mass. (*The Letters of Theodore Roosevelt,* Elting E. Morison, ed.); The Johns Hopkins Press, Baltimore, Md. (*Manifest Destiny: A Study of Nationalist Expansionism in American History* by Albert K. Weinberg); P. J. Kenedy & Son, New York (*Catholic Directory, Almanac and Clergy List* [Milwaukee 1900-1906], also 1907); Regnery Company, Chicago (*The Great Crisis in American Catholic History* by Thomas T. McAvoy, C.S.C.); and St. Anthony Guild Press, Paterson, N. J. ("Mother M. Annunciata" *Superior-Generals: Centenary Chronicles of the Sisters of the Holy Cross, 1841-1941*).

It should be noted that this biography stems from my doctoral dissertation at the University of Notre Dame. Scholars interested in a more extensive, technical study of Zahm's life and contributions will find this account available at the University of Notre Dame Library.

Manuscript sources are abbreviated as follows:

AASP—Archives of the Archdiocese of St. Paul, Minnesota.
ACUA—Archives of the Catholic University of America.
CA—Archives of the Diocese of Covington, Kentucky.
LC—Library of Congress.
PA—Province Archives of the Congregation of Holy Cross, South Bend, Indiana.
UNDA—Archives of the University of Notre Dame.

Contents

PREFACE   vii

I   THE EDUCATION OF AN ENTHUSIAST   1

II   AN ENTHUSIAST IN CATHOLIC EDUCATION   11

III   VICE-PRESIDENT AND TRAVELER   32

IV   FAMOUS APOLOGIST FOR SCIENCE AND CATHOLIC
     DOGMA, 1892-1896   53

V   AN AMERICAN IN EUROPE AND AT NOTRE DAME   94

VI   PROVINCIAL OF HOLY CROSS   129

VII   EXPLORER, AUTHOR AND CRITIC, 1906-1921   180

APPENDIX   199

INDEX   207

Notre Dame's John Zahm

I

The Education of an Enthusiast

"Quiet, Scholarly and Correct"

The occasion was the golden jubilee, in 1888, of Father Edward Sorin, founder of the University of Notre Dame; the speaker, as reported in the June 2 Notre Dame *Scholastic,* was Father John A. Zahm, Vice-President of the University:

> I love to see in our Notre Dame of to-day the promise of the potency of a Padua or a Bologna, a Bonn or a Heidelberg, an Oxford or a Cambridge, a Salamanca or a Valladolid. It may be that this view will be regarded as one proceeding from my own enthusiasm, but it matters not. I consider it a compliment to be called an enthusiast. Turn over the pages of history and you will find that all those who have left a name and a fame have been enthusiasts, and it is because our venerable Founder has been an enthusiast—I use the word in its primary signification—that he has been able to achieve so much.

To the conservative mind the word "enthusiast" connotes too much of the impetuous and irresponsible. There were not a few present at the dinner who would have been more comfortable had it not been used to describe their ageing Superior General. But, all agreed that in speaking of himself, Zahm had chosen the right word.

The second of fourteen children, John Zahm was born June 11, 1851. His father, Jacob, had been brought as a

1

child to America when his grandparents emigrated from Alsace in the eighteen-twenties. His mother, Mary Ellen, daughter of John Braddock and grandniece of Major General Edward Braddock, was born in Pennsylvania and later moved to New Lexington, Ohio, where she and Jacob Zahm met and married. John Zahm's boyhood in New Lexington until the age of twelve was characterized by strict discipline, thrift, perseverance, and a love for literature. His formal schooling began in a one-room log school where elementary studies were taught at times which did not conflict with farm chores. One of Zahm's classmates during these early years was Januarius Aloysius McGahn who later became a famous war correspondent before the turn of the century.

Like their parents before them, Jacob and Mary Ellen Zahm, with their eight children migrated westward and in 1863 settled on a two-acre plot of fertile soil a few miles north of Huntington, Indiana. Gradually the venturesome family prospered, which enabled the father, a carpenter-farmer by trade, to buy additional acreage. John, the oldest son, was never idle, and here too he continued his formal schooling at SS. Peter and Paul School.

In 1867, then fifteen years old, John decided to resolve his thoughts concerning a vocation to the priesthood. Writing in mid-October to his aunt, Sister M. Praxedes, who had become a Holy Cross Sister a few years earlier at St. Mary's College near Notre Dame, he inquired about the religious life and asked that she give his letter to Father Sorin at Notre Dame. Sorin replied promptly and asked Zahm how far he was in his Latin studies, what studies he had taken in English and German, and finally, what sum his parents could pay yearly for his education at Notre Dame.[1]

Zahm's answers were satisfactory, for a short time later Sorin wrote: "As you seem so anxious to come & try yourself here, I am willing to accept your offer viz.: on your paying $50 to keep you for five months in the College. You may come anytime your parents will deem it expedient."[2]

Relieved, after months of indecision, Zahm began the hundred mile journey northward soon after fall harvest. His luggage filled with the required clothing and the "1 table-knife, 1 fork, 1 teaspoon, 1 tablespoon" specified in the *Catalogue*,[3] he arrived on campus, December 3, 1867. The cluster of yellow brick buildings bordering the lake appeared imposing, especially the Main Building which served as classroom building and dormitory. The campus appeared busy too as students dashed hither and yon shortly before the annual holy-day, the Feast of the Immaculate Conception. It was fitting that Notre Dame's future inspirer should begin his college education at this time.

The University, not much older than Zahm at the time, was still under the dynamic leadership of Sorin. This missionary priest, born at La Roche, France, in 1814 and ordained in 1838 at Le Mans, France, joined the newly formed Auxiliary Priests of Father Moreau in 1840. At the urgent request of Bishop de la Hailandière, Sorin with six Brothers sailed on the *Iowa* for America one year later and arrived at Vincennes, Indiana. Some months later, the bishop gave Sorin money and Father Stephen Badin's former Indian mission property near South Bend, Indiana, in order to found a college. By November, 1842, the Holy Cross members took over their new property near the south bend of the St. Joseph River and began the difficult job of establishing a school.

Our Lady's University developed rapidly in the years that followed as brick buildings arose on the wilderness campus: in 1844, the State of Indiana gave Sorin a university charter. So well did the institution expand its enrollment, buildings, and financial programs, that Sorin, fifteen years after the founding, assessed Notre Dame's monetary value at $159,047.15.

St. Louis University provided the model for the University's plan of studies as Sorin instituted a simple but thoroughly practical curriculum under two departments in 1848 —the Classical and Commercial. The two programs were theoretically identical except for the fact the Commercial

students substituted bookkeeping and commerce courses for
Latin and Greek. By the spring of 1868, University officials
listed thirty-one subjects with ninety-one classes.[4] In addition, they reported that their program of studies, in which
each subject was taught separately and each class divided
according to one or more divisions (based upon the enrollment and students' proficiency), surpassed the European program of eight invariable classes and was done with a view
to saving American students the useless review of matters
already studied, together with time and money. These
French religious had become Americanized quickly!

Recognizing the heightened interest in the physical and
natural sciences, Notre Dame authorities added a physical
and natural science program to the curriculum during the
Civil War, and assumed a position of leadership among
American Catholic colleges after Appomattox. A survey of
sixty Catholic colleges in 1866 shows that thirty-five others
taught natural philosophy; thirty-four others, chemistry;
thirteen, geology; and twelve others, botany.[5] Notre Dame
taught all these subjects.

By modern standards, Notre Dame was a small school. Its
grammar, high school, and college departments, during the
school year 1867-1868, numbered a faculty of 39 and a student body of 448. At Commencement that year, three A.B.
degrees, three B.S. degrees, thirty Commercial and five Medical certificates were awarded.[6] Tuition costs fluctuated during the Civil War; however by 1867, they were set at one
hundred and fifty dollars per semester (five months) for
board, bed, bedding and tuition. Fringe services such as
washing and mending of linens, doctor's fees, medicine, and
nursing care were also included in this fee. Primarily for
the benefit of prospective students' parents, school authorities emphasized that the University was located at some
distance from the nearest town and hence the students were
not distracted; furthermore, the "stern though mild" discipline riveted the students' attention to their studies. Although the semester began in the first week of September,
a new student was welcome whenever he could come—the

Director of Studies discussed his previous schooling with each applicant and assigned the proper sequence of courses.

Because of his interest in the priesthood, Zahm enrolled in the Classical Course, which involved a program of studies similar to that still pursued in B.A. programs in many present day Catholic colleges and universities. The scholarly progress Zahm exhibited was recorded in the Honorable Mention Table, a kind of scholar's bulletin board, which was published in almost every issue of the Notre Dame *Scholastic,* a weekly student newspaper. Shortly after his arrival he received mention for fourth algebra, and during the remainder of the school year he took honors in first grammar, third German, and seventh Latin. In the May 16 issue he was honored for having obtained six certificates for improvement in studies during the previous two months.

His rhetoric notebook, now in the Provincial Archives, reveals the wide variety of his compositions: "The Crusades," "Discovery of America," "Concerning the Right of Young People to Judge Their Elders," "The Blessings of Christianity," and "Do Savage Nations Possess a Right to the Soil." His essay on wealth, "The Safest Way to Become Wealthy," reflected America's optimism about capitalistic enterprise so current after the Civil War. He wrote that the desire of becoming wealthy was so strong and widespread that it must have been intended by God for man's greater good. To become wealthy, he continued, a man must be honest, orderly, thrifty, and friendly with his neighbors. In this manner, a man could become rich enjoyably and with a clear conscience. Thus, too, tranquillity of soul would be his highest happiness and "worth more than all the riches that he could possess."

Zahm's semester examination grades in the middle of his sophomore year, published in the *Scholastic,* February 6, 1869, gave little indication of a great academic future for he failed mathematics and German! The problem was reflected in a letter he received from Sister M. Praxedes in which she said she was pleased he would stay on longer in college and urged him to persevere.[7] The temporary indecision over, he achieved a coveted place at the Table of Honor by the end of the semester.[8]

A better picture of Zahm's intellectual and personal development is drawn from his extra-curricular activities. The St. Aloysius Philodemic Society, the Scientific Association, the Archconfraternity, the Student Choir and the Juanita Baseball Club were important to his education. The St. Aloysius group publicized in the *Scholastic* of June 11, 1870, that it had sponsored debates on sixteen questions, two lectures, and twenty-one declamations during the preceding year; and that the library for its twenty members numbered over one thousand books, magazines, pamphlets, and newspapers. Soon after his arrival on campus, Zahm became an officer and librarian of this stimulating group. In debates, his earnestness and logic brought him student respect. More than this, however, Zahm mastered the art of public speaking on popular topics which ranged from "That Poland has suffered more from oppression than Ireland" to the necessity for Latin language study. A fellow student wrote the best description of Zahm during these years when he commented that Zahm's essay on "Truth" was like its author, "quiet, scholarly, and correct." [9]

Founded a few months after Zahm's arrival, the United Scientific Association, restricted in its membership to honor students, became an energetic organization under the directorship of Father Joseph C. Carrier. This man exerted a great influence on Zahm.[10] Born *circa* 1833 in France, Carrier was teaching physics at Ferney College near Geneva when Bishop Joseph Cretin of St. Paul, Minnesota, encouraged him to leave in 1855 and study for the priesthood at St. Paul. Following the death of Cretin, Carrier transferred to Notre Dame in 1860 and was ordained a priest in the Congregation of Holy Cross in 1861. After a chaplaincy in Sherman's army, Carrier returned to Notre Dame's science department.

As Director of the Science Museum and Professor of Chemistry and Physics, Carrier developed the science curriculum despite the hesitant acceptance of this curriculum by some Notre Dame professors. One of these men, Joseph A. Lyons, carried the controversy into print when he wrote that scientific studies claimed an undue preference to the harm of classical studies. The former, he said, afforded little mental discipline and "open the mind to no knowledge of human nature and social duties." [11] Notre Dame, he admitted, had a scientific course for those whom divine Providence had given a special aptitude for science; however, "she prefers the classical and, as much as in her lies, exhorts her children to the same preference." [12] Carrier had a different view for he explained in the columns of the *Scholastic*, January 30, 1869, that a study of science, especially zoology, trains the intellectual powers and is therefore, "worthy of the reverent exercise of the highest faculties of the human mind." He also emphasized in his lectures that the first chapter of the Book of Genesis did not conflict with historical geology.[13]

Zahm worked closely with Carrier in the Scientific Association as his essay reprinted in the *Scholastic* on May 27, 1871, indicates. Entitled "Thoughts on Science and the Age in which we live," Zahm noted that progress and general enlightenment characterized the nineteenth century for the ancient philosophers studied theoretical rather than practical science. In declaring Watt's steam engine, Morse's telegraph, and the invention of printing the truly great discoveries, Zahm sounded much like John Quincy Adams, who had said twenty-five years earlier: "Fulton and Morse have done more by their discoveries, for their country and the human race, than any two hundred Presidents in succession could be expected to accomplish." [14] Zahm's essay ended on a typically late nineteenth-century American glorification of Progress by declaring science "is now and deservedly so, regarded as the only talisman of wealth, prosperity and happiness; as the highest exponent of power and intellectual superiority; as the primary index of the material and social condition of mankind, and as the most reliable touchstone of the progress and tendency of the age in which we live."

Commencement marked the end of college studies for

Zahm, not quite four years after his enrollment, on June 21, 1871, when he received his Bachelor of Arts degree in a graduating class which numbered one other A.B. student, three LL.D., one M.S. and one M.A., thirty Master of Accounts and four Medical Certificate students.

For Zahm, the graduation ceremonies terminated only one phase of his formal schooling since he had finally resolved his doubts concerning the priesthood. Consequently, on September 11, 1871, he was received into the Congregation of Holy Cross and entered the novitiate at Notre Dame. Because of financial reasons and a shortage of staff, the Congregation assigned its seminarians to teach in the college in addition to pursuing their studies in the seminary. Practically every other Catholic college with a source of seminarians available followed this practice.[15] During the first year Zahm taught regular classes in Greek and grammar. A year later, he became Carrier's Assistant in the Science Department and the *Twenty-ninth Annual Catalogue* listed him as Assistant Librarian, Curator of the Museum, Assistant in Chemistry, Physics, and Natural Science! In spite of the manifold duties, Zahm found the life satisfying and therefore made his religious vows on November 1, 1872. And at the end of that school year he received his Master of Arts degree.

When Carrier was appointed president of St. Mary's College, Galveston, Texas, in 1875, Zahm, a subdeacon and only twenty-three years old, became Professor of Chemistry and Physics, and Co-Director of the Science Department. Moreover, he became Director of the College Library (which opened at 3:45 P.M. each day), Curator of the Museum and a member of the Board of Trustees.

With typical enthusiasm, Zahm followed in the footsteps of Carrier in many ways. For example, on October 25, 1874, the *Scholastic* reported his purchase of several hundred dollars' worth of physics equipment with the comment, "It is quite a sight to see this gentleman's room with instruments and machines of all kinds in it." Succeeding Carrier to the directorship of the St. Aloysius Society in 1874, Zahm, according to the students, gave the group "tone and dignity by his presence, as well as edification by his wise and instructive counsel." [16] He became president of the Scientific Association in 1875. The Minims, Notre Dame's grade school students and Sorin's favorite young friends, shared Zahm's enthusiasm as he thrilled them with sparks of fire from a Leyden jar and lantern views of Rome.

As June 4, 1875, and ordination to the priesthood approached, Zahm could reflect on a busy seven and one-half years at Notre Dame. Still outwardly serious and formal, a notable characteristic in his public life, he presented a youthful physical appearance. He was of medium height and slender, with light brown hair, a high forehead and oval face. His physical characteristics contributed only a fair indication of tremendous nervous energy. The youth from rural Huntington, Indiana, had matured quickly during these years. His deep interest in classical studies combined with fine ability in scientific work gave promise of a well-balanced teacher. Many extra-curricular responsibilities developed his administrative talents while the busy "jack-of-all-trades" seminary years prepared him for the future role of developing a young religious congregation and an expanding American Catholic university. That these were pioneering days in Catholic education, he personally realized. Elevated to the priesthood on June 4, Zahm accepted the responsibilities of the future. Scholarly, outwardly quiet, enthusiastic, he was anxious to develop a congregation and university of saints and scholars.

NOTES TO CHAPTER I

1. Sorin to Zahm, October 20, 1867. Albert Zahm Collection, UNDA.
2. *Ibid.*, November 14, 1867. Albert Zahm Collection, UNDA.
3. *Twenty-fourth Annual Catalogue of Notre Dame University, 1867-68* (Notre Dame, 1868), p. 14.
4. Notre Dame *Scholastic,* May 23, 1868.
5. Sebastian Anthony Erbacher, *Catholic Higher Education in the United States, 1850-1866* (Washington, 1937), p. 89. Only thirty-five of them had charters with permission to grant degrees. Burns and Kohl-

brenner, *A History of Catholic Education* (New York, 1937), p. 266.

6. Burns Collection, PA.

7. Sister M. Praxedes to Zahm, January 12, 1869. Albert Zahm Collection, UNDA.

8. The personal approach to education was emphasized, for at weekly faculty meetings honor students were chosen for special seats of honor in the refectory.

9. *Loc. cit.,* December 3, 1870.

10. Years later, Carrier confided to Professor James Edwards that Zahm failed to give him sufficient credit for the science department —"I am afraid that Fr. Zahm is not over unselfish, nor over just in his appreciation of what he may owe to me—little as that may have been. The disciple is now made famous by the conspiracy of—no doubt, well deserved—world-wide publicity; while the master . . . is content to remain ignored, or well-nigh so." Carrier to Edwards, March 3, 1895. Edwards Collection, UNDA.

11. Joseph A. Lyons, *Silver Jubilee of the University of Notre Dame* (Chicago, 1869), p. 49.

12. *Ibid.,* p. 50.

13. *Loc. cit.,* February 11, 1871.

14. As quoted in Carleton Mabee, *The American Leonardo, A Life of Samuel F. B. Morse* (New York, 1943), p. 186.

15. Edward J. Power, *A History of Catholic Higher Education in the United States* (Milwaukee, 1958), pp. 92-93.

16. *Loc. cit.,* January 17, 1874.

II

An Enthusiast in Catholic Education

"The Popular Style of Lecturing"

Writing a personal note to Orestes A. Brownson in the fall of 1875, Zahm revealed his concern over the future education of English-speaking Catholic students as he urged Brownson to publish the various articles from the *Review* in book form:

> As yet English-speaking Catholics have but few volumes of Essays & Criticisms by Catholic authors. The Protestants are far ahead of us in this department of literature, and it is a pity that our youth should be obligated to have recourse to such works on similar subjects by Catholic writers. I for one particularly felt this want during my college course; not only myself but many also of my Catholic fellow students . . . certainly nothing is more needed, or better calculated to supply the want so long felt by our more advanced students in philosophy & general literature.[1]

In a sense Zahm was writing a platform for his own activities during the years following his ordination as he sought to improve Catholic higher education by exceptional teaching and superior science facilities at Notre Dame. Finally, his apologetical essays on a wide range of topics reached a large audience.

His educational crusade in the decade after ordination included Carrier's practice of giving popular science lectures for students at Notre Dame and at St. Mary's College, a school for young ladies conducted by the Holy Cross Sisters, located a mile west of Notre Dame. In addition to the duties of Librarian, Curator of the Museum, Professor of Chemistry and Physics in the academic year, 1876-1877, he also held the posts of Vice-Chancellor, Vice-President, Director of students, director of the St. Aloysius Philodemic Society, assistant director of the St. Cecilia Philomatheon Association, president of the Scientific Association, and president of the Lemonnier Boating Club!

Lectures with experiments, or science education with visual aids, had been inaugurated successfully at Harvard in 1850 by Professor Josiah Parsons Cooke, a master in this form of education.[2] As their popularity increased during the next two decades, others followed his leadership. In March, 1876, Zahm presented the first chemistry lecture in the Scientific Series, inaugurated by him, on "Water." In it, he demonstrated with an electric battery that water was composed of oxygen and hydrogen; moreover, he exhibited an oxy-hydrogen blowpipe, the electric arc, and suggested that machinery might be run off power from the latter.

The audience termed his lecture brilliant and the *Scholastic* on March 11, urged its readers to procure their tickets for the next five lectures immediately, since they would never have such a fine opportunity for learning about Physics and Chemistry. Pleased with the reception, Zahm continued the Series with lectures on heat, light, chemical affinity, sound transmission, static electricity, magnetism, and optics. That this activity was becoming an integral part of Notre Dame's education may be inferred from the statement in the *Thirty-fourth Annual Catalogue:* "They are intended mainly for those students who cannot or do not wish to take up the Scientific Course, but who nevertheless desire to have a general knowledge of the leading facts and principles of the Physical and Natural Sciences."

Using the magic lantern, he presented travel lectures periodically to the campus audience. Scenes of ancient and modern Europe ranging from the ruins of Pompeii and Egypt to St. Peter's Basilica in Rome were shown. With showmanship and a rather rare display of humor, he delighted the students with slides of the faculty and ended a typical program with comical illustrations such as "the bad effects of getting up at half-past 5 o'clock" and "coffee as a cure for fits."

Acquisitions for the Science Department and science shows continued. Like Carrier, Zahm believed a knowledge of science was indispensable to an educated man; and good equipment was absolutely necessary for the study of science. As a result of a buying trip along the Atlantic seaboard in 1876, Zahm added equipment for the Physics Department such as a stereopticon, a microscope for projection, a galvanometer and self-condensing gas cylinders. However, the prize purchase he made during the tour of the Philadelphia Centennial Exposition was Rudolph Koenig's device which graphically illustrated the tone of sound by means of manometric flames.[3] An historian of education has said the Philadelphia Exposition gave new vigor to science education:[4] this proved exceptionally true at Notre Dame. Again during an eastern tour the following summer, Zahm purchased additional equipment: optical devices for studying double refraction and polarized light together with Helmholtz and Lissajous sound machines. In 1876 he bought expensive microphones and a phonograph—the students were amazed when he demonstrated the latter machine at a campus convocation.

Notre Dame's museum, by 1876, contained four thousand species of birds, stuffed quadrupeds, and color lithoes of animals, plants and minerals. They had been collected under the direction of Carrier. Zahm, eager to develop a first-rate collection, purchased quantities of shells, minerals and salt-water fish during one of his eastern tours. Upon his request, Father William Corby, President of Notre Dame, authorized the purchase in 1877 of an extraordinary collection of specimens which had been exhibited at the Chicago Exposition. After convincing the University council that the Science Department should be expanded, Zahm had little difficulty in urging them that this collection of skeletons—human, monkeys, horse, wolf, birds—should be purchased for $5,000.[5]

A few months later, again at Zahm's request, the Council voted to exchange a house in Chicago for the J. M. Veasey collection of zoological and mineral specimens valued at $6,000.[6] This collection of Rocky Mountain animals, including buffaloes, mountain sheep, and antelope, prompted the South Bend *Tribune* to report:

> In securing this collection Notre Dame has shown her enterprise, as in other things, and her knowledge of the wants of the present generation—the facilities for acquiring a thorough scientific education . . . we can, without being a prophet, foretell, that the scientific department of Notre Dame will at no distant future be recognized as one of the centers of science in our country.[7]

With the addition of the Veasey collection, which required ten large wagons for the transfer from the railroad station to the campus, the natural history museum was moved from Phelan Hall to the fourth floor of the Main Building—a move dictated by space requirements but regretted when the latter building was destroyed by fire less than a year later. Meanwhile Zahm promised the students in the pages of the *Scholastic,* May 11, 1878, that Notre Dame would have one of the nation's best museums: "It will not be a mere repository of curiosities, but a systematic working collection of such specimens, preparations, etc. as will be of most value to the student in the prosecution of his scientific studies."

In accord with the administration's decision the previous fall to expand the Science Department, Zahm left on June 4, 1878, for a careful inspection tour of European science laboratories preparatory to constructing a new science building on campus. After an unpleasant voyage, because of seasickness, Zahm stopped off in Liverpool, England. While exploring the Museum of Natural History there he recorded in his diary in great detail the room dimensions and the precise measurements of the display cases, and noted as well that the various specimens were grouped artistically.[8] Traveling on, he inspected the Royal Museum at The Hague, and noted incidentally, that the Dutch were plain, quiet and industrious. Turning southward, he toured Cologne before going on to Bonn University. At Bonn and eager to learn the latest scientific advances, he attended the physics lectures of Professor Kelleler and Professor Schliiger in paleontology: very precise notes and sketches of the University's mineralogical cabinets, physical and chemical lecture rooms and equipment were faithfully recorded during the ten-day visit. The boat ride down the Rhine River valley and a tour through Coblentz and Mayence provided a pleasant interlude before he resumed his intellectual pursuits at Heidelberg. There he attended lectures on theoretical Chemistry and electro-magnetism and discovered that Heidelberg's collection of scientific materials was not as complete as that at Bonn. A week later, he arrived at Karlsruhe and the Royal Polytechnic School, famous for its physics equipment. Following tours of Oldsberg, Holzem, and Brussels, he turned southward to Paris and visited the Exposition during the latter days of July. He was surprised to find that the equipment on display did not equal that shown at the Philadelphia Exposition.

The young, relatively unknown priest visited Rudolph Koenig in Paris and worked with him on some acoustical experiments. Moreover, he attended a meeting of the French Society of Physics and observed carefully the electrical apparatus on display. With unconcealed pleasure, he accepted its invitation to membership.[9] Too, the electric lights strung along the Rue de l'Opera gave him further enthusiasm for future Notre Dame projects.

After a Baedecker-type tour through Paris, its environs, and the discovery of the *Père La Chaise,* "the most wonderful cemetery in the world—a real *ville des morts,*" he returned to England and studied the facilities of the British Museum before embarking at Liverpool for the return voyage by way of Southern Ireland. In a characteristic style, begun as a reporter on the Notre Dame *Scholastic,* Zahm described the visit to the "Greenland of Catholicism" in a manner which pleased the Irish-American readers of the *Catholic Columbian*. In this account, the first of his "newspaper letters," he predicted that Ireland's great moral power and the force of public opinion would effect what fire and the sword had hitherto failed—independence.[10]

Zahm's European tour proved to be a "growth" investment for Notre Dame as his imagination and project-planning took on new proportions. When he returned to the class room in the third week of September, he was enthusiastic with new plans for Notre Dame's development. Also, he had reason to be proud of the advances in equipment and facilities his department had made in the three previous years. His desire to provide a superior science education was finding fulfillment; and gradually the museum was becoming first rate. The *Scholastic* on April 19, 1879, journalistically patted Zahm on the back by stating that the numerous additions to the museum collection were excellent. Four days after this report appeared, the total museum, except for three stuffed specimens, was destroyed in the "Great Calamity!"

This $200,000 conflagration, lasting three turbulent hours, began in the Main Building at eleven o'clock on Wednesday morning. Hastily-formed bucket brigades had little effect as the fire destroyed the Main Building, Minim Hall, Music Hall, the Old Men's Home, and most of the Infirmary. The following day's Chicago *Times* described the destruction succinctly: "Hot Havoc—Vast Libraries and Innumerable Scientific Treasures Consumed or Ruined." The University closed its college year one day later, transferred the Minims to Phelan Hall, and began reconstruction. Friends, alumni, and students were urged to send donations for the new Notre Dame. Zahm went to Fort Wayne on one of the fund-raising tours; this visit together with others he made, netted the building fund over two thousand dollars in cash and pledges.[11] He personally began rebuilding the museum collection by requesting friends and former students, especially those living in mining districts, to send specimens of minerals, fossils, stuffed animals, skeletons, shells, coins, corals, and Indian relics.

The fire of '79 failed to diminish Notre Dame's progressive spirit; in fact, witnesses reported that Father Sorin looked years younger and more energetic in building the University a second time! Indicative of this resurgence, the new Main Building opened for classes in September, five months later!

Zahm, a major force in this new drive, enlarged his program for rebuilding the science facilities and equipment. His request for specimens was answered with large shipments of minerals from South Dakota and the Rocky Mountain region, copper from the Lake Superior region, minerals and shells from Iowa, coins from South Bend, and quartz crystals from Alabama. Despite the recent extraordinary expense, he secured Sorin's permission to begin a construction fund for a new Science Hall. In a letter dated October 23, 1879, Sorin stated: "Our Father Zahm is hereby fully authorized to keep for the building of the eastern wing, as marked in the place, for a Scientific Hall, all donations and moneys he may, from this day, solicit and receive for that purpose." [12]

Characterized by strong determination, Zahm began new ventures for acquiring funds for the proposed building. With an eight-hundred-pound electro-magnet built according to his specifications by Charles Reitz, he commenced a lecture tour which opened at Notre Dame shortly after Christmas. The next stop on his schedule, a few weeks later, was the South Bend Opera House. The South Bend *Daily Register* reported on January 8, 1880:

> Father Zahm is youthful in appearance as he is in years, but a man of fine presence, and carries a head on his shoulders that rises to an intellectual dome of unusual height. His language was well suited to the popular style of lecturing, through its simplicity and succinctness, and the lecture was so profusely illustrated by experiments that the audience was kept awake to every point introduced.

Two weeks later, Zahm went to Fort Wayne and again drew congratulatory reviews. The Fort Wayne *Sentinel*, January 21, said his audience "had the pleasure of witnessing some of the most brilliant and interesting experiments in connection with the subject-matter of the lecture."

Determined to prevent another fire, University authorities appointed Zahm campus fire chief, shortly after the Main Building was completed. Under his direction, a fire pump was installed which filled strategically-located water tanks around the perimeter of the campus. A cautious and competent man, he installed still another fire pump in the basement of the boiler house, and this pump, by drawing water from the lake, could fill the cistern and four tanks in the college and surrounding buildings in one hour—a job which previously required a full day. Two years after the fire, the installation of hydrants and outlets within the buildings completed the fire insurance program. In June, 1881, a fire drill was held and eight heavy streams of water were directed on the Main Building within five minutes. Apparently his new fire-fighting system encouraged a certain lethargy, for the "Council Minute Book" noted on November 17, 1882, that a fire department would be organized, and one month later, "It was decided . . . to get the fire company to practice."

The *Scholastic* reported on October 29, 1881, that Zahm had purchased a dynamo-electric machine which, when connected to the steam plant, powered a lamp of 2,500 candles. This arrangement permitted the Sorin Cadets to drill at night in the Junior Yard; and a few evenings after this unprecedented innovation, the Minims played a game of night football. For Commencement ceremonies the following June, he used the equipment for spotlighting the Main Building, the Academy of Music and the college grounds. A few months later Zahm made arrangements with the Vanderpoel Electric Light Company of Chicago to build a new Notre Dame electric light plant which would be used for outdoor lighting. All this activity prompted one newspaper to comment:

It seems to us that the learned gentlemen at Notre Dame are making scientific advancement pretty rapidly for people who are supposed to live mainly in the mists of the middle ages.[13]

The first phase of campus electrification ended with the installation of an electric crown on the sixteen-foot statue of the Blessed Virgin on top of the Golden Dome in 1884.

Zahm's fund raising took on a new aspect with his trip to Columbus, Ohio, in the summer of 1880 as he began recruiting students for Notre Dame. Moreover, he secured reduced rates from the Pennsylvania Railroad for the new students' trip to Notre Dame. The next summer, he again advertised the University in southern Ohio and returned with a student contingent in the fall. In 1882, Zahm turned westward and spent the first of many summers in the West—Mexico, New Mexico, Colorado, and Wyoming—in exploration for museum specimens and new students. His diary of the journey, now in the Provincial Archives, lists the promises by Albuquerque parents to send their sons to Notre Dame and their daughters to St. Mary's. Discounts of 10 per cent less than catalogue prices were promised for two students from the same family and 15 per cent, for three or more. Railroad fares were set at one-half the usual rate. Although in 1870 Notre Dame had only one student from New Mexico and none from Colorado, approximately twenty-five new students from the Denver area returned with Zahm on a special palace car in 1882. His diary listed precise feeding instructions, and also financial ones, for some of his charges. The contingent's arrival in South Bend was declared one of the most picturesque events of the season as the eager students and their two lively burros left the train. Without question, the priest-promoter had a shrewd eye for publicity and money-raising projects. He had learned, as he told his brother Albert, "Keep yourself before the public always—if you wish the public to remember you or do anything for you."

Zahm returned in the summer of 1883 to the Southwest and after exploring the Rocky Mountain area with his brother Albert, went south into Chihuahua, Mexico, to study the Zuni and Accoma Indian customs and gather rare mineral specimens. Albert enjoyed serving as assistant to his brother for the two respected each other. Albert, eleven years younger, enrolled at Notre Dame in 1878 and like his brother, although registered in the Classical Course, took great interest in the study of science, especially aeronautical research. Eager for Albert's advancement and recognizing his brother's inventive ability, Zahm encouraged Albert to use the science laboratory during the evenings and weekends. The Zahm brothers were a spirited team on Notre Dame's campus as they complemented each other's study and personality. As Albert remarked later: he was the inventor, his brother the popularizer of science: one the "Twainish" humorist, the other the serious professor. Like his older brother, Albert joined the Scientific Association at Notre Dame; he presented the results of his pioneering experiments in aeronautics, constructed steam engines, and developed the first wind tunnel in order to study the influence of wind currents. This last study proved invaluable for the Wright Brothers' Kitty Hawk flight in 1903.[14]

In September, the Zahm brothers, after diligent recruiting, escorted a large group of new students back to South Bend. Father Zahm headed the contingent from Denver, Colorado, in a special railroad car which was identified with the large banner, "Students for Notre Dame University," while Albert escorted the group from Chihuahua. The eighty excited passengers, including some mothers of the Minims and young ladies for St. Mary's, paraded to the campus in twenty carriages. This "Western Contingent" resulted in the announcement that for the first time in its history Notre Dame had over four hundred students during the first month of school.

At Christmas time, Zahm returned again to Chihuahua for two months, and this time carried a supply of colorful advertising circulars which pictured the route from Mexico City to Notre Dame and described in Spanish the University's many advantages. The trip netted ten more students who accompanied him on the "First International Train from Mexico City to Notre Dame." Subsequent summers brought larger western contingents which added to Notre Dame's growing enrollment. A student debate on the topic, "Is Colorado more interesting than any other state in the Union" lasted four hours and one proud son spoke from his prepared manuscript of 122 pages! Zahm also presented travel lectures on Colorado to Notre Dame audiences and his first pamphlet, "Colorado, Its Past, Present and Future," published at Notre Dame in 1883, was a Baedecker-type description of the Centennial State.

During this year, his lectures, which previously had covered science topics and travel descriptions in an expository fashion, became apologetic and Catholic in tone. For example, in a travelogue on "The Great Southwest, Its Attractions, Resources and People" given in 1883, Zahm appealed for a form of cultural Pan-Americanism which would recognize the Catholicity and dignity of South Americans and the Indians in southwestern United States. Critically he wrote:

> Notwithstanding the fact that nearly all the Indians of the Southwest are Catholics, as have been their forefathers for upwards of three hundred years, and in spite of their earnest and repeated protests, they have, in consequence of one of Grant's celebrated Civil Service Reforms (!) been handed over to the care of teachers they know not . . .

nor love nor trust.[15] Continuing this bitter and accurate criticism, he wrote that these benighted Indians had been denied their Black Robe friends and American friendship. Similarly he complained about the popular newspaper portrayals of the typical Mexican as a "greaser." With some exaggeration, he insisted that the Spanish-Mexicans in Mexico and the United States had been more misrepresented and less understood than any other people. They were not lazy, ignorant, dishonest, immoral or strangers to a cultured life. Such unjust descriptions resulted, he thought, from the actions of certain criminals who fled from justice in the

United States and Europe, and made their homes in Mexico. Even more responsible, however, were the ignorant and bigoted newspaper correspondents and tourists whose experience of the Spanish-Americans was limited to views from barroom stools and hotel lobbies. In conclusion, he said that Mexicans, if not a better people, were certainly no worse than other nationalities.

At this same time Zahm moved into a study of the relationship between religion and science, a study which would gradually absorb his interest during the next fifteen years and bring international fame together with a specific warning from Rome for his advanced position on evolution. This topic, fraught with strong emotional and theological implications, won for him large listening and reading audiences. The bitterness, misunderstanding, and the theological controversy engendered in discussions of the topic after 1865 produced serious dogmatic conflict among Christian churches and hampered science education in America.

Darwin's ideas in his *Origin of Species* in 1859 and *Descent of Man* in 1871 caused mixed reactions in the United States among scientists and theologians. Louis Agassiz, Professor of Geology and Zoology at Harvard, remained a steadfast opponent of Darwin's theories until his death in 1873, for he opposed, on scientific grounds, the transmutation of species. Like Orestes Brownson he opposed extreme Darwinists who refused recognition of a divine agent.[16] However, Asa Gray, Professor of Botany and Natural History at Harvard, accepted the evolutionary theories and told religious men that religion was not harmed by these new studies because derivation could be theologically acceptable. Yale's geologist, Charles Dana, the third member of America's leading scientific trio, accepted a middle position only after considerable reluctance.

American Catholics took a reasonably tolerant attitude toward evolution around 1865. The most difficult problem for Christians centered on the manner in which the theory of evolution could be harmonized with the traditional Christian explanation for the world's origin and development.

Some American Catholic writers kept pace with the startling advances of scientific theory and offered complex judgments on Darwinian evolution. Others rejected and journalistically scoffed at the theories while attributing them
simply to Comte's positivism, bad logic, and atheistic tend-
encies. Too often the adverse critics struck at the infer-
ences of evolution and refused to evaluate it as a specific
theory on the mechanism of biological change. The famous
Catholic convert and editor, Orestes Brownson, believed that
only faithful Catholics could be great scientists: that nineteenth-century scientists knew nothing of value that was unknown to the early Church Fathers. He judged evolution
to be unworthy of belief for it lacked a Christian philosophy and led to a denial of God as a Creator.[17] Another
Catholic writer claimed English scientists were deliberately
prostituting science in order to undermine the religious convictions of ordinary people.[18] Incensed at this general state
of affairs, Father Edward McSweeny struck at Tyndall's rau-
cous laughter at prayer and Huxley's ridicule of the Mosaic
account rather than the exact doctrine of evolution. Furthermore, he wrote that evolution as a theory could not
explain changes in the moral and intellectual spheres, for
while there was growth within individuals, races, and nations there was also climax and decay. Concluding the
pointed attack, he explained,

> We say nothing about its repugnance to the conclusions of
> metaphysics, nothing about the destruction of morality which
> is a necessary outcome of the system, when it is not content
> with evolving the body of man from the brutal form, but
> claims that even his mind and soul are mere developments
> of corresponding (?) [sic] constitutional parts of lower ani-
> mals.[19]

Another journalist attacked Darwin and stated that his implications were subtleties—"Like the devil, he sometimes as-
sumes the garment of light, and puts in an appearance of
virtue." [20] Continuing with unwarranted accusations Smith
wrote, "He sets aside revealed truths. He knows nothing

about the simple but sublime narrative in the first chapter of Genesis." [21] These writers represented a group which, for lack of scientific training, failed to evaluate Darwin's specific proposals. For this reason and because Darwin himself had abandoned religion they leaped to inaccurate conclusions and thought the theory of evolution was harmful to Christianity, and the proponents of evolution totally agnostic or atheistic.

A more moderate but unsigned appraisal of Darwinism appeared in the *Catholic World* in 1873. The author distinguished between radical scientists and radical theologians —both of whom did not understand the other's position. He pointed out that Darwin and Huxley were aware that they had only a hypothesis.[22] Further, he explained that the English Catholic convert and biologist, St. George Mivart, in his book *The Genesis of Species* (1871), gave Darwin's theory its full measure of praise. He agreed with Mivart who said evolution and creation were not necessarily contradictory—a Catholic could accept evolution. While closing with the theme that Darwin's teaching on the origin of the soul contradicted the Catholic doctrine, he counseled patience while science tried to prove the facts of the hypothesis.

From England, Professor St. George Mivart, accentuated a moderate approach to Darwin's theory and assumed leadership among those Catholics holding a similar position. This English convert, brilliant professor and biologist, admitted the possibility of evolution in general but urged a distinction between organic and inorganic forms. He wrote that evolution by the action of an internal force or "psyche" was possible and that this internal force could be stimulated or modified by external conditions.[23] This theory, he contended, left room for the divine creative act as St. Augustine had noted earlier.

Alexander M. Kirsch, then a seminarian and assistant to Zahm, appeared the most vocal critic of evolution on Notre Dame's campus during these early stages. As reprinted in the *Scholastic*, September 16, 1876, his essay soundly denounced Professor Lorentz Oken for his theory that every

living being came from the sea and agreed with Agassiz
that man "is the crowning work of God. . . . He may sink
as low as the lowest of his type, or he may rise to a spiritual
height that will make that which distinguishes him from
the rest a far more controlling element of his being than
that which unites him with them."

Professor Huxley's popular lecture tour in the United
States during the fall of 1876 brought severe criticism from
the pen of Kirsch in an essay published in the *Scholastic*.
He claimed that Huxley lost his way when lecturing in
philosophy and theology. "I repeat, it is not out of religious
spite that we come to such a conclusion, but it is our honest
conviction, strengthened by the reading of works like that
of Mr. Mivart's 'Genesis of Species' or 'Lessons of Nature.' " [24] Zahm's assistant concluded with a reassuring note:

> Evolution in its broadest sense may be accepted, and will be,
> probably, as far as it goes, when proved logically . . . the
> theory of evolution need alarm no one. A little patience will
> clear the ground . . . we hope that at the end a principle is
> evolved which is not on the one hand, unscientific, and on
> the other conflicting with Catholic doctrine.

Moreover, Kirsch believed Professor Huxley did not have
to travel 3,000 miles merely to censure the notion that Nature had been all along in the same state, nor to correct
the poetical account given in Milton's *Paradise Lost*. Huxley's third lecture brought forth an important statement
from Kirsch:

> for our part, we believe strongly in a derivative creation:
> namely, that God created many species, not in *actu*, but in
> *potentia*, to be produced by natural powers into their differ-
> ent forms. Some Catholics will be startled probably at this
> doctrine, but if they consult Suarez and many other theolo-
> gians they will find that such is really the case, and that there-
> fore we may accept this view since it is reasonable and is not
> contrary to religious teaching.[25]

Without doubt, Kirsch did startle some American Catholics, especially the complete rejectors of Darwinism; how-

ever, his approach to evolution offset certain radical Catholic writers' repudiation of Darwin's theory.

Notre Dame students agreed with the position taken by Kirsch. One *Scholastic* reporter on November 29, 1879, editorially soothed a Chicago *Times* writer who feared that a Catholic, Professor Procter, was heretical in declaring millions and millions of years were mere trifles in the world's growth. The reporter concluded that the Mosaic accounts of creation permitted an unlimited time for the creation of the world. When Darwin wrote in his last edition of the *Descent of Man* that he had probably attributed too much to the action of Natural Selection or the Survival of the Fittest, the Notre Dame school paper commented on September 23, 1882: "These utterances are examples of the fine intellectual honesty by which Mr. Darwin was distinguished, and it is a pity that all his followers do not emulate his candor."

Zahm first publicly entered the controversy over evolution with a sermon at Denver, Colorado, March 26, 1883, repeated later at Notre Dame and St. Mary's and printed in pamphlet form that same year. Reprinted in the French newspaper *Cosmos: Les Mondes,* this lecture marked the beginning of his international reputation. After restating that there was no real conflict between the Church and scientific truths, Zahm explained he was not speaking as an apologist, for the Church had no need of one. In fact, however, he did speak as one. When discussing the geologists' contention that the world was older than some theologians said, Zahm said the Church had never defined the age of the world ". . . and most probably never will, as the age of the world has nothing whatever to do—at least as far as I can see—with the object of her teaching, viz.: faith and morals." [26] Zahm also explained that Scripture did not state the age: therefore, scientists were permitted all the latitude they required. Although, he said, some commentators said six thousand years, this was not the official teaching of the Church. "If this distinction between opinion and doctrine, between theory and demonstration, were always borne in mind, we should hear less of so-called conflicts between science and religion." Rather, he wrote, it should be called a conflict between individuals. Objections raised by scientists to the "days" mentioned in Scripture were declared foolish. The "days" did not necessarily mean twenty-four hours but might be interpreted as indefinite periods of time as St. Augustine, St. Thomas, and St. Albertus Magnus believed.

Zahm warned that evolution was only a hypothesis and it rested upon the assumption of the nebular hypothesis (that the earth and celestial bodies existed in a state of incandescent vapor and after a long period of time condensed into solid orbs): the assumption of spontaneous generation (necessary, since life could not exist on the globe during the gaseous stage) which even Darwin considered absolutely inconceivable; and the assumption of transmutation of species of either plant or animal into another. This last assumption had no evidence, reported Zahm, and even Professor Huxley admitted this fact. These three assumptions must be proved before the theory of evolution might be considered valid, Zahm specified.

Let it be supposed, however, that the necessary postulates for evolution were shown—then what? After stating that Catholics could not accept the theories of the atheistic and agnostic evolutionists, he cautiously suggested, like Mivart before him, that Catholics might accept a theory of theistic evolution.

I trust you will not consider me as proclaiming a novelty, or as giving expression to a heterodox opinion, when I state it as my belief that there is not [anything contrary to Scripture or the teachings of the Catholic faith]. According to the words of Genesis, God did not create animals and plants in the primary sense of the word, but caused them to be produced from pre-existing material. "Let the earth bring forth, Let the waters bring forth," He says: showing clearly that creation in these instances, was only secondary or derivative.[27]

Thus, the theistic evolutionist merely believed God did *potentially* what many Scriptural interpreters believed He did directly and distinctly. Nor did the Church condemn evolution as contrary to faith. As for the Doctors and Fathers of the Church, St. Augustine held that plants and animals were brought into existence by natural causes. The Church Fathers taught that "As the seed contains invisible within itself all that is found in the full-grown tree, so also the world, after its creation by God, contained all the germs of the various forms of life that were afterwards produced." [28] St. Thomas and Suarez, he said, also held this doctrine of derivative creation.

Zahm rejected evolution of the soul. He observed that Mivart defended the theory of the human body's evolution and added: "The hypothesis may be rash, and even dangerous, but I do not think that, considering it simply in its bearing on dogma. [sic] anyone could pronounce it as certainly and positively false." [29]

Concluding his discussion on evolution, Zahm noted that men would probably never know whether theistic evolution occurred, for it would remain a mystery. He agreed with Mivart who said that certain men in the name of science propagated conflict in order to kill religion. In a final statement Zahm emphasized that there could be no genuine conflict between true science and the Catholic Church since both lead to God.

This pamphlet was the first of his writings on a topic which would some years later mark him as the leading Catholic writer and speaker on the relationship between Catholicism and Natural Science. Gradually he assumed the mantle of Catholic apologist after 1883 as he increasingly described the attitude of the Church towards Science in the past and the present. For example, in a subsequent lecture series during these early years, entitled, "What the Church Has Done for Science," reprinted in the first three issues of the March, 1885, *Scholastic,* he contended like Count de Maistre had earlier, that the Church through its universities and scholars had historically led the progress of science. To her, the western world owed, therefore, an immeasurable debt. This type of apologetics together with others gave Zahm an influential leadership of national and international proportions. Indeed, without Darwin, Zahm's work would have taken a considerably different direction, possibly less rewarding, certainly less exciting.

Meanwhile, on the campus at Notre Dame, another Zahm project, begun with his European journey in 1878 and steadfastly continued with fund-raising lectures, pamphlet writing, and student recruiting trips, came to completion. The Science Building, a symbol to his aggressive leadership in education, opened its doors to Notre Dame students at a ceremony led by Father Thomas Walsh on December 14, 1884. Incorporating the latest designs in lecture rooms and laboratories, this two-story Romanesque, yellow-brick building housed the departments of the physical and natural sciences together with the photography laboratory and the mechanical engineering department. The University, proud of this latest sign of progress, featured the building's floor plan in its 1885 *Catalogue*.

As the 1884-85 academic year drew to a close, Zahm could look back on a decade of progress in the field of science at the University. His apparently boundless energy in raising funds, popularizing science, and recruiting students, laid the "brick and mortar" foundations for Notre Dame's success in the study of science. On the national and local scene, he taught Catholics to view evolution calmly, and with persevering study, to investigate the theory. As a Catholic priest and scientist he gave courage to those who feared the advance of science would destroy the Church; but more than this, he interpreted the theories of evolution in theistic terms. His work promised a much better education for Catholic students.

NOTES TO CHAPTER II

1. Zahm to Brownson, October 14, 1875. John Zahm Collection, UNDA.

2. Charles Loring Jackson, "Chemistry 1865-1929," in Samuel Eliot Morison, ed., *The Development of Harvard University* (Cambridge, 1930), p. 259.

3. *Scholastic,* November 11, 1876.

4. Ellwood P. Cubberly, *The History of Education* (New York, 1920), p. 799.

5. The asking price was $8,000 but Notre Dame offered $5,000. University Report, PA.

6. *Ibid.*

7. As reprinted in *loc. cit.,* April 6, 1878.

8. Zahm's diary is in the Provincial Archives.

9. *Loc. cit.,* September 21, 1878; May 7, 1892.

10. Clipping from the *Catholic Columbian* for 1878. PA.

11. A few of Zahm's notebooks which list the amount of money and/or work promised for rebuilding the college are in the Provincial Archives.

12. As quoted in Patrick J. Carroll, "Mind in Action," *Ave Maria,* 63 (January, 1946), 82.

13. *Ypsilanti Sentinel* as reprinted in *loc. cit.,* December 16, 1882.

14. Albert received his A.B. (1883) and M.S. (1890) at Notre Dame, M.E. at Cornell (1892) and Ph.D. (1898) at Johns Hopkins. He served as Professor of Mathematics and Mechanics at Notre Dame before attending Cornell; later, he was in charge of mechanical and aerodynamic research at Catholic University. Following careers as Chief Research Engineer for Curtiss Aeroplane Co. (1914-1917) and Chief of U. S. Navy Aerodynamic Laboratory (1917-1929), he became Chief of the Aeronautics Division (Guggenheim Chair), Library of Congress. He died at Notre Dame in 1954.

15. John A. Zahm, *The Great Southwest, Its Attractions, Resources, and People* (Notre Dame, 1883), p. 31.

16. Cf. Bert James Loewenberg, "The Reaction of American Scientists to Darwinism," *American Historical Review,* 37 (July, 1933), 687-702, for a discussion of Agassiz, Gray and Dana.

17. Cf. John L. Morrison, "A History of American Catholic Opinion on the Theory of Evolution, 1859-1950," (Unpublished doctoral dissertation, University of Missouri), p. 54.

18. X.C.S.P., "Positivism and Evolution," *American Catholic Quarterly Review,* II (October, 1877), 613. The *Civilta Cattolica* in 1865 attacked evolution theory as an invention of the materialists. Morrison, *op. cit.,* p. 40.

19. Reverend Edward F. X. McSweeny, "The Logic of Evolution," *American Catholic Quarterly Review,* IV (July, 1879), 561.

20. F. Smith, "More About Darwinism," *Catholic World,* 17 (August, 1873), 641.

21. *Ibid.,* 17, 646. He continued the attack to the last paragraph where he admitted that there was a germ of truth in the theory of evolution but failed to explain what it was!

22. "The Evolution of Life," *Catholic World,* 17 (May, 1873), 148.

One historian of the period notes that in this year, the *Catholic World* became more tolerant of evolution theory partially because of the split between its editor, Father Hecker, and the arch foe of evolution, Orestes Brownson. Morrison, *op. cit.*, p. 76.

23. St. George Mivart, "The Soul and Evolution," *American Catholic Quarterly Review*, VI (July, 1881), 416-17; also his article, "A Limit to Evolution," *ibid.*, VIII (April, 1883), 192-222.

24. *Loc. cit.*, November 25, 1876. The articles on Huxley were substantially reprinted in the October, 1877 issue of the *American Catholic Quarterly Review*. His article, "Professor Huxley and Evolution" won mention in Andrew D. White's classic, *A History of the Warfare of Science with Theology in Christendom* (New York, 1898), I, 86 (fn.): Dr. White believed it to be "remarkably fair-minded, and in the main just, as to the Protestant attitude, and as to the causes underlying the whole action against Galileo." *Ibid.*, I, 162 (fn.).

25. *Loc. cit.*, February 3, 1877.

26. John A. Zahm, *The Catholic Church and Modern Science* (Notre Dame, 1883), p. 6.

27. *Ibid.*, p. 13.

28. *Ibid.*, p. 14.

29. *Ibid.*, p. 15.

III

Vice-President and Traveler

"A Padua or a Bologna"

At the golden jubilee celebration for Sorin in 1888, as described earlier, Zahm declared his belief that Notre Dame held the promise of becoming a truly fine university, equal to the best in Europe. Unquestionably, too, he agreed with Archbishop John Ireland who spoke out for the man of action. The *Scholastic,* August 25, 1888, reported Ireland's sermon at Notre Dame:

> I despise the many who worship success and who are ever ready to censure failure. Failure, when not the result of culpable imprudence, obtains my sympathy, and the effort that preceded it, my approval. The safe conservatism which never moves lest it fail, I abhor: it is the dry-rot in the Church, and my heart goes out to the man who never tolerated it in his calculations. Safe conservatism would have left the Apostles in Palestine.

Zahm did not typify the man of "safe conservatism" in his efforts to make Notre Dame a distinctively superior university with an intellectually strong student body. The seven years after 1885 found him enlarging the foundations of a home for scholars and obtaining a national reputation for the University and himself.

Although named to the post of Vice-President of the University in 1885, Zahm continued as the head of his beloved Science school. Likewise, he drove himself and those around him with characteristic vigor as he aimed for the improvement of Notre Dame's enrollment, reputation, and educational facilities. Each September, as over the three previous years, Zahm personally guided a contingent of western students to both Notre Dame and St. Mary's College campuses via specially reserved railroad Pullmans replete with delightfully entertaining service. The Southwestern United States proved to be a fine recruiting ground for these midwestern schools and Zahm's determination won the hearts of parents and students alike—"With Coloradans Father Zahm is the most popular educator in the country," reported the Denver *News* on January 8, 1887. School newspaper reports such as the one on September 19, 1891, noted that the trip's entertaining manager provided the colleges with students who arrived eager and even happy to begin the long, tedious school year. In 1887, the thirty-six hour journey over Union Pacific or Burlington lines provided Notre Dame and St. Mary's College with more than fifteen per cent of their enrollment.[1]

Each September enrollment increased at the fledgling Notre Dame: the modern Science Hall south of Washington Hall experienced a larger share of the new enrollees as interest in science spread throughout the world and, more especially, as Zahm promoted this study of science. The daily roll call in science subjects was estimated by the *Scholastic* on February 19, 1887, at 200 students—young men whose studies and experimentations ranged from the Departments of Chemistry through microscopy and Physics to practical mechanics. One faculty member, exclaimed that Zahm was the University's happiest man because his plans for teaching the sciences, and, as well, for completing the large electric light plant on campus had been achieved.

The friendly Buffalo *Union and Times* boastfully stated that Notre Dame rivaled Harvard "and [has] a scientific 'plant' second to none in the country." [2] Famed Dr. Rudolph Koenig judged that Zahm's collection of acoustical apparatus was one of the best in existence.[3] The Providence *Telegram* informed its readers that Notre Dame, while one of the greatest universities in the United States, was certainly the greatest in the West; and judged the science college, "one of the best-equipped institutions of the kind in the world." [4] Closer to home, the South Bend *Tribune* continued to laud the scientific improvements dotting the campus and more especially the completion of the Edison Electric Light Plant in 1885.[5] In its columns, the New York *Electrical Review* credited Notre Dame with being the first college to be lighted by electricity by explaining that in 1881, the arc light was employed successfully on the campus and the Edison incandescent lamp was introduced in 1885.[6] A gift from the New York Edison Light Company of a complete electric light plant together with a high-speed steam engine from the Providence Armington and Sims Engine Company, both gifts probably engineered by Zahm, helped the college authorities to complete the electrification of all campus buildings.[7] With a burst of local but unsubstantiated pride, the South Bend *Register* on February 10, 1886, claimed that Notre Dame's Science Hall "has no equal in all the educational institutions of the land." Zahm was proud of these reports of his efforts to build a true Catholic University at Notre Dame.

In 1888, Notre Dame began a new era in American Catholic higher education. Increased enrollment in the renovated law school, directed by Colonel William Hoynes, and in the collegiate department, together with the desire to attract older Catholic college students, brought Notre Dame authorities to risk a departure from the practice of housing students in the traditional dormitories. The precise role of Zahm in this radical departure from standard Catholic college practice in the United States is not clear. Albert Zahm, whose memory was remarkably accurate, claimed that his brother formulated a plan for private rooms in a residence hall but Father Thomas E. Walsh, President of Notre Dame, refused to consider it. Albert said Zahm then interested the Superior-General, Father Sorin, in the plan, and the latter sent Walsh to Europe for the 1888 meeting of the International Catholic Scientific Congress. During the two months Walsh was gone, Zahm had the building designed and the cornerstone laid. As far as written evidence is concerned, only the following facts can be verified. Walsh left for Europe to attend the International Scientific Congress on March 14, 1888, and on April 28, 1888, the *Scholastic* announced that Mr. W. J. Edbrooke was designing a new structure to be named Sorin Hall. Furthermore, it said that Sorin was eager to have the building completed as soon as possible. The cornerstone dedication led by Sorin and Zahm took place on May 27, and Walsh returned from Europe two days later.[8] Thus, Zahm's exact role remains an interesting conjecture; however, Albert's recollection was probably correct as it appears strange that the cornerstone dedication took place two days before the University's president returned!

The University authorities became concerned over the parents' reaction to this innovation. The *Forty-fourth Annual Catalogue* cautiously explained the Sorin Hall arrangement to parents of prospective and returning students. It told how for the previous four or five years private rooms had been furnished to advanced students who desired them and assured the readers that the results had been extremely encouraging: neither inferior work nor disciplinary problems resulted. For younger boys, the dormitory and study hall system was pronounced best; however, the lads in their junior and senior years and also law students who were "earnest, industrious, intelligent, and well-disposed young men would find the private rooms more conducive to good study." A year later, even students below the junior year who were exceptionally industrious and studious could obtain space in Sorin Hall in return for a fee of $100 a year. The aristocracy of age continued for older students and they received the privileged rooms at no extra cost.

Father James Burns, at Notre Dame at the time, and an authority on Catholic education in the United States, approved the private room system and said it would mark the end of the traditional discipline of the Catholic college because it destroyed the theory and practice of uniform college discipline and life. Also he reported that while conservative faculty members opposed it, students enjoyed the freedom and enrollments increased. With great accuracy, he also stated that intercollegiate athletics was the second factor which changed the Catholic college because the games took the college out into the world and brought the world into the college.[9]

As director of Sorin Hall, Father Andrew Morrissey took charge on January 1, 1889, when qualified students, returning from the holidays, moved into the building which contained sixty resident rooms. Each room was deemed large enough for study, yet small enough to discourage visiting! The left wing had quarters for Hoynes' law department and the right wing contained a chapel. The basement had smoking and reading rooms. Strong though typical optimism colored a *Scholastic* reporter's story on January 2 when he suggested that May 27, 1888, should long be remembered and some commemoration held each year in honor of the Hall's cornerstone dedication on the day "on which Notre Dame entered on a new era that will in time make her the foremost American University." Actually the hall proved so popular that a month after the formal opening, the *Scholastic* on February 16 urged the construction of a similar structure twice the size to accommodate all the applicants.

In 1890, Maurice Francis Egan, former editor of the *Freeman's Journal* and then English professor, poet, and critic at Notre Dame, explained the basis for Sorin Hall in an article in the February *Catholic World* entitled, "A New Departure in Catholic College Discipline." Actually, he wrote, the common dormitory system in which all sleep "like patients in the wards of a hospital" was intensely disliked by American Catholic students. These young men, hungry for independence, wanted rooms of their own. Catholic colleges which would not provide them, he prophesied, would either suffer decreased enrollments or become mere preparatory schools for junior students. Egan then told of the very real fears experienced in planning and building Sorin Hall at Notre Dame—conservatives feared "that any recognition of modern prejudices against the dormitory system, even for students in senior grades, meant anarchy." However, more than a year of experimentation proved the venture a success. Seventy-five more rooms were scheduled for the new addition to the existing building. The discipline, order, and cleanliness pleased all the originators of the plan. More important, the quiet environment absolutely necessary for the life of a student, resulted from this experiment. The author concluded that Notre Dame had led the way and shown how to bring older students to its university with this important experiment—"The success of Sorin Hall marks an epoch and the beginning of a synthesis between traditions and the demands of the present time."

The work on Sorin Hall was barely finished before Zahm initiated still another project. Finding the Science Hall, constructed a few years earlier, inadequate for the mechanical department, he made plans for a building which would be erected just south of Science Hall. Excited over the project, he wrote Albert:

> I want the mechanical dept. of Notre Dame to be equal to any in the U.S.—without exception, & I want you to do here what Thurston has done at Stevens [Institute] & at Cornell —develop the dept. & give it a national reputation. You can write books and thus indulge your library tastes & can show also that Catholic colleges need not be behind sectarian or government institutions. My ideas may seem Utopian but I am thoroughly in earnest & have never been more sanguine of success in anything I have undertaken.[10]

Shortly after ground was broken for the building in February, 1890, Zahm confided in Albert who was studying at Cornell: "Everyone here is perfectly dazed at the new departure. All they can say is 'What next?' " [11] Moreover, delighting in mystery, he said no one at Notre Dame yet knew the size of the building; nevertheless, the project itself is so daring "it has taken the breath away from everyone. I cannot imagine what the average looker-on will say when he gets his second wind." The building, paid for by a friend of Zahm in Chicago, was two stories high in front: this area housed the wood and metal working machines and provided classrooms as well; the rear of the building was reserved for the foundry and blacksmith shops. In conclusion, Zahm wrote, "Our intention is to not simply equal Cornell, but to eclipse it both in buildings and equipment."

Fortunately for the students, Zahm remained close to the science laboratory and the lecture rooms where he explained the latest findings in the field of physics. Too, he purchased the latest European scientific apparatus for the chemistry and physics laboratories. His "Great Experiment" —Foucault's pendulum experiment which demonstrated the earth's rotation—was called by the student body a huge success when performed in Science Hall. The astronomy lectures to the students, which included stereoscopic views showing the motion of the planets, together with Kodak pictures of local persons and places familiar to the viewers, brought loud applause.

Some of the students asked the versatile priest to recommend a list of 100 best books. His list (see appendix) of the classics in literature was not, as he explained in the Scholastic, May 21, 1887, for every student, since there was as much difference between the advanced and beginning scholar as between the Summa Theologica and the catechism. In addition to these books, he thought every student should have a set of Appleton's American Cyclopedia and a dictionary in his library. Quite in character, Zahm endorsed the Cyclopedia, while accurate and reliable, particularly because Appleton's employed Catholic writers to treat of Catholic subjects. His selection does not resemble the Hutchins-Adler Great Books; rather it contains predominately Catholic books on the subjects of Theology, Religion, Science, History, Biography, Art and Music, Poetry, Travel and Fiction. Without question, his insistence upon a fair treatment of Catholicism only mirrored Catholic journalism and Catholic public opinion generally. This religious minority group did not hesitate to defend its theological and educational structure.

The students appreciated Zahm's manifold contributions to Notre Dame. On March 20, a Scholastic reporter described the annual St. Patrick's Day party in 1886 and the honors bestowed upon Zahm with the statement:

> No one connected with the University is held in higher esteem among the students and alumni of Notre Dame than is Father Zahm. He has been identified with the progress and growth of that institution as an instructor for the past fifteen years. His travels . . . and his labors in the Department of Science of the University have won for him an enviable reputation.

The reporter concluded his compliments with a mention of Zahm's Alaskan trip and the illustrated pamphlet which described the journey.

The Alaskan trip mentioned by the reporter took place during the summer of 1885 when Zahm, after returning the western students to Denver, continued westward to San Francisco and then voyaged northward to Alaskan waters. His Alaskan letters [12] began with an historical, social, and economic description of William Seward's purchase, written in news story style. After castigating President Polk and his secretary, James Buchanan, for the inept 1846 treaty with Great Britain concerning the 49 degrees parallel of latitude and, as well, lauding the true American patriots who demanded "54 40 or fight," the critical author presented an interesting sketch of society and customs in Alaska.[13]

To his disgust, he found few Americans but literally a sea of Chinese huddled in the pioneering settlements along the coast, and this race, he predicted, would soon be world rulers rather than world servants. He complained bitterly that they fastened themselves like a cancer on the richest and fairest parts of the two most important cities west of the Sierras—San Francisco and Portland.[14] Unfairly, though in the American fashion of the eighteen-eighties, Zahm considered them a blight on the cities they infested and he urged stricter immigration laws:

> It is well for Eastern sentimentalists to talk about the equality allowed by the Constitution to all men, but I venture to say that if these same utopians were to make a study of the

'heathen Chinee,' as he is found in California or Oregon, or even here in Alaska, their ideas regarding anti-Chinese legislation would be wonderfully modified.

Further, he agreed with those Pacific coastal leaders who had demanded the cancellation of reciprocal immigration privileges in the Burlingame Treaty of 1868. The Chinese labor exclusion act of 1882 which prohibited the immigration of Chinese laborers for ten years apparently pleased Zahm and it seems he backed this restriction which became a permanent feature in American immigration law. Actually it seems that the well-meaning priest played the role of an overly patriotic American in his fear that Oriental immigrants would eventually control the United States: as such he accurately reflected at least one aspect of the strong Anglo-Saxon cult in the latter nineteenth-century America and at the same time he recognized the apparent failure of non-Caucasian assimilation in the United States, especially along the Pacific coast. Nevertheless his views are strange for a man who denounced the unjust American treatment of Mexicans, Alaskan Indians, and Hawaiian natives.

Zahm shared with his readers a strong sympathy for the pitiful plight of the Indians in Alaska. As he had emphasized in his Mexico messages, the Indian unfortunately contracted in large measure the white man's vices and acquired none of his virtues. To Zahm it seemed the "only hope, apparently, of ever successfully educating and Christianizing him is to keep him isolated from those who should be his helpers, but who, in reality, are his destroyers."

Prone, as ever, to think of things in terms of science, he pictured a glorious future for Alaska because of its rapid progress in utilizing steam and electricity. That territory, like the Great American Desert, could eventually be settled and become prosperous through railroad development. His Alaskan writings concluded with an optimistic prediction that the northern territory would soon be one of the most highly prized gems in Columbia's crown.

The Hawaiian Islands attracted Father Zahm during the following summer and his letters from those sunny lands accurately forecasted the economic and political fortunes awaiting U.S. investors in Hawaii.[15] Continuing to write in the fashion of an American expansionist, he promised that because of American investments the United States would convince other rivals of her right to ownership of the islands and her ability to enforce these rights. Congress should renew the Reciprocity Treaty of 1876 for it would assist the beautiful though struggling little kingdom. Finally, he thought San Francisco would be seriously harmed if any "mole-eyed policy on the part of our legislators should allow the rapidly increasing trade with the Hawaiian Islands to be deflected to any other mart."

His reports sympathized with the plight of the Hawaiian natives. Zahm found that the native population was declining seriously because of the white man's diseases and encroachments. As in his Alaskan letters, he complained that the white man who should be giving example and encouragement in righteousness were failing in their obligations— "flattery is substituted for advice, and the wineglass is proffered in lieu of sage counsel."

However, he thought the education of the natives excellent and estimated 90 per cent were able to read and write. Since their compulsory education included science, he believed they would reach a high degree of proficiency in mechanical arts and engineering unless, however, because of climatic conditions, they might remain a somewhat listless and indolent race.

His final report from Hawaii traced the history of leprosy and the heroes who treated the victims of this dreaded disease. After noting its beginning in Hawaii around 1837, he went on to applaud the government's scientific work on Molokai Island and, more especially, the sacrifice of Father Damien. Concluding his observations of the pitiful toll of human life and the horrible disfigurement caused by the disease, he warned that there were many cases of leprosy reported among the San Francisco Chinese and urged the United States government to abandon its ostrich-like complacency.

Believing firmly in Manifest Destiny and, as well, that whoever controlled these islands controlled the North Pacific, Zahm predicted "the Hawaiian Islands are destined at no distant day to become the prized tropical gardens of the western portion of our great and growing Commonwealth."

During the summer of 1887 Zahm again visited the Southwestern United States and found the almost completed railroad between Denver and the Gulf of Mexico a harbinger of prosperity for the regions it served. He suggested to the readers of the Colorado *Rocky Mountain News* on September 4 that their state would profit from a state board of advertising which would publicize the beauties of its territory.

On the last day of October, 1887, Sorin telegraphed his protégé and requested that they meet in Rome for a trip to the Holy Land.[16] On November 18, Notre Dame's founder and Zahm left Rome on the first leg of a pilgrimage to the Holy Land via Naples, Brindisi and Cairo. The ready chronicler delighted in the Mediterranean scenes along the way. Drawing upon his earlier travels, he thought the villages surrounding Port Said were strangely similar to the pueblos in New Mexico while the little gardens seemed to be cultivated like those in Hawaii. He thought the Suez Canal was a truly wonderful monument to Count de Lesseps. Incorrectly, he predicted the same courage would enable the Frenchman to complete the Panama project. Sight-seeing in and around Cairo during the latter days of November preceded their trip to Alexandria, Jaffa and Jerusalem. Readers of the Leadville *Chronicle* on August 21, 1888, read his report that the Turkish government did little to provide and enforce law and order in Jaffa. But Zahm praised the inhabitants for abstaining from all forms of liquor.

Leaving Sorin in Jerusalem, he made the average four- or five-day trip to the Dead Sea on a borrowed Arabian pony in almost record time. As the New York-published *Pilgrim of Palestine* reported: "Rev. Father Zahm made the trip to the Dead Sea all alone, like a true American, doing the whole business going and coming, in the remarkably quick time of thirty hours." [17] After visits to Jordan and Jericho, the two priests returned to Jaffa on December 14 and then to Rome by Christmas day, just in time for the Golden Jubilee Mass of Pope Leo XIII.

In a letter dated Rome, January 2, 1888, and published in the *Catholic Review,* Zahm described the colorful pageants marking this jubilee celebration. He wrote that the Holy Father's pale, emaciated appearance because of his seventeen years as a prisoner of the Vatican, was in strong contrast to the happy, excited throngs filling St. Peter's Square. Moreover, all the large governments had joined in sending congratulations except

> poor, forlorn, unfortunate, outcast Italy, the Government that despoiled the Pope of his possessions, and that for nearly twenty years, has kept him a prisoner in his own palace. The robber Government realizes its awkward and unenviable position, but pride and despotic brutality will not allow it to make the only *amende honorable* that simple self-respect would permit the Pope to accept.

He aimed other harsh statements at the Italy of Prince Cavour's creation and quoted Herr Ludwig Windthorst, the last prime minister of Hanover before Prussian annexation in 1866, as saying that the Catholic world has the right to demand the Pope's freedom. Optimistic, Zahm believed the "prisoner of the Vatican" would soon be freed. From Rome, Zahm went to Geneva and purchased "magnificent" equipment for Notre Dame: an apparatus for condensing gases at high pressure, an hydraulic press, and other machines which he believed would be "without superiors" in America.[18]

The two Holy Land visitors arrived back at Notre Dame in January: Zahm, with breviary sets purchased in Rome for his colleagues, Fathers Morrissey, Kirsch, and Stoeffel. Sorin, especially proud, told his associates that the University was held in high esteem among the educated and religious leaders in Rome and other European centers of learning. Zahm took to the lecture platform with a whole new series based on his recent travels; and during the next four years various audiences shared in his observations. In Washington Hall, Notre Dame students viewed Jerusalem, Jaffa, Damascus, and other cities. St. Mary's young ladies saw the Holy Land and Egypt as pictured with stereopticon views. Denver audiences applauded his lectures on the Middle East. As reported in the *Scholastic*, February 7, 1871, students believed that "With Father Zahm as *compagnon de voyage,* no journey could fail of interest."

Notre Dame's small Lemonnier Library profited from Zahm's trips. He donated a treasury of history, religion, and topography books purchased in Alaska, Mexico and the Hawaiian Islands. Another donation in 1888 consisted of several hundred volumes in Spanish by Mexican and Spanish authors.

The subject of religion and science continued to involve Catholic writers and scientists after 1885. Writers still sought to describe the relationship, made difficult by agnostics and atheists, between the two exacting studies. The founder of Notre Dame's Biology Department, Father Alexander M. Kirsch, after his studies in biology at Louvain, wrote again on this subject. He emphasized that previous to the nineteenth century, religion had been attacked on its own ground, that is, philosophy, scripture, or theology. However, some men under the name of science sought to explain religious events and beliefs by purely physical formulas. Objecting to the bitter Biblical criticism, he complained that Renan removed God's divinity by philology; Semler and Eichborn explained miracles with physics; Lyell called Moses a poor historian on the basis of geology; Huxley stated that life was a property of some matter called protoplasm, and Tyndall predicated that matter had the potential of every form and quality of life.[19] In the name of science, Kirsch rejected these warped views, and in succeeding articles, he noted the blind faith that people foolishly posited with certain scientists. Regarding Darwin's thesis, Kirsch believed that different causes may have accounted for the origin of species—that natural selection, survival of the

fittest, and struggle for existence were not the only possible
choices.

Realistically, Kirsch concluded his ideas on the relations
of science and theology by stating that the best remedy for
counteracting the evil influences of the materialistic scientific doctrines

> is for the defenders of orthodox doctrines in science to rise
> to a level with the intellectual scientific standard of their op-
> ponents and when thus completely prepared, let the battle be
> fought on purely scientific grounds—religion has nothing to
> do with the question. Until this mode of warfare be adopted,
> we shall have to dread and deplore the fatal ravages caused
> by misinterpreted science.[20]

It was this method of defense that Zahm followed in his
lectures and writing on science and religion. He sought to
answer the involved questions with a scholarly objectivity
both scientific and historical, and in so doing, he became
for many, a popular defender of the Catholic Church.

The Indianapolis *Journal* credited Zahm with being the
first Catholic priest to have lectured on the Sunday Lecture
Program at the University of Indiana. After a personal invitation from Dr. Louis Jordan, President of the University,
he spoke on "The Catholic Church and Modern Science."
Zahm's remarks followed the pattern of his earlier written
work on this subject—that the Church and true science were
not opposed and the great conflict was between scientists.[21]
The newspaper, Bloomington *Progress,* reviewing the lecture, praised his scholarship and as well, the Catholic
Church, because of the excellent training which it provided
for her clergy. With rather critical words, the newspaper
continued, "Unlike many a Protestant minister, Father
Zahm knew what he believed, where he got his belief, and
how to sustain himself in the same." [22] Too, it congratulated the Church and its disciple for allowing no conces-
sions to infidelity, skepticism or the vagaries of science; and
finally, it judged that "this is the secret of the power and
advancement of the Catholic Church."

Notre Dame audiences learned more of modern science

and its errors through Zahm's discussions in his Science Hall. Discarding the previous talks on physics and chemistry, he turned with vigor to the field of scientific dogmatism. Most of the lectures first presented on the campus later became magazine articles. In April, 1887, Zahm told his student audience that many modern scientists had not been guided by Revelation and metaphysics and therefore, men like Charles Darwin and Ernst Haeckel oftentimes gave only provisional theories or nebulous conjectures in their scientific accounts of the world's growth. Rather carefully, he contrasted their ideas and teaching with those of Christian scientists and thanked the latter for their realistic judgments.[23]

In July, 1890, Zahm, for the first time, reached a large Catholic national audience with an article, "Catholic Dogma and Scientific Dogmatism," published in the *American Catholic Quarterly Review*. With historical perception, he offered the premise that the Catholic Church was the friend, defender and guide of science, since of all religious denominations, it alone could teach the truths of faith without contradicting the definitive declarations of science. Zahm went on to say that Catholic scientists from Galileo and Pascal to the present decade realized the limits of inductive philosophy and accepted Christian metaphysics and divine revelation as more trustworthy teachers. Tyndall, Huxley, Darwin and Haeckel, he found, were merely using the principles of the Protestant Reformers in their denial of authority. Sharply, he dismissed Tyndall as an intellectual pigmy and wrote that although Huxley, Darwin and Haeckel were excellent observers of facts and phenomena, they were extremely unskilled logicians. Their disciples and followers were likewise impoverished by a lack of fundamental logic.[24]

Zahm wrote, however, that he was much more concerned with the great reputation of infallibility that these teachers and apostles of science possessed in matters of philosophy and religion. These men were teaching a science which subverted morality, religion, the immortality of the soul, and the existence of a personal God. Too, he feared the acceptance of Darwin as a messiah and Darwinism as the "Gospel of Modern Times." His vehement attack on the generals of science concluded with a final barrage at those who shamelessly exchanged a person's faith for atheism. This essay was noteworthy in that it placed the warfare between science and religion completely on the Protestant field of battle. With only partial accuracy, he attributed all the errors of modern science to the sixteenth-century reformers and insisted that the Catholic Church was innocent of any of these philosophical and scientific mistakes. In another article three months later, he more distinctly stated his principle:

> The friends of the Church, of revelation, of sound doctrine, have ever been the friends of true science. On the other hand, science has known no greater foes than these who have actively opposed the Church, denied her dogmas, or called in question her divine origin.[25]

Using historical evidence, Zahm noted how reforming theologians had weakened education and true science and how French and Italian scientific academies were more free of this stigma than the Royal Academy in England.[26]

As a result of his first book, *Sound and Music,* published in 1892, Zahm's reputation as a physicist grew by leaps and bounds with the reading American public and the Catholic hierarchy. The book was the product of his study of acoustics and the physical basis for musical harmony. Preliminary plans for his series of illustrated lectures on acoustics at Catholic University were made during the latter months of 1890 after an invitation from Bishop John J. Keane, rector of the newly-founded graduate school. Delighted with the recent arrival of over two thousand dollars' worth of superb sound apparatus from Paris, he thought this addition, together with what he had already had in his physical cabinet would make the lectures interesting and instructive. As he wrote to Keane:

> I think I can now safely say that I have the most complete collection of acoustical apparatus in the United States. I am

sure you will be pleased with them and I trust my hearers
will be equally pleased with my lectures. I shall do my best
to give the latest results of the researches conducted in the
domain of physical acoustics and musical harmony.[27]

He realized the possible dullness of the topics he would
cover; however, he promised that though "The subjects look
dry and uninteresting, I feel certain that when illustrated
by experiments they will be the very opposite." [28] And thus,
though he dreaded the task, he began the difficult job of
crating the expensive and delicate instruments for his show.

In April, 1891, Zahm traveled east to Washington, D.C.,
confident that the lectures would be well received. He was
correct. The *Catholic Standard* of Philadelphia wrote:

> Father Zahm's reputation as a scientist and a lecturer is well
> established in non-Catholic as well as Catholic circles; and
> the fact that in him we possess one of the best equipped
> scientists in the country to-day is one of the strongest refu-
> tations of the charge that our Catholic educational institu-
> tions do not keep pace with the scientific progress of the
> age.[29]

The Boston *Republic* and the Washington *Post* also congratulated Zahm.[30]

In publishing *Sound and Music,* Zahm gave his readers
an exact knowledge of the principles of acoustics and a brief
exposition of the physical basis of musical harmony. Privately, he wrote Keane that he also sought honor for Notre
Dame and Catholic University.[31]

Many reviewers praised the book and critics of leading
magazines and newspapers thought its author a skilled man
of science. Boston's *Literary World* believed that the volume
was on a par with Professor Tyndall's lecture on Sound.[32]
The *Scientific American* found it to be "an extraordinary
book by one of our foremost workers in science." [33] The
Musical Courier of New York endorsed the book, "the most
complete book of its sort in English—Helmholtz up to date,
in fact." [34] The *Atlantic Monthly's* review told its readers
the book was, in effect, highly satisfying and the author

more humble and less autocratic than most acousticians![35]
The Chicago *Tribune* believed "No one will question that
'Sound and Music' is the most elaborate and exhaustive
work of its kind American musical scholarship has yet produced."[36]

Out of the maze of reviews, perhaps the critic of the
North-Western Chronicle of St. Paul, Minnesota, saw the
wider implications of this study, for he wrote:

> The work reflects honor on the author, the well-known Uni-
> versity of Notre Dame, and the Catholic priesthood; espe-
> cially in our advanced age and country, it is of great con-
> sequence that Catholic priests should in all departments of
> science be found in the foremost ranks of the leaders of true
> modern progress.[37]

It was a wise evaluation for it measured the needs of American Catholicism at that time.

Almost self-consciously, the American Catholic hierarchy
congratulated him. Bishop Spalding of Peoria praised him
and wished for more American priests to take up scientific subjects in such a thorough and impartial manner.
Archbishop Ireland thought the author gave great honor
to the Church and her clergy by the complete investiga-
tion. Others, such as Bishops Keane, Elder, Katzer, and
Ryan, also thanked him for their copies of *Sound and Music*. By 1896, over 750 had been sold. It went into a second
edition in 1900.[38]

The year 1892 not only marked the publication of *Sound
and Music;* it also bordered the end of an era in Zahm's
world. His enthusiastic endeavors at Notre Dame ceased
temporarily. In that year Father Andrew Morrissey replaced
him as Vice-President of the University. Then, too, the student trips which he had inaugurated in Ohio in 1880 and
directed to the Southwest since 1882 were no longer under
his personal command. During those years he had, with one
exception, personally supervised each September and June
trip. In June, 1892, Father Thomas E. Walsh made the arrangements for the students' return under the guidance of

two faculty members. In September, Morrissey and Professor C. Neil brought the students from Colorado.[39]

Finally, the appearance of *Sound and Music* made Zahm's reputation more national in character. As a Catholic priest, writer, and lecturer, he proved himself a popular and learned man: before the ranks of American Catholics he took on leadership, nation-wide in appeal, and primarily constructive in emphasis. And at the same time his awareness of earthly progress through applied science marked him as a skilled observer of his times. The tedious making of a "Padua or Bologna" and of a popular apologist moved ahead.

NOTES TO CHAPTER III

1. *Scholastic,* September 14, 1889. St. Mary's College enrolled twenty-four Colorado students. *Ibid.,* September 14, 1889. The Denver *News,* September 8, 1887, story as reprinted in *ibid.,* September 17, 1887, stated that approximately fifty-one students for Notre Dame and nine for St. Mary's College departed. It is estimated that there would be about seventy-five students after the delegations at Colorado Springs, Pueblo, and La Junta joined the group. Notre Dame's enrollment at this time was about four hundred. *Ibid.,* March 12, 1887.

2. *Ibid.,* March 29, 1890.

3. *Ibid.,* May 7, 1892.

4. Reprinted in *ibid.,* January 4, 1890.

5. Reprinted in *ibid.,* November 21, 1885.

6. Reprinted in *ibid.,* March 26, 1887.

7. *Ibid.,* January 9, 1886.

8. *Ibid.,* June 2, 1888.

9. Reverend James A. Burns, *Catholic Education: A Study of Conditions* (New York, 1917), pp. 150-52.

10. Zahm to Albert Zahm, November 8, 1889. Albert Zahm Collection, UNDA.

11. Zahm to Albert Zahm, February 26, 1890. Albert Zahm Collection, UNDA.

12. These letters were printed in *loc. cit.,* October 17, October 31 and November 7, 1885, and also in pamphlet form. Father Zahm may have gone with Charles Warren Stoddard to Alaska although neither of them mentioned the other as a companion. Cf. Charles Warren Stoddard, *Over the Rocky Mountains to Alaska* (St. Louis, 1899). Reverend Kerndt M. Healy, "Father Zahm, Priest and Scientist." *America,*

26 (December 13, 1921), pp. 154-56, noted that the two of them made the trip together.

13. This was a rare public political statement by Zahm whose father was a fervent Democrat. Interview with Pius Zahm, March 28, 1954. Zahm was in good company in his criticism: John Quincy Adams thought Americans could till the soil better than the Englishmen; Theodore Roosevelt said: "We were the people who could use it best, and we ought to have taken it all . . ." as quoted in Albert K. Weinberg, *Manifest Destiny: A Study of Nationalist Expansionism in American History* (Baltimore, 1935), p. 158.

14. *Loc. cit.,* October 31, 1885.

15. These letters were printed in the *Rocky Mountain News* during the summer of 1886 and later reprinted in the Notre Dame *Scholastic,* December 11, 1886; January 22, 1887; February 5, 1887; February 12, 1887; February 19, 1887; February 26, 1887 and also reprinted in pamphlet form as *Letters from the Hawaiian Islands* (Notre Dame, 1887).

16. *Loc. cit.,* November 19, 1887. Zahm's diary of the trip is in the Provincial Archives. The *Rocky Mountain News* published his travel reports in early 1888.

17. Reprinted in the Notre Dame *Scholastic,* February 18, 1888. Also see Leadville *Chronicle,* August 21, 1888, and Zahm's diary of the trip in PA.

18. Zahm to Albert Zahm, January 8, 1888. Albert Zahm Collection, UNDA.

19. Notre Dame *Scholastic,* January 23, 1886.

20. *Ibid.,* January 30, 1886.

21. Indianapolis *Journal* as reprinted in *ibid.,* January 23, 1887.

22. Bloomington *Progress* as reprinted in *ibid.,* February 19, 1887.

23. *Ibid.,* April 30, 1887. This lecture, it appears, became his essay, "Catholic Dogma and Scientific Dogmatism," in the July, 1890, issue of the *American Catholic Quarterly Review.*

24. One of these disciples was Paul Bert. Previously Zahm had noted Bert's lack of Christianity in an introduction which he wrote to Maurice Egan's translation of Bert's *First Steps in Science* (New York, 1889). Zahm praised Egan's interpretation of science for it was truly Christian. Bert's book had lacked this orientation.

25. Reverend John A. Zahm, "The Friends and Foes of Science," *American Catholic Quarterly Review,* XV (October, 1890), 630.

26. Zahm even employed Andrew D. White's book, *History of the Warfare of Science with Theology in Christendom* (New York, 1898), to prove some of his assertions. A far different view of this celebrated book and its author was taken by the *Scholastic,* August 25, 1892, when it urged Dr. White to take his book with him to Russia for it would "be a relief to his fellow-citizens."

27. Zahm to Keane, January 7, 1891, Microfilm Copy, ACUA.

28. Zahm to Keane, March 19, 1891, and March 30, 1891, Copy, ACUA.

29. Reprinted in the Notre Dame *Scholastic*, May 16, 1891.

30. Boston *Republic* article reprinted in *ibid.*, April 11, 1891; and Washington *Post* story reprinted in *ibid.*, April 25, 1891.

31. Zahm to Keane, May 1, 1892. Copy, ACUA.

32. Reprinted in *loc. cit.*, April 29, 1893.

33. As quoted in *ibid.*, February 18, 1893.

34. As quoted in *ibid.*, February 13, 1893.

35. *Atlantic Monthly*, 72 (October, 1893), 560.

36. As quoted in *loc. cit.*, February 18, 1893.

37. As reprinted in *ibid.*, May 13, 1893.

38. McClurg Publishers to Zahm, July 8, 1896. PA.

39. *Loc. cit.*, September 17, 1892. The following June trip was reported merely as "Shorty took the 'Denver Crowd' home." *Ibid.*, June 24, 1893. This report was a great change from the days when the trip rated at least a full page story written by one of the returning students.

IV

Famous Apologist for Science and
Catholic Dogma, 1892-1896

"A Great Mission Before Me"

Writing from St. Patrick's Cathedral rectory in New York City, as the guest of Archbishop Michael A. Corrigan, Zahm proudly reported that his articles on faith and science in the *American Catholic Quarterly Review, Donahoe's Magazine* and the *North American Review* had attracted wide attention in the East among Catholics and Protestants alike and were considered good advertisements for Notre Dame. The *North American Review*, the best magazine of its class in the world, he continued, gave him an audience of a half-million readers and as a result he was getting numerous requests for contributions to Catholic and non-Catholic magazines. Zahm concluded his letter to the Superior General with prophetic words.

> I . . . am beginning to feel that I have a great mission before me in making known to the Protestant world the true relation of Catholic dogma towards modern science—this is surely a fertile field to labor in, & I trust I may be given the health & strength necessary for the work.[1]

With the zeal of Urban II, Zahm began an energetic crusade of education; teaching Catholic dogma in the light of recent scientific discoveries, and as well, publicizing famous scientists who were exemplary Catholics. During the four years, 1892-1896, Zahm reached the peak of his production as a lecturer and writer on science-religion subjects [2]—he lectured before thousands of Catholic Summer and Winter School students, was publicized in dozens of Catholic and non-Catholic magazines and newspapers while his learned books touched off a bitter controversy. Even amidst the roar of heated arguments concerning temperance and the American Protective Association and the countless columns in magazines and newspapers covering these controversial topics, he was heard and judged newsworthy. During these years, Zahm became the most widely known American Catholic priest engaged in investigating the theology of evolution. While his popular investigations distressed and alienated many conservative Catholics who accepted only the traditional interpretation of dogma, he won the approval of most liberal students during this nervous age of skepticism.

On May 21, 1892, it was formally announced that Zahm had been invited by the Catholic Summer School Committee to deliver a course of lectures on "Science and Revealed Religion" to a hoped-for assembly of four hundred students. Cardinal Gibbons and Archbishop Corrigan had also been invited. However, at the request of Sorin, Zahm refused the offer and shared the summer with his Superior at Nantucket, Massachusetts, where the sea air and warm sunshine brought about the relaxation sought by the ageing Superior General. Zahm also spent his days on the seashore and planned some tentative summer school courses. He was not very familiar with the objectives of the new movement, as was indicated in his letter to Father Joseph H. McMahon in which he asked whether the lectures should be on the popular level.[3]

Probably he became interested in the Catholic summer school movement, which was modeled after the Chautauqua success, through the influence of Maurice Francis Egan. A New York *Tribune* article said that Egan was probably the first to suggest an institution for Catholics similar to Chautauqua.[4] Egan had come to Notre Dame in 1888 at the express invitation of President Thomas Walsh as Professor of English Literature. Born in Philadelphia, 1852, he became associate editor of the *Freeman's Journal* in 1881, and in

1887, editor and part owner.[5] During his Notre Dame career, he enjoyed the stimulation of intellectual discussions held at his home, "The Lilacs," with Fathers Walsh, Hudson, and Zahm.

In an organizational meeting held in New York City during May, 1892, Reverend Morgan F. Sheedy of Pittsburgh was chosen president of the projected Catholic Summer School by George F. Lathrop, John A. Mooney, Brother Azarias and Reverend John Talbot Smith. Reverend John F. Mullaney of Syracuse, Reverend Joseph McMahon of New York City, Mr. Thomas McMillan, Warren Mosher and George Hardy also devoted themselves to inaugurating this Catholic coeducational venture in adult education.

Warren E. Mosher, editor of the *Catholic Reading Circle Review* and secretary of the Catholic Chautauqua movement, had organized the Catholic Educational Union with the express idea of a summer school assembly.[6] With favorable coverage from the Catholic press and clergy, Mr. Mosher called the first summer school into session at New London, Connecticut, in 1892. Notre Dame's only faculty representative that summer was Egan who lectured on Shakespeare to students of varied intellectual levels. Shortly after the close of this session, Zahm was officially notified that he had been appointed Dean of the Faculty of Science for the projected Catholic Winter School. However, as it happened, the first Winter School did not meet until 1896.

Almost five hundred people from sixteen states gathered together on Sunday, July 16, 1893, when the Catholic Summer School, using Weed's Theatre and St. John's Church, was called into session at Plattsburg, New York. Zahm presented five lectures on Science and Revealed Religion.[7] As it happened, these lectures touched off his rise to fame and began the heavily publicized association of his name with the science and religion controversy in America. Other lecturers at the second annual summer session included Reverend James A. Doonan, S.J., Very Reverend Augustine F. Hewit, C.S.P., Thomas Harrison Cummings, Richard Malcolm Johnston, and Major John Byrne. However, the Notre

Dame priest, publicized as the friend of Pasteur, was considered the star lecturer and "Mivart of America" because
of his advanced position regarding the relation of science
and theology. Rabbi Veld, pastor of Temple Emmanuel, a
wealthy and influential Reformed Jewish Congregation in
Montreal, attended the opening lectures because of his scholarly interest in the subjects offered; after he heard the lectures of Doonan, who was from Boston College, and Zahm,
he decided to remain for the entire session. He related during an interview with a reporter of the New York *Sun:*

> In listening to Father Zahm's exposition of the relation of
> science to revealed religion I frequently said to myself that
> the Messianic period is not only at hand, but we are almost
> in the midst of it. I could see how critically Father Zahm had
> examined many of our old Hebrew authorities, especially the
> Talmudists. So deeply impressed am I with Dr. [sic] Zahm's
> researches that I have been impelled to pay tribute to his
> erudition by delivering next Saturday in the Plattsburg syna-
> gogue a sermon which I have called 'Dr. Zahm Endorsed.' " [8]

Zahm was very pleased with the thrilling teaching experience at the summer session. He confided to his young
protégé, newly-ordained Reverend James A. Burns, C.S.C.,
that "My audiences increased daily & the last lecture was
the occasion of quite an ovation. More than this a large
number wanted me to repeat the course, or continue lecturing on a similar subject." [9] In an interview with a *Catholic Times* reporter, Zahm replied, when questioned on his
liberal views, that only people who were backward in Biblical studies or had neither heard nor read his lectures would
hint that he was "advanced." Rather, he continued, "The
conclusions of my articles in the *American Catholic Quarterly Review* and at the School have been familiar to
me and to every Catholic Biblical 'scientist' . . . for many
years. I have simply restated them and grouped old opinions and new illustrations about them." [10]

A reporter for the *Sun* wrote that Zahm had startled his
audience on the morning of July 21 when he denied the

universality of the Flood and gave arguments for proof: then this reporter quoted at great length from Zahm's lectures defining this position.[11]

In a Sunday editorial on July 23, 1893, the editor of the New York *Daily Tribune* wrote that the priest's lectures were extraordinary and showed how "profoundly even Catholicism is being affected by modern thought." The editor also thought the lectures proved that Catholicism had awakened to modern research with its concurrent scientific problems. Zahm's ideas on the Deluge, that it was local, was opposed, said the editor, to the almost unbroken tradition of the Church—"One might suppose that in a Church as conservative as the Catholic, which pays so much deference to traditional teachings, there would be no attempt made to modify the ancient views on this question in order to make them conform to the conclusions of science." Continuing with this fundamentalist philosophy, the writer thought that Catholicism was revealing a strong desire to be on sympathetic terms with modern thought and, as such, the Church was attempting to revise and restate non-dogmatic doctrines in the light of present knowledge. Therefore, he said, the more intelligent Christians would not be alienated by the ignorant rantings of clergymen intent upon destroying straw soldiers. Zahm's lecture on the Deluge, he concluded, clearly exemplified the advanced thinking:

> The dead matter and surplusage of past ages is being dropped or worked over. At times there are conservative protests; but the tendency is so irresistible that no opposition can stop it. As we see it, it is actively in operation in the most conservative of all the Churches.

Many others who attended the lectures during the warm July days called him the "St. George Mivart of America"—especially because of his views on the Deluge and the antiquity of man.[12] The name was to stay with him during the three years that he participated in the Catholic summer and winter school circuit. Thus, his first lecture series at Plattsburg brought him into the national spotlight among both Catholics and Protestants, and for that matter, those of the Jewish faith. Exhausted and bound for Europe a week after his lectures, Zahm wrote that his ideas had evoked considerable heat—"Didn't I stir up the bears? All enthusiastic over them, but they considered me very daring & ultra liberal. Probably the smoke shall have cleared away by the time I return." [13] It was satisfying to be heard as a learned Catholic priest and apologist of the Church. As he believed, his mission in making known the true relation of Catholic dogma towards modern science had indeed commenced at Plattsburg.

Students in the summer school courses were in many instances different from those in college. At first, Zahm overestimated their ability, even after the Plattsburg lectures, for he suggested in a letter, published in the *Catholic Citizen,* August 18, 1894, to the editor, Humphrey J. Desmond, that a future summer school should introduce studies in art, ancient history, literature, and the famous research by Pasteur, Gilmary Shea, and Garcia Icazbalceta. Desmond, more aware of the students' talents and purpose, thought Zahm's topics were too learned for the average man and woman on a "summer jaunt," especially since few lecturers compared with Zahm in combining profound scholarship with popular exposition.

Some other editors were downright pessimistic about the students' ability and the whole summer school movement. For example, William Henry Thorne, a caustic critic of the summer school movement, and of almost every other phase of modern religious and national life, cynically predicted that like the bicycle fad, the summer school fad would run itself out. "Both are evolutions of modern genius, and the one bears about as much relation to Catholic culture as the other—that relation being, as near as I can see, a minus quantity, or, at best, a giddy absurdity on wheels." [14] With exaggeration, Thorne wrote that the summer schools were a "spendthrift temporary fad, with courtship and matrimonial bureau attachments." Rather, he said, the money could be better used by him and the *Globe* to make it a highly respectable magazine for the intelligent American Catholic citizens.

Despite the criticism displayed by Thorne and others, summer school proponents sought to expand the venture. The birth of a Western Catholic Summer School took place in the late spring of 1894. The originators, Zahm, Desmond, and Egan, were very optimistic. According to the *Catholic Citizen,* July 28, 1894, many Middle Western Catholics had appealed to Zahm and Egan for just such a school, carefully explained as a twin but not a rival to distant Plattsburg. Rather than compete with the Eastern Summer School, the new school, according to Zahm, would increase interest in such education, for the United States was large enough for three or four summer schools. At a meeting held in Chicago on June 14, 1894, Catholic laymen and religious leaders convened to plan the Western Summer School: with interest they listened to the financial and scholastic plans for this venture as explained by Zahm and Egan.

A few months later, Zahm consented to serve on the executive committee and was formally appointed, along with Bishop Sebastian Messmer of Green Bay, Father Michael Hughes, S.J., of St. Louis, Maurice F. Egan and Conde B. Pallen of St. Louis.[15] The Committee on Studies for the Columbian Catholic Summer School met again in Chicago at the Columbus Club on December 28, 1894. Present when Chairman Messmer called the meeting to order were Reverend James F. X. Hoeffer, S.J., rector of St. Ignatius College, Chicago; Conde B. Pallen; Reverend P. J. Agnew, Chicago; William A. Amberg, President of the Columbus Club; Charles A. Mair and William J. Onahan of Chicago; Desmond, and Zahm. Zahm had just returned from Europe and the Brussels International Catholic Scientific Congress. He gave assurance of cooperation in the new venture by the Chief of the Bollandists, Reverend Charles De Smedt, S.J., and Marquis de Nadaillac. The decisions by the committee, according to the *Catholic Citizen,* January 5, 1895, included an invitation to Msgr. Satolli to preside at the opening session on Sunday, July 14; to Archbishop Ireland to give the opening sermon, and to Bishop Maes, the evening sermon. Ticket prices for the full session were set at five dollars; or twenty-five cents per single lecture. The last major decision concerned the school's location. After considering various large cities in Michigan, Illinois and Wisconsin, the committee chose the latter state's capital, Madison, because of its location in a cool pleasant lake area, the availability of libraries and especially its proximity to Milwaukee and Chicago.

On July 14 at the inaugural session of the Columbian Summer School at Madison an audience estimated at almost four hundred, mostly young women, listened to the message of blessing and approval of the school sent by His Holiness, Pope Leo XIII.[16] Formal welcoming ceremonies continued during the next day from the stage of the Fuller Opera House with Messmer, William J. Onahan and Charles A. Mair, together with former Attorney-General J. L. O'Connor and John V. Leary of Madison, participating. In reply to the greetings extended by Governor W. H. Upham and Senator William Vilas, Messmer said humorously, as reported in the *Catholic Citizen,* July 20, that the school most definitely was not going into politics. Also, aware of the tensions of the time, he asserted: "Our Summer School will issue no declarations of war against science and modern theories of progress. Our Church is in favor of all this. Our presence here is a proof that she has gauged her part in the intellectual movement of the day."

Three comprehensive lectures that first Monday to over four hundred students began with Reverend Patrick J. Danehy, Professor of Scripture at The St. Paul Seminary in Minnesota, who spoke on "The Origin and Development of the Canon" at the 9 A.M. session. Zahm delivered his, on "Some Scientific Errors" at 10:30 A.M.; and Reverend Eugene Magevney, S.J., of Detroit concluded the day's series with a lecture on education. It was clearly apparent that Zahm's Plattsburg's fame and the honorary doctor's degree, bestowed by Pope Leo XIII in February, made him the "star attraction." [17] His comprehensive lecture questioned

the understanding of evolution in modern society, he unequivocally stated that Darwinism was not evolution but
rather only one *modus operandi*. To his questioning audience, he again clearly emphasized that the contradictions re-
volving about faith and evolution resulted from the misap-
prehension of terms or from attempts by some to exploit
their pet theories at the expense of religion and dogma.
Repeatedly, he urged his audience to consider carefully the
reasonable position of science.[18]

A larger student body attended the second day's sessions
to hear Danehy's liberal lecture on "The Inspired Record
of Revelation" in which he surprised some summer school
enthusiasts by noting that the Church accepted some Books
as inspired that were previously rejected by early saints and
philosophers, but that the Church also rejected some they
had accepted previously. John G. Ewing, Professor at Notre
Dame, pleased an evening audience with his historical
topic, "The Magna Charta and the Church." His friend and
fellow professor, Zahm, chose as his topic, "Agnosticism,"
and in the course of the lecture he described the major
proofs for the existence of a Creator on the basis of order
and design in the universe.[19]

Lectures during the first two days provoked little discussion as the summer school operated smoothly. The calm
broke on Wednesday, however, with Zahm's third lecture,
"Contemporary Evolution," and subsequent publicity emphasized his statement that the theory of evolution was not
in contradiction with the Church's position on the development of man. The story in the July 18 Milwaukee *Sentinel*
was headed with large bold-face type, "Dr. Zahm on Evolution":

> This is a novel stand for a clergyman, especially one of the
> Catholic faith to take, and it was considerable surprise to
> many high dignitaries of that Church present at the lecture.

Actually the lecture was largely an historical review of
the views on evolution held by early churchmen and philosophers such as St. Gregory of Nyssa, St. Augustine, and St.

Thomas Aquinas. According to Zahm's lecture, these saintly scholars all accepted theistic evolution and taught that God created primordial and inorganic matter in various forms. Rocks, crystals, and minerals were created by secondary causes. These liberal, to some, novel, thoughts were probably the topic of considerable discussion during the next day, Thursday, which was formally termed as Excursion Day.

On Friday, a large, curious audience crowded around Zahm's lecture platform, and perhaps a few recalled the popularity of Galileo's discourses. They were not disappointed for Zahm had chosen to speak on one of the most delicate aspects of the whole evolution question—"The Simian Origin of Man." Undoubtedly some were surprised when he announced that there was nothing in dogma to preclude the view that man was descended from an anthropoid ape or another animal. Some listeners objected and thought him too radical: they rebelled further when he explained that St. George Mivart wrote that the evolution of man's body and the subsequent infusion of a rational soul by God was not antagonistic to the teaching of St. Thomas. Carefully, however, Zahm related that this position involved some obstacles in the domain of Biblical exegesis and metaphysics. Wishing to quiet the skeptical, he emphasized that Mivart's theory as first developed in his book, *Genesis of Species*, published in 1871, had never been condemned, and furthermore, the book had not been placed on the Index as dangerous or heretical. Further, according to the July 27 *Catholic Citizen*, he told his listeners it was conceivable that with the development of more delicate instruments of observation, it might be possible to show that spontaneous generation not only could, but did occur daily in millions of cases in minute forms of life. Continuing, he said that the soul was directly and immediately created by God and whatever verdict science may have regarding man's body, it could not be in opposition to Catholic dogma.

On Saturday, summing up his position on evolution, he again emphasized that evolution was not a new theory, that it had been spoken of in the days of Aristotle; modern research had only added details and illustrated the theory.

Properly understood, evolution could be a strong and useful ally of Catholic dogma.[20]

Zahm, reported the Chicago *Time-Herald* on July 27, had "rippled the sea of religious discussion and . . . his liberal views startled his audiences because they came from a learned Roman Catholic scholar." Although acquaintances had said he was somewhat exclusive, the reporter said he presented "most affable manners and a pleasing character, free from the airs and affectations of men who become suddenly noted in the public eyes and, at the same time, in their own." Another reported that Zahm was thoroughly courageous in his convictions and though conservative, did not hesitate to destroy prejudice and false tradition. Moreover, in the patriotic decade of the nineties, Zahm's Americanism was very impressive.[21]

Without question, these Madison lectures produced some sensational reports in the secular press as well as in Catholic discussions. A friendly Catholic observer on the scene reported that the priest was credited in the secular press with a more extreme position than he had actually taken; however, he continued, when his manuscript was examined, it would be found that he had made all the precise qualifications that were necessary to keep him within orthodox limits.[22] Adverse criticism of his ideas was attributed by some self-styled judges as resulting not so much from his liberality of thought on evolution as to his liberal interpretations of the writings of St. Thomas.[23] Some bitter comments were published. Reverend J. W. Vahey of Chicago, in an open letter to the editor of the *Catholic Citizen,* published August 17, termed Zahm an agnostic scientist!

To the defense of the Holy Cross priest rushed his friend Reverend John Gmeiner, who shared a number of Zahm's ideas. From his office in St. Thomas Seminary, St. Paul, Minnesota, the former professor at St. Francis Seminary in Milwaukee proclaimed in the *Catholic Citizen* on August 24:

Years ago I already held, and still do hold the views advocated by Dr. Zahm with which Father Vahey finds fault. These views I maintained in a paper read before the Catholic International Scientific Congress held at Paris in 1888, and I have still to hear that any real Catholic scientist who is abreast of the science of the age has found any fault with my views.

Concluding this defense, he asked the readers to study his own book, *Mediaeval and Modern Cosmology,* for a substantiation of his views and then put him in company with Dr. Zahm as an agnostic, heretic or what not!

Another Catholic newspaper was friendly to Zahm's ideas. The editor of the *Catholic Sun,* describing his livid opponents as making "monkeys out of themselves," haphazardly dismissed the young and old defenders who rushed to protect the Church from imagined dangers—"They pronounce Zahm a heretic because he did not take a load of the musty tomes of the Fathers with him to the Summer School and tell the people that St. Augustine held this opinion but he was contradicted by St. Ambrose who held the opposite opinion." [24] An echo of those famous hectic summer school days was heard when some months later, Mr. John Nader from Madison wrote that Zahm's lectures were "an exhibit far in advance of most of our best thinkers; yet withal, he was, on account of misrepresentation, subject to criticism amounting to indignity." [25] Accurately, he judged that too many people, uneducated in theology and science, criticized with neither knowledge nor understanding during those celebrated days of the first Columbian Catholic Summer School in Madison, Wisconsin.[26]

Less than two weeks after his lectures at Madison, Zahm spoke at the Plattsburg Summer School and again attracted large audiences with his lectures, thus competing successfully with Colonel Richard Malcolm Johnston's discussion on "The Novel" and Abbe Hogan's lectures on "French Literature." This fourth week of the eastern summer school opened, said the New York *Daily Tribune,* July 30, with a boom when Reverend Herman J. Heuser spoke on "The Bible" and Zahm on "Evolution." Again, Zahm spoke of theistic evolution; however, he let it be known rather quickly that "It is not my purpose to write a treatise on the subject, but merely to indicate . . . that there is nothing in evolution, properly understood, which is contrary to Church doctrine.[27] On Friday, August 2, he concluded his lectures and with them closed the most successful week of the 1895 session.

On August 4, 1895, the Sunday edition of the New York *Herald* carried a page five story designed to be sensational and headlined, "Is Dr. Zahm a Heretic?" Under eye-catching sub-headings such as "Lectures of the Eminent Catholic Divine at Plattsburg School Create a Sensation," "Defender of Evolution," "He says the Conclusions of Modern Science Are Not Hostile to Church Dogmas," and "Another St. George Mivart," the reporter wrote an account of the popular lectures. Admitting that the Notre Dame professor came out of the West with a well-established reputation for extreme liberalism, he continued his report by noting that some of the more conservative Catholics "breathe hints of heresy" and a few would even be disappointed if the apologist's alleged unorthodoxy did not become the basis of a Church trial and dogmatic scandal. The *Herald* reporter then wrote that some unfriendly observers stated that Zahm, like St. George Mivart, who had also received a Ph.D. *motu proprio* from the Vatican (Pope Pius IX gave him the degree in 1876) and was later reprimanded for his unorthodox utterances, would likely be called to task; however, Zahm did not fear this possibility. Similar to other summaries of the lecturer's position, the report emphasized that Zahm's ideas were not new or startling in the world of science; rather, they commanded attention because they came from an eminent Roman Catholic priest who obviously enjoyed the favor of the Holy See. Thus, Zahm accepted certain conclusions of science and affirmed that they were not at variance with legitimate interpretation of the divine record as seen by the studies of St. Thomas Aquinas and St. Gregory of Nyssa. Too, Zahm said that even the seven days of Genesis were not days of twenty-four hours each, the Deluge was not universal, but local, and the history of man on earth began more than six thousand years ago. Finally, these "novelties," according to the reporter, included the priest's insistence that the theory of evolution was far more rational than the theory of special creation; more important, it was in accordance with the teaching of the Church Fathers and Doctors. Lengthy extracts from the lectures, as personally and officially revised by Zahm, covered the latter half of the newspaper account:

> Whether, then, the germ of life was specially created for each individual creature or whether matter was endowed with the power of evolving what we call life by the proper collocation of the atoms and molecules of which matter is constituted, was from their [Church Fathers and Scholastics] point of view immaterial so far as dogma was concerned.

And though no "missing link" or evidence for it has been found

> Analogy and scientific consistency would seem to require us to admit that man's bodily frame has been subject to the same law of evolution, if evolution there has been, as has obtained for the inferior animals. There is nothing in biological science that would necessarily exempt man's corporal structure from the action of this law.

Continuing with carefully guarded observations, Zahm admitted that this theory of evolution of man's body from some inferior animals and the subsequent endowment in this body by God of a rational soul was not antagonistic to any dogma of faith and even would be shown to be in harmony with the teaching of St. Thomas—even though there were grave, although surmountable, difficulties in the area of metaphysics and Biblical exegesis.

> To say evolution is agnostic or atheistic in tendency, if not in fact, is to betray a lamentable ignorance of what it actually teaches, and to display a singular incapacity for comprehending the relation of a scientific induction to a philosophical—or, more truthfully, an anti-philosophical system. Never in the history of science have thoughtful students felt more the necessity of recognizing a personal creator, a spiritual, intelligent, first cause than at present. Never has the

divine character of the book of books been so gloriously manifested as it is now after the many and furious onslaughts
made on it in the name of science and the higher criticism.
The very investigations and discoveries which it was fondly
imagined could completely nullify all its claims to being divine revelation, far from destroying such claims, have but
strengthened them and rendered them more logical and consistent.

Thus ended the most complete newspaper report of Father
Zahm's summer school lectures at Plattsburg and, although
not its purpose, the story probably caused further concern
to conservative Catholics and many Fundamentalists who
watched these ideas being publicized in this large New York
journal.

The New York *Freeman's Journal* in a feature story date-
lined August 3, 1895, said Zahm's lectures had been the
sensation of the week and noted that some conservatives
thought he might be reprimanded by Rome because of his
very liberal views. A recent acquaintance of the Notre Dame
priest and editor of the Cincinnati *Catholic Telegraph,* Dr.
Thomas F. Hart, wrote, "The wide advertisement you received in the secular and religious press had added wonderfully to your drawing powers, and you are now one of the
cards of the lecture platform." [28]

These somewhat unpopular explanations of evolution
were the topic of heated discussions among many ecclesias-
tics on the Cliff Haven (Plattsburg) campus. So controversial
was the issue that Father Thomas Conaty, President of the
Summer School, and later Bishop Keane's successor as second Rector of the Catholic University and Bishop of Los
Angeles, felt obliged to announce to the full assembly that
the Catholic Summer School was not responsible for Zahm's
views.[29] And at a reception for Bishop Burke of Albany
held during the session, Conaty said that his school was a
place for Catholic truth—not a field whereby lecturers could
exploit their theories in the interest of sensational notoriety.
Plainly irked by the publicity and excitement, he stated:

"We hope to teach [only] the sound conservative well defined truth of the Catholic Church." [30]

The *Wisconsin Patriot,* an A.P.A. publication, took a dim
view of all this. It believed that in order to please the scientific men at the State University in Madison, the Jesuit [sic]
Zahm told how liberal the Romish Church was and then
later, the Jesuit [sic] Conaty pleased the conservatives in the
Romish Church by denouncing Zahm.[31]

The widely read accounts of Zahm's popular lectures and
supposedly radical departures from Catholic tradition almost halted the western summer school movement. Bishop
Sebastian Messmer, president of the Columbian Catholic
Summer School, wrote in mid-January, 1896, to Father
Thomas O'Gorman and objected to Zahm's arrangement
whereby the Catholic University professors, Father Edward
Pace and O'Gorman, would lecture at the coming summer
school. Messmer related that Zahm as Chairman of the Committee on Study had overstepped his power in assigning
them to this session: rather, the Board of Directors made
decisions of this nature. As well, last year, he wrote, a rule
was formulated that no professors of the Catholic University
could be invited to lecture! As president and a member of
the hierarchy, Messmer apologized for his own sensitivity
and explained that

> having been exposed to a great deal of incrimination last
> year on account of Dr. Zahm's expression on the evolution
> of man, we have to be more careful this year to have no the-
> ories or opinions put forth from our boards which would not
> find acceptance with all.[32]

Actually, the "liberal" O'Gorman had just been appointed
Bishop-elect to Sioux Falls, South Dakota. Messmer, not
certain that newspaper reports of the appointment were
true, offered in a letter to Zahm a compromise whereby
Father O'Gorman might lecture on some non-controversial
topic.[33]

In another letter, Messmer offered Pace no compromise
and unequivocally told him not to lecture at the summer

session because so many American Catholics looked with disfavor upon Catholic University, its Rector and Professors.[34] Add to the names of O'Gorman and Pace, those of Reverend Louis A. Lambert and Mr. Humphrey J. Desmond, complained the Green Bay prelate, and the C.C.S.S. would have the cry of liberalism shouted at it from all sides.[35] Zahm urged Pace to give the lecture and revealed that only Messmer and a layman on the Board of Directors opposed Pace's appointment. If Pace failed to lecture, it would have a bad effect on the Catholic University.[36]

Despite Messmer's concern, Desmond's *Catholic Citizen* for January 25, 1896, confidently publicized that Pace would lecture on "Psychology" and the Bishop-elect of Sioux Falls, O'Gorman, would speak on "The Church and Society in the Middle Ages." Other lecturers and their topics on the preliminary schedule were Reverend P. J. Danehy, who would speak on Sacred Scripture, Colonel Richard Malcolm Johnston, Spanish and French Literature; Reverend Eugene Magevney, S.J., on the History of Education; Reverend John M. Poland, S.J., "The Church and the Social Question"; and Maurice Francis Egan on English Literature. Messmer would lecture on "Pope and Emperor."

Troubled greatly, Messmer wrote again to Zahm and said the situation concerning Pace and O'Gorman had worried him so much that he considered calling a board meeting and resigning: "I stated last year, that with the hour when Liberalism *in any form or shape* [sic] would come into the C.C.S.S. I would step out." [37] He revealed that he was compromising only to help Zahm out of a difficult position. This letter also contained the report that the rector of St. Ignatius College in Chicago and one of the Columbian School's founders, Father James F. X. Hoeffer, S.J., of Chicago, had resigned in protest. Messmer feared that all the Jesuits would follow his lead.

The stern reply that Zahm mailed Messmer left no doubt about his own personal position in this highly sensitive problem which, asserted Zahm, could have been solved if Messmer had abided by the decision reached in the recent board meeting.[38] In logical fashion, Zahm replied that the Board of Studies had sought to choose men of ability and scholarship who would attract large audiences and,

> Speaking for my single self I never knew, until I received your letter, that Drs. O'Gorman & Pace, Fr. Lambert & Desmond were regarded as 'liberals'—Surely the Holy Father would not have made the first a bishop if there had been any doubt about his orthodoxy.

Obviously irked, he wrote that Pace was scrupulously orthodox and so was Desmond who had been Vice-President since the school's beginning. The label of liberalism puzzled him: "I have no disposition to boycotting any man or body of men, because forsooth, he or they may on controverted questions, entertain views different from my own & I think it is a grave mistake that the issue was ever raised." Thus, with that good liberal principle, Zahm concluded his letter. That summer, Pace and O'Gorman lectured at the Madison school.

The last direct experience Zahm had with the popular Catholic adult season schools began at New Orleans, February 16, 1896, at the first Catholic Winter School. Zahm gave substantially the same popular lectures he had delivered the previous summer at Madison and Plattsburg. According to the March 7, *Catholic Citizen,* he was introduced to the large audience as "the best-abused man at the school." Most likely, the news story continued, he would tend to monopolize that title for in spite of his clear explanation of the relations between dogma and science, "he is still obliged to argue many points with individual sceptics as he descends from his rostrum; but his unfailing serenity is bound to prolong his life and preserve him for many years to Notre Dame University." Pleased with the lectures, Zahm returned to Notre Dame extremely enthusiastic about the Winter School in theory and practice.

Although Zahm's fame spread quickly during this time, his writings during these same years brought more lasting acclaim, and in one case, notoriety, than did the popular podium. During these four years, he wrote five books, four pamphlets and twenty-one articles! His theme was twofold: to publicize men who were both faithful Catholics and excellent scientists such as Pasteur; and secondly, to show there was nothing in evolution, rightly understood, to trouble Catholics. Whether his ideas were accepted or rejected they were printed in almost every major Catholic publication and such secular publications as the *North American Review* and the *Popular Science Monthly*.

Of these numerous writings, certain ones stand out as landmarks in Zahm's progress toward a rapprochement between Catholicism and modern science. The whole issue of the March, 1894, *American Ecclesiastical Review* was given over to Zahm's articles, and this rare feat, as he told Albert, produced a sensation at Notre Dame and elsewhere. The articles in the *Review* together with a number of others were printed in a well-documented book entitled, *Bible, Science and Faith*. This book, which tells the story of Creation as found in Genesis and viewed in the light of modern science, presents Zahm's ideas as he first expressed them in 1893 at the Plattsburg summer school, and emphasizes that Moses' cosmogony contained the spirit of Revelation in its every line. Moreover, in this book, Zahm emphasized that Moses' account of creation was in accord with all the certain declarations of science for, according to both sources, God created primitive matter and, after an indefinite period of time, proceeding from the simpler to the more complex, made innumerable forms of the organic and inorganic worlds. As authorities for these assertions, Zahm explained the ideas of St. Gregory of Nyssa, and St. Augustine, especially the latter's belief that God created primordial matter and by action of His physical laws, all forms of terrestrial life resulted: "days," according to St. Augustine, represented the beginning and end of God's work rather than morning and evening.

Dwelling on the alleged universality of the Deluge, Zahm explained that it had not been authoritatively interpreted; therefore, students were free to question it. He doubted its universality and believed instead that it probably affected only Western Asia. Conservatively, Zahm estimated the age of the human race at nine to ten thousand years.

Friendly critics reviewed the book in phrases similar to that in the October, 1894, issue of the *Catholic World* which deemed it a godsend and Zahm, just what "intelligent and inquiring Catholics need, namely, a guide who can be trusted as safe, so that they need not fear to be led astray from faith and orthodoxy." Archbishop Ireland, in characteristic fashion, wrote in a personal letter: "There are many things in common between us, upon which I would love to chat with you. Your books I admire very much—even if some deem them venturesome—perhaps all the more, because they are venturesome." [39] Zahm related that some readers told him they regretted the book had not appeared in the eighteen-sixties; and while a few labeled him a sensationalist, he wished more would do so because then the average American could read his ideas and realize that harmony was possible between religion and science. This book, *Bible, Science and Faith,* became for American Catholics a pivotal summation of ideas on the relationship between the Church and science.[40]

The vast amount of study, lecturing, and writing claimed its toll on Zahm's nervous system. Exhausted after the Plattsburg lectures in 1893, he toured France and Spain hoping for rest and relaxation. Returning in the fall to Notre Dame after the brief interlude in Europe, he plunged back into teaching, planning the Columbian Summer School, and further writing. During the next summer, Dr. Horwitz, Medical Director of the United States Navy, examined him and wrote an alarming report which prescribed complete mental rest:

> The mental pabulum that you need is to be found in travel, change of scene, & change of climate. And above all, do not go near any religious establishment. For recreation try horseback exercise, theatres, the opera . . . You should be out of the U.S. at least two years.[41]

The diagnosis made by the competent Medical Director was that the priest suffered from extreme nervous prostration with a tendency to paralysis brought on by over-work and too conscientious attention to duty. The thorough report concluded with a firm injunction, "He requires *entire and absolute* rest for a period of at least two years; during time [sic] he should not indulge in mental labor of any kind." And travel in foreign countries should speed the recovery.

The priest left a few days later for a three-month stay in Europe and to participate in the Brussels Scientific Congress: the warnings of the doctor were largely disregarded. The conscientious essayist maintained his exhausting pace of explaining Catholicism, Scriptures and science.

World-wide fame attended the well-publicized Zahm at the International Catholic Scientific Congress which brought notables in science from throughout the world for the third triennial sessions beginning on September 4, 1894. According to the *Catholic Citizen* of July 28 he was selected as a delegate from the United States because he was the leading Catholic scientist in the country: the delegate in turn was reported as considering the Congress the most momentous event of its kind since the Vatican Council, 1869-1870.

The scheme of using international Catholic scientific congresses as weapons in the warfare between religion and science originated at Rouen, France, in 1885. The first Congress, composed of six sections, Religion, Philosophy, Law, History, Anthropology and Mathematics, Natural and Physical Sciences, was held with Papal approval in Paris, 1888, under the sponsorship of Bishop Perraud of Autun. The second Congress met in that same intellectual center in 1891.[42]

After arriving in Europe Zahm hastened to Rome where, among other visits, he examined the Vatican Observatory in preparation for a future essay. Shortly before leaving for Brussels, he was received in a special audience by Pope Leo XIII: he personally carried the Holy Father's benediction to the Brussels Congress.[43]

Over two thousand members attended the sessions of the Congress held at the Palais des Académies and the Institut Saint-Louis during September 4-7. More than two hundred learned papers which covered all topics except theology and politics were read and discussed.[44] Famous European churchmen and scientists entered into the lively exchanges: the Cardinal Archbishop of Mechlin, Msgr. Pierre Goossens, President of the Congress; Msgr. Jean Abbeloos, Honorary President; Dr. Lefebvre, President; Reverend Van Den Gheyn, S.J., Secretary; Professor E. Pasquier, Treasurer; also Albert de Lapparent, professor of geology; historian and archaeologist Paul Allard of Rouen; Reverend Charles De Smedt, S.J., Chief of the Bollandists; Msgr. Désiré Mercier, President of Louvain; and Reverend David Fleming, O.F.M., Provincial of the English Franciscans. American representatives included Bishop John J. Keane, Reverend John Gmeiner and Zahm. Bishop Keane addressed the Congress on the controversial "Parliament of Religions" held in Chicago in 1893; Gmeiner of the diocesan seminary at St. Paul, Minnesota, who had attended the first Congress in 1888, read a paper, "Primitive America," before the anthropological section.

Zahm's address before the entire Congress, on the fourth and last day, at the Palais des Académies, dealt with the failure of seminaries to instruct their students in the latest methods and findings of science. He stated that it was absolutely necessary to improve the facilities and studies in order to arm their graduates for the warfare against agnosticism.[45] The bitter warfare which had existed between Catholicity and Protestantism was ended; instead, agnostics were the true foes of the Church. Likewise, he added, priests must provide their people with an *intelligent* faith. "If we were to devote as much time to science as we do to Classics, we could exhibit better results," he concluded.[46]

Zahm and Keane were praised for their lectures. The *Catholic Review,* October 6, 1894, quoted a French bishop who, after hearing the two of them, said, "It takes the Americans to teach us how to move forward. Verily these Americans are wonderful people." The Rome correspondent for the New York *Sun* observed with fervor: "It is from the United States, it is from that progressive Church, seeking for a new ecclesiastical type, that come to us words of reform, of light, and of power." [47]

Zahm believed the Brussels' address was his greatest triumph and the last step to the doctor's degree which was awarded him in February, 1895, by Pope Leo XIII. It likely was.[48] On a return visit to the Vatican six weeks after the Conference Zahm had a private audience with the Holy Father and presented him with a copy of the address, beautifully printed in French and bound in white silk. When the Pope asked about the Vatican Observatory, Zahm commended it: he also praised the Pope's encyclical, *Rerum Novarum*. Enthusiastic after the audience, Zahm wrote "Leo XIII is decidedly the greatest man of the century." [49]

Archbishop Francesco Satolli sent a brief conferring the degree, Doctor of Philosophy, on Zahm on February 24, 1895. It was awarded in the hope it would serve as an incentive for him to labor even more wholeheartedly for the development and propagation of Christian science.[50] The award surprised Zahm, as he wrote, "So far as I know, Leo XIII has given this degree only to two persons—both heretics —Mivart and Zahm!" [51]

In the months that followed the litany of magazine articles under Zahm's name continued. In the *Catholic World* he described a new system of writing for the blind, and a short time later, *Rosary* magazine published his biographical sketch of the famous Catholic and scientist, Monsignor Charles De Harlez. The August, 1895, issue of the *North American Review* led off with a bitter attack on Catholicism by W. J. H. Traynor, president of the American Protective Association, entitled, "The Menace of Romanism." A few pages later, Zahm's article, "Leo XIII and the Social Question," provided an antidote. This essay ranks as one of Zahm's best, for he revealed a clear understanding of the society created by the Industrial Revolution and universal education. While recognizing the great contribution made by *Rerum Novarum,* he also paid tribute to Bishop von Ketteler, Cardinal Gibbons, Archbishop Ireland, and Bishop Keane for their roles in the workingman's crusade for justice.

Zahm, though the most notable American Catholic author to discuss the problems involving evolution, science and religion, was not the only writer to do so in American Catholic magazines. An able contributor who discussed evolution was St. George Mivart, the man whose name Zahm "won" during the summer school lectures and whose two books Zahm listed in the "One Hundred Best Books." As described previously, Mivart was an irregular contributor to the *American Catholic Quarterly Review* after 1860 and his views on scientific matters were most welcome in this journal of intellectually precise articles. A convert to Catholicism in 1844 at the age of seventeen, St. George Mivart led many Catholics to survey the fields of science intelligently. His deep interest in science brought him to the frontiers of evolution and with his *Genesis of Species,* published in 1871, he was marked as an evolutionist. He was not a Darwinist for he rejected the hypothesis of Natural Selection. Also, he emphasized the creation of the human soul and consistently asserted the great differences between inanimate and animate, animal and rational. In 1874 he was appointed to the Chair of Biology at the new Catholic University at Kensington. Two years later Pope Pius IX awarded him a Doctorate of Philosophy. He continued to be a powerful antagonist to Darwin on scientific grounds, and as a result of many controversies he gained Darwin's intense dislike.[52]

Mivart was extremely hopeful that the studies in evolution would bring about a return to Aristotelian metaphysics; thus during his years as a neo-scholastic philosopher he aided the Jesuits in their struggle against post-Cartesian philosophy. In 1894 he was awarded an M.D. degree at Louvain and remained there as Professor of Natural History. Difficulties arose over his views on philosophical and theological questions; five of his imprudent articles in the *Nineteenth Century* between 1885 and 1892 were placed on the

Index. Thus, for example, he complained at the failure of Pope Leo XIII to criticize the bitter animosity towards the Third Republic shown by French Catholic Royalists in the celebrated Dreyfus case. One of his condemned articles, "Happiness in Hell," was an attempt to liberalize the doctrines concerning those punished to eternal hell-fire.[53] Finally, his two articles, "The Continuity of Catholicism" in the January, 1900, issue of the *Nineteenth Century,* and "Some Recent Apologists" in the *Fortnightly Review,* that same month, brought his orthodoxy into grave question.

Instead of signing a profession of faith as demanded by Cardinal Vaughan on January 18, 1900, Dr. Mivart refused and was accordingly forbidden the sacraments. He died on April 1, 1900, still under the ban of excommunication. Four years later, his case was reopened and friends proved his refusal to sign the profession of faith resulted from ill health. His body was moved to a Catholic cemetery. Mivart's researches into evolution were thoughtful and the articles he mailed to the *American Catholic Quarterly Review* were clear presentations of his advanced position. In a highly interesting article published in 1883,[54] he described the limits of evolution and emphasized that matter received life from a higher agency in the beginning; thus spontaneous generation was clearly impossible. He was emphatic in his assertion that man was more than an evolved ape.

Other Catholics such as Cardinal Gibbons, W. H. Thompson, Father George Searle and William Seton also wrote articles for the *Catholic World* and the *American Catholic Quarterly Review* during this time. They belong to what may be termed the liberal writers on the relationship between science and Catholicism.

In 1896, Zahm's most controversial book, *Evolution and Dogma,* a summary of his studies on evolution, was published. With this book, the conservatives' clamor increased in volume as laudatory reviews appeared in many weekly and monthly publications. The book itself provided American Catholic students with a tentative summary on the relationships of evolution and Catholic doctrine presented in an orderly fashion and based upon considerable research.

In October, 1895, along with a partial manuscript for *Evolution and Dogma*, Zahm mailed a note to Reverend Augustine F. Hewit in which he requested that this leading Catholic editor and scholarly apologist review his study. Further, Zahm wrote of his intentions for a great mission:

> My object is not to prove that the theories discussed are true, but that they are tenable, that they are not the great bugbear they are sometimes declared to be. I wish to show that Catholics have no cause for alarm even should certain theories by which modern scientists set such store be proved to be true. I wish to have your comforting opinion that I am 'safe' & not temerarious. My desire is to quiet the doubts of many Catholics who are now sorely puzzled about certain questions to show them that there is no possibility of conflict between science & religion, & that in controverted questions the Church allows her children the utmost liberty. Our people have suffered much in consequence of having presented them only the non-Catholic side of the subjects examined. I have tried to exhibit this Catholic view . . .[55]

Thus, Zahm again, though privately, stated his intention of educating thoughtful Catholics on the boundaries of freedom within Catholicism.

Hewit replied less than a week later that after a careful reading of the study relating to the evolutionary character of Adam's body he feared Zahm's ideas might well awaken opposition and, unless it was very important, he suggested it should not be published. The question of evolution was presently at rest, as was that of the transmission of species, and it seemed certain that Dr. Mivart's hypothesis was tenable for now—"Whether it is consistent with the true interpretation of Genesis is another matter, and it may yet be condemned as contrary to Scripture."[56]

A few months later, in an article for the *Catholic World*, Hewit further delineated his position regarding the Simian anthropoid or ape-man. He wrote that the Simian hypothesis, that is, the "first man, Adam, made by the creation of a rational soul and its infusion as the substantial form of a body which was this offspring of anthropoid parents" was not against faith; however, it had not yet been decided whether it was consistent with Scripture.[57] Thus, it could be considered as tolerable and tenable as an opinion more or less probable by any Catholic without harm to faith, provided, of course, that the holder would willingly submit to the judgment of the Holy See which might later be promulgated. Personally he could not accept it:

> I will say, frankly, at the outset, that this hypothesis, in my opinion, is not only, as all admit, without a scintilla of positive evidence, but also destitute of even a slight probability, on any other line of reasoning. Moreover, I think there are conclusive reasons which prove it to be absolutely false, if not absurd.[58]

Disregarding Hewit's suggestion, Zahm proceeded with his plans for publication.

Unfortunately, an overly enthusiastic advertising circular preceded the distribution of *Evolution and Dogma*. It included sensational quotes from newspaper reviews in praise of the author's intellectual position and it suggested that his ideas were in the realm of the questionable and suspect: therefore the book should be purchased quickly.[59] Zahm had no share in preparing or approving the advertisement; rather it was the project of his publishers, D. H. McBride and Company.[60]

The key ideas in *Evolution and Dogma,* published in 1896, had been originally covered in summer school lectures at Madison and Plattsburg, and the Winter School at New Orleans. In the introduction, Zahm explained his position relative to the all-absorbing problem of evolution—"It is because Evolution contains as large an element of truth, because it explains countless facts and phenomena which are explicable on no other theory, that it has met with such universal favor." [61] What was necessary, he continued, was that Christians take this truth from its unnatural alliance with Monism, Materialism and Pantheism and convert it into a power for righteousness and the exaltation of the Holy Faith. Still anxious to "baptize" the theory of evolution, Zahm credited St. Thomas and St. Augustine as important teachers for the understanding of transformism. Moreover, he said, the Jesuit T. N. Harper in his *The Metaphysics of the School*, and the Dominican Cardinal Gonzales in his *La Biblia & la Ciencia*, taught a prudent view of evolution. Personally, Zahm explained, he was committed to no theory as to the origin of the world: his sole purpose was to "remove misconceptions, to dispel confusion, to explain difficulties, to expose error, to eliminate false interpretation, to allay doubt, to quiet conscience, to benefit souls." [62] Probably recalling the stormy summer school sessions, he noted that a similar season of doubts and cries of heresy had set in when the Copernican and Newtonian theories were introduced.

The author carefully traced the history of evolutionary theories from the ancient beliefs of Thales, Empedocles and Aristotle to St. Thomas, Albertus Magnus, Cuvier and Darwin. Further, he offered the theory that the world could have been in existence for many millions of years.[63]

In his historical treatment of theories on evolution, Zahm explained that although Aristotle, St. Augustine and St. Thomas believed in spontaneous generation or abiogenesis, Francisco Redi of Florence published his ideas in 1668 to the effect that there could be no life without antecedent life. This theory was generally accepted when it had been reinforced by the experiments of Pasteur. The advance of science pointed towards some process of evolution and the impression became popular that the changes and developments on earth were the result of a single creation with a uniform process of evolution under definite and immutable laws rather than a series of separate creative acts.

Furthermore, a litany of great scientists believed in various phases of evolution: Lord Bacon thought the transmutation of species possible; Descartes believed in a continual process rather than special creative acts; Immanuel Kant accepted the idea that a specific mutability could result from selection, inheritance, adaptation and environment. Also to give perspective, Zahm noted that Erasmus Darwin, grandfather of Charles, popularized evolution. More especially, Zahm said that the evidence of embryology favored the view

. . . of a God who inaugurates the era of terrestrial life by the creation of one or more simple organisms, unicellular monads . . . and causing them, under the action of His Providence, to evolve in the course of time into all myriad, complicated, specialized and perfect forms which now people the earth.[64]

The evidence from geographical distribution and geological succession, continued Zahm, made the evolution theory at least highly probable although it did not have the force of a demonstration. In fact, he added, the theory of evolution rested upon as firm a foundation as did Newton's theory of universal gravitation. It would merely be a question of time until it was as popular as Copernicus' solar system theory.

Realizing that many Christians were skeptical, even fearful, of the theory because it appeared that there existed a strong kinship between the holders of Darwinism and atheism, Zahm reassuringly answered that Asa Gray, a good Christian and scientist, accepted both Christianity and evolution. Further, he criticized the Monist school under Ernst Haeckel, the "German Darwin" and professor at the University of Jena, and the agnostic schools taught by Thomas Huxley and Herbert Spencer. These schools lacked genuine theology and philosophy. He concluded that the Christian ideas on creation involved the postulate that God created the world out of nothing; He could, however, create matter and through the operation of natural laws and in virtue of powers originally conferred upon this matter, produce all the diverse phenomena of the physical universe indirectly or by the operation of secondary causes. This theistic evolution, as explained by St. Gregory of Nyssa, St. Augustine and St. Thomas, was consistent with Scripture and science.

Without question, Zahm remarked, physical science was

incompetent to pronounce on primary creation for it lay outside the sphere of science, being a metaphysical problem. Catholics, Zahm repeated, had the liberty to accept a theory of evolution as to the various forms of animal and plant life; in effect, he asserted, this theory contributed a more noble conception of the Deity than did the traditional view of special creation. Disregarding Hewit's views, he readily agreed with Mivart's theory that the body of man could have been created indirectly: however, the soul of man was created directly. He recalled that Cardinal Gonzales favored a moderate view in which Adam's body was partly a result of evolution and partly the direct work of God; philosophically, however, Zahm thought this approach was unnecessary.

In the concluding chapter of *Evolution and Dogma,* the author posited sincere faith in the dictum that evolution as a theory was in accordance with science, scripture, and with patristic and scholastic theology. He predicted that it would soon be the generally accepted view.

Thus ended *Evolution and Dogma,* a scholarly and controversial American contribution to the often misunderstood relationship between religion and science. It was a sincere attempt to summarize the Catholic platform of theology in relation to evolution and science. Unquestionably, it was the most important volume on evolution written by a Catholic and published in America during those troubled years.

Many private and printed reactions to *Evolution and Dogma* were quite favorable; only a few reviewers found minor faults. The world-famous French scientist, Monsignor Nadaillac, thanked the author for a gift copy and added:

> Even if on some points I disagree with you, it is impossible not to admire the immense science of the book and I am very glad that a French translation will enable my countrymen unfamiliar with the English language to read it and learn much by it.[65]

A leading American magazine of science and philosophy, the *Popular Science Monthly,* judged that Zahm's approach was

clear, temperate, and readable.[66] Two Notre Dame publications varied in their views of the book. Farther Hudson's
conservative magazine, *Ave Maria,* announced the publication of the book in a few sentences.[67] Austin O'Malley,
Maurice Egan's successor at Notre Dame, praised the book
in an enthusiastic review published in the Notre Dame
Scholastic. He heartily endorsed the book and added: "A
mere amateur in science cannot but observe that theistic evolution is too well established at present to be slighted, and
it will break no church windows." [68] The *Catholic World* advocated the careful study of the book and the acceptance of
its ideas.[69] The reviewer, likely Reverend Herman J. Heuser,
in the well-written *American Ecclesiastical Review* believed
Zahm was quite safe from heresy in his presentation of this
timely problem.[70] Furthermore, the reviewer continued,
while Zahm did not commit himself once in the 450 pages,
readers should object to the fact that whereas *Evolution and
Dogma* showed one *may* believe in evolution, it also concluded one *should* do so.

A good deal of futile discussion has been caused regarding
the view of Dr. Zahm expressed in his lectures on evolution.
The consequent reclame is due no less to exaggerated blame
than to praise for wrongly assumed originality. As a matter
of fact, the topics and views of Fr. Zahm have been taught
in the schools of Germany, France and Italy for many years.
Hence, we should find nothing to controvert in the volume,
which not only collates many scattered shreds of knowledge
and weaves them into a consistent whole, but supplies the
judicious reader with excellent weapons to confute atheism,
materialism, and the various assumptions of false science.[71]

However, the writer feared that the readers of *Evolution
and Dogma* would fail to distinguish or read carefully what
had been written. Finally, the critic thought that to say the
theory of immediate creation was less reasonable, therefore
less honorable to the Christian intelligence, was a sensational
exaggeration.

The book review of Reverend David Fleming, O.F.M.
in the *Dublin Review* was extremely interesting. Fleming

wrote that *Evolution and Dogma* was a noteworthy contribution to the evolution controversy,[72] and that Zahm, a convinced evolutionist, wrote well from scientific and theological viewpoints. As things stood at present, he explained,

> the theory of evolution has passed from the state of being *merely possible* to the state of probability—that is, when misconceptions are cleared away and monstrous and glaring errors are set aside.[73]

This Franciscan theologian found no incompatibility between evolution and the doctrine of the soul's spirituality and separate creation. However, he thought Zahm should have emphasized the Thomistic ideas that the soul's union with the body must be substantial and that this union included a substantial change in the body. Consequently, a man's body, if evolved, was prepared by God before the reception of the soul. In conclusion, Fleming pointed out a few minor errors by Zahm, largely in his choice of words.

A Milwaukee newspaper, the *Catholic Citizen,* rated *Evolution and Dogma* as the "book of the year" for American Catholics and continued:

> It is possible that Dr. Zahm has a *cacoethes* for shocking the sensibilities of the old fogy by indulging in a sort of blank cartridge sensationalism; the learned doctor is not only a good rhetorician, but an acute student of proper effects for an audience. His latest work evinces a most discursive acquaintance with the great scientific literature which has come into being since 1859.[74]

The *Catholic University Bulletin* liberally praised this controversial study and remarked that its author presented very well the theory that God created primordial elements out of nothing and then gave them latent energies to be developed with time. Also, the book explained how God created the rational soul directly and infused it into the body. Clearly sympathetic, the reviewer concluded: "His conclusion is that, while the process of evolution must be admitted, the 'ideal theory' belongs to the future. He is

neither Darwinian nor Lamarkian: he is simply expect-
ant." [75]

A number of Catholic magazines and newspapers opposed the theory of evolution. For example, *Donahoe's
Magazine* (although it had published one of Zahm's articles
on evolution in 1893) rejected the hypothesis of evolution
as did the *Messenger of the Sacred Heart.* The *Review,* a
weekly newspaper edited by Arthur Preuss and consistent
in its opposition to liberal views, took a similar position and
printed extended articles which rebutted Zahm's view that
St. Augustine and St. Thomas espoused the doctrine of evolution.[76]

Evolution and Dogma appeared in February, 1896; one
month later Zahm, plainly troubled, replied to certain critics
in the Preface of a new book, *Scientific Theory and Catholic
Doctrine.* He stated he was not a Darwinist or a "Huxley-
ist" and that, like Mivart, he had little faith in natural selection. In this *Apologia,* he said he had attempted to show
that there was truth in portions of their studies—that Darwin, Huxley, and their followers had contributed very much
"towards a wider and truer knowledge of nature and nature's laws." [77] After noting the old adage, "In essential
things, unity; in doubtful things, liberty; in all things, charity," Zahm recalled that even Bishop Sebastian Messmer had
said it was wise and expedient to have current topics such
as evolution studied at the Western Summer School. In a
plea for intellectual charity, Zahm then related that the
International Catholic Scientific Congress had discussed
evolution in 1888, 1891 and 1894; further, that this august
body of scientists had stated:

> there is nothing in Evolution which should trouble the faith
> of Catholics and nothing which justifies unbelievers in using
> the theory as an engine of war against the Church.[78]

Catholics, he emphatically stated in this preface, must be
shown a sense in which evolution could be accepted and
also shown that there had been nothing contributed by un-
questioned evidence which negated the declarations of Holy

Writ or detracted from the Christian concept of God as Father and Creator. Two weeks after writing this preface, Father Zahm confessed to his brother, Albert: "The critics have received 'Evolution & Dogma' most favorably—especially those of the secular press. I have certainly struck the right note this time, & you will hear its reverberations for some time to come." [79]

In April, 1896, a few critics believed that Rome was initiating action against an erring son when it announced that Zahm was going to the Eternal City. An interview, which the Preuss *Review* reprinted, said there was absolutely no question of his being called to Rome—rather, he was being sent for disciplinary reasons. In reply to these reports, Zahm stated prophetically:

> I have never been 'disciplined,' as they put it, and it is not likely that I shall be. The trouble is that we have a great many pious persons in America who are more orthodox than Leo XIII, and the Holy Office. My views may not be looked upon with favor by all in Rome. I do not expect so much, and I really do not care for the approval of everyone. But I know that every eminent man of science throughout Europe is in perfect sympathy with my views. I venture to say that the twentieth century will not be very old before nine out of every ten thinkers and students will be evolutionists, as opposed to believers in a special creation.[80]

Despite this reply, the unbelieving Arthur Preuss thought the transfer resulted from a decision by his superiors to have him imbibe the pure fresh air of Catholic orthodoxy in Rome. After all, he concluded, "The evolution bacillus is a dangerous thing."

An additional report of an interview with Zahm prior to his departure for Rome revealed the priest's feelings after the months of harping criticism. He said the new assignment was something of a promotion and then distinctly he asserted:

> I have been criticized for holding views which are hostile to religion. But the old views can no longer be held. They were good enough to explain during the middle ages questions

which are still in controversy and which are not 'of faith,' but the researcher of modern science has made a thousand discoveries in biology, paleontology, and archaeology, which throw new light on these questions and suggest solutions which never could have occurred to mediaeval scientists.

It is amusing to study the different points of view taken by my censors. In America they unite in denouncing me as a liberal and a radical, and yet I read a fortnight ago in one of the most prominent Catholic reviews of Europe that I am entirely too conservative, almost an old fogy! [81]

When questioned about his Superior-General's views on *Evolution and Dogma*, Zahm replied that he did not know but imagined that his superior liked it. In any event, his Superior-General had the utmost confidence in the author. Also, although he had several more books in mind, he did not know if he would have time to write on the topic of evolution while in Rome.

Despite the fanciful imagination of the *Review*, Zahm's assignment to Rome was decided entirely by other considerations. On February 10, 1896, the Provincial Council at Notre Dame discussed the Superior-General's request that either Father Linneborn or Zahm be appointed to the Office of Procurator-General, which had been recently vacated by the Very Reverend Dion who had been appointed Provincial of Canada. The General, Gilbert Français, preferred Zahm, and the Council formally acquiesced in his choice although it realized that it would be difficult to find a replacement for the Chair of Physics. [82]

Actually it was with great surprise that Zahm read the letter from Français upon his return from the New Orleans Winter School, March 4, and learned, somewhat to his dismay, that he had been appointed Procurator-General. Although caught off guard by this new assignment, he was pleased to read: "Your grand influence will be utilized for the fundamental interest of the Congregation." [83] He was assured that in this post he could help the Sisters of Holy Cross secure their definitive approbation and that he was *persona grata* in Rome; also, while there he could write of

Rome to the American newspapers. Despite these words of encouragement he was reluctant to go and apparently asked Father Morrissey, President of Notre Dame, to keep him at Notre Dame.[84] One observer on the scene, Father James Burns, wrote that it was certain Father Morrissey could have kept Zahm if he had desired; however, he was happy to release him.[85]

Thus, with a heavy heart Zahm accepted the new assignment to Rome. He said to one interviewer: "I shall be sorry to leave America, for I am an American in heart and soul, and I shall be glad when it is permitted me to return to my native country and my college home, old Notre Dame." [86] With regret he recalled the mission to educate American Catholics in dogma and evolution undertaken almost three years previously. Now it must be terminated or at least interrupted. Though at the peak of popularity or, with some, notoriety, he would have little time in Rome for research in science and Scripture.

During these last four fruitful years, he, as scientist, historian, and journalist, had publicized the lives of leading Catholic scientists and a liberal approach to the theory of evolution. His American crusade for intelligent Catholic participation in the discussions on science and evolution was nearly finished. Understandably, in view of the seeming alliance of science and godlessness, his mission during these years was considered advanced, rash, and deserving of censure. But the man had been made—he had become one of the most famous evolutionists produced by the American Catholic Church.[87] The formal end of the crusade would come after the interlude in Rome.

NOTES TO CHAPTER IV

1. Zahm to Sorin, September 6, 1893. PA.
2. He was still at Notre Dame; however he no longer entertained the students with travelogues or lectures. Though Professor of Physics, his maximum efforts were in the science-religion studies. When asked in 1893 about his book, *Sound and Music*, he replied that the subject

had small interest for him now. *Catholic Times* clipping in Zahm Scrapbook, PA.

3. James A. White, *The Founding of Cliff Haven* (New York, 1950), p. 30.

4. Reprinted in the Notre Dame *Scholastic,* October 1, 1892.

5. He joined the Catholic University faculty in 1896, resigning in 1907 when he was appointed by President Theodore Roosevelt as Minister to Denmark. He resigned from this post in 1918 because of ill health and died in 1924. Cf. Maurice Francis Egan, *Recollections of a Happy Life* (New York, 1924).

6. White, *op. cit.,* p. 24.

7. *Ibid.,* p. 74; also the Notre Dame *Scholastic,* September 23, 1893. Zahm's book, *Bible, Science and Faith* (Baltimore, 1894), contained the lecture material from the Plattsburg sessions. Cf. John J. O'Shea, "The Catholic Chaplain," the *Catholic World,* 57 (September, 1893) 853-62; also "The Columbian Reading Union," the *Catholic World* 57 (July, 1893), 590-93; *Catholic Citizen,* July 23, 1893.

8. Reprinted in the *Catholic Citizen,* August 19, 1893. Zahm did not receive his doctorate until 1895.

9. Zahm to Burns, August 13, 1893, John Zahm Collection, UNDA. Zahm also congratulated him on his recent ordination to the priesthood and wrote that gifts were on the way to him and Mr. Cavanaugh (later Father John Cavanaugh), his two favorites among the seminarians.

10. Clipping in Zahm Scrapbook. PA.

11. *Ibid.,* PA.

12. Milwaukee *Sentinel,* July 18, 1895, and *Catholic Citizen,* July 20, 1895.

13. Zahm to Albert Zahm, July 28, 1893. Albert Zahm Collection, UNDA.

14. William Henry Thorne, "Summer Schools and Catholic Culture," *The Globe,* VI (May, 1896), 105.

15. *Catholic Citizen,* October 20, 1894; December 1, 1894.

16. *Ibid.,* July 13, 1895.

17. *Ibid.,* July 20, 1895, and the Milwaukee *Sentinel,* July 16, 1895. Zahm, described as of medium height, ruddy complexion, clear piercing blue eyes and an American through and through, was rated alongside Father Magevney, S.J., as being the best lecturer in the first week. Mr. Egan and Father J. J. Conway, S.J., received that rating for the second week's session, and during the third week, Bishop Messmer and Professor Joseph S. La Boule took top honors. *Catholic Citizen,* July 20, 1895.

18. Milwaukee *Sentinel,* July 16, 1895; *Catholic Citizen,* July 13, 1895.

19. Milwaukee *Sentinel,* July 17, 1895.

20. *Ibid.*, July 21, 1895.

21. *Catholic Times* clipping in Zahm Scrapbook. PA. The Notre Dame *Scholastic*, September 14, 1895, saw no cause for concern in Zahm's Columbian School lectures.

22. *Catholic Citizen*, July 27, 1895.

23. *Ibid.*, August 24, 1895.

24. Reprinted in *ibid.*, September 14, 1895.

25. Published in *ibid.*, March 28, 1896.

26. Total enrollment for the three week school was over twelve hundred students. Forty lectures were given. *Ibid.*, August 10, 1895. Members of the Catholic hierarchy who participated in the sessions were Bishop Schweback of La Crosse, Wisconsin; Bishop Watterson of Columbus, Ohio; Archbishop Elder of Cincinnati, Ohio; Bishop Rademacher of Fort Wayne, Indiana; Archbishop Kain of St. Louis, Missouri; Bishop Horstmann of Cleveland, Ohio; and Archbishop Ireland of St. Paul, Minnesota; as noted previously, Bishop Messmer of Green Bay, Wisconsin, was President of the Summer School. *Ibid.*, July 13, 1895.

27. New York *Daily Tribune*, August 1, 1895.

28. Hart to Zahm, September 25, 1895. John Zahm Collection, UNDA.

29. "Criticisms and Notes," *The Ecclesiastical Review*, 73 (August, 1922), 210-14. This recollection—thirty years after the event—was published by the critic, likely Father Herman J. Heuser, in a review of George Barry O'Toole's book, *The Case Against Evolution* (New York, Macmillan Co.), 1925.

30. *Catholic Citizen*, August 17, 1895.

31. Reprinted in *ibid.*, August 31, 1895.

32. Messmer to O'Gorman, January 20, 1896. UNDA. Also see Patrick Henry Ahern, *The Catholic University of America, 1887-1895: The Rectorship of John J. Keane* (Washington, 1948), pp. 157-58.

33. Messmer to Zahm, January 20, 1896. UNDA. O'Gorman's topic was "The Church and Society in the Middle Ages," *Catholic Citizen*, January 25, 1896.

34. Ahern, *op. cit.*, p. 156. Messmer wrote: "Whatever one's private opinion may be, the fact cannot be denied that the Catholic University, its professors and Rector are not looked upon with favor by many of our Catholics." Quoted in a letter of O'Gorman to Zahm, January 27, 1896. John Zahm Collection, UNDA.

35. Messmer to Zahm, January 20, 1896. John Zahm Collection, UNDA.

36. Zahm to Pace, January 27, 1896, as cited in Ahern, *op. cit.*, p. 159. Also see Ahern, *The Life of John J. Keane* (Milwaukee, 1955), p. 175, where Zahm in a letter to Pace termed Messmer and Father Michael Hughes, S.J., "two self-constituted inquisitors."

37. Messmer to Zahm, January 31, 1896. John Zahm Collection, UNDA.

38. Zahm to Messmer, February 1, 1896. John Zahm Collection, Copy, UNDA.

39. Ireland to Zahm, February 2, 1895. John Zahm Collection, UNDA.

40. Ulrich Albert Hauber based many of the statements in his book, *A Catholic Opinion on the Evolution Controversy* (Davenport, 1925) upon this book.

41. Dr. P. J. Horwitz to Zahm, July 23, 1894. John Zahm Collection, UNDA.

42. John A. Zahm, "The International Catholic Scientific Congress," *Donahoe's Magazine,* XXXII (November, 1894), 459-67. The magazine announced that Zahm was its official correspondent for the meeting. "Notes," *ibid.,* XXXII (September, 1894), 348.

43. *Moniteur de Rome,* August 30, 1894, as reprinted in *Catholic Citizen,* September 22, 1894.

44. *Catholic Review* (New York), October 6, 1894.

45. Reverend John A. Zahm, "The Warfare with Agnosticism," *Donahoe's Magazine,* XXXII (September, 1894), 255-76. Reverend Joseph Selinger, Professor of Theology at Milwaukee's St. Francis de Sales Seminary, gave qualified approval of Zahm's plan in "Should a Priest Be A Scientist," *Donahoe's Magazine,* XXXIII (March, 1895) 315-20. Archbishop Ireland's St. Paul Seminary, partially because of Mr. James Hill, the institution's financial father, had the natural sciences enthroned side by side with theology. James Michael Reardon, *The Catholic Church in the Diocese of St. Paul* (St. Paul, 1952), pp. 309-13.

46. Reverend John A. Zahm, *Science and the Church* (Chicago, 1896). His address became Chapter Six of this book.

47. Dateline Rome, November 12, 1894. Clipping Zahm Scrapbook, PA.

48. Chicago *Times-Herald,* July 27, 1895. However, in an interview with a Denver newspaperman, Zahm stated that Pope Leo XIII was so pleased with *Bible, Science and Faith* that he awarded him the degree. Zahm Scrapbook, PA.

49. Zahm to Albert Zahm, October 25, 1894. Albert Zahm Collection, UNDA.

50. Satolli to Corby, February 24, 1895. Corby Collection, UNDA.

51. Zahm to Albert Zahm, March 1, 1895. Albert Zahm Collection, UNDA.

52. Sister Mary Frederick, *Religion and Evolution Since 1859* (Chicago, 1934), pp. 64-65.

53. "Editorial Notes," *Catholic World,* 56 (January, 1893), 585: the editor found it an adequate answer for those who find the Church's doctrine on hell a stumbling block!

54. St. George Mivart, "Limit to Evolution," *American Catholic Quarterly Review*, VIII (April, 1883), 193-222.

55. Zahm to Hewit, October 2, 1895. Photostat. UNDA. Original copy in Paulist Fathers' Archives.

56. Hewit to Zahm, October 7, 1895. John Zahm Collection, UNDA.

57. Reverend Augustine F. Hewit, "The Simian Anthropoid," *Catholic World*, 62 (January, 1896), 526.

58. *Ibid.*, 62, 527.

59. For example, "There are fogies—like some of the French royalists who piously pray that Leo XIII may soon be taken to heaven—who think that with Mivart and Zahm thus honored the Church faces a deluge. She has survived a deluge of ignorance." From the Milwaukee *Catholic Citizen*. Another account related that Zahm's opinions were almost generally tabooed in Catholic groups because ". . . they are not thought conducive to the strengthening of dogma among the common people." From the Brooklyn *Daily Times*.

60. Zahm to Albert Zahm, February 5, 1896. John Zahm Collection, UNDA.

61. Reverend John A. Zahm, *Evolution and Dogma* (Chicago, 1896), p. xviii.

62. *Ibid.*, p. xxv.

63. *Ibid.*, p. 38. Later he claimed that geology, physical geography and paleontology showed that the earth's age must be reckoned in millions of years; maybe even tens of millions. *Ibid.*, p. 51. It should be recalled that he made an estimate of about ten thousand years only two years earlier in *Bible, Science and Faith*.

64. *Ibid.*, p. 122.

65. Nadaillac to Zahm, October 10, 1897. PA.

66. *Popular Science Monthly*, XLIX (July, 1895), 414-15.

67. *Ave Maria*, 42 (April, 1896), 468-69.

68. Notre Dame *Scholastic*, March 21, 1896.

69. "Review of Evolution and Dogma," *Catholic World*, 63 (April, 1896), 130-33.

70. *American Ecclesiastical Review*, 14 (June, 1896), 568-70.

71. *Ibid.*, 14, 568.

72. Reverend David Fleming, "Review of Evolution and Dogma," *Dublin Review*, 119 (October, 1896), 245-57.

73. *Ibid.*, 119, 250.

74. *Catholic Citizen*, April 11, 1896. A few months later, the editor reproved the *Messenger of the Sacred Heart* for terming Zahm's writing a disgrace. *Ibid.*, July 25, 1896.

75. *Catholic University Bulletin*, II (April, 1896) 237-38.

76. "St. Thomas and Evolution," *The Review*, April 30, 1896: "St. Thomas and Evolution," *The Review*, May 21, 1896: "St. Augustine and Evolution," *The Review*, June 4, 1896. An article from *The Sacred*

Heart Messenger reprinted in *The Review*, June 25, 1896, stated that the prevailing ideas on evolution were unchanged by Father Zahm's book. Also see *The Review*, July 2, 1896. Msgr. Joseph De Concilio's unfavorable criticism of Zahm's theories (he termed Zahm a "blustering scientist") as printed in the *Freeman's Journal*, March 21, 1896, was reprinted in *The Review*.

77. Reverend John A. Zahm, *Scientific Theory and Catholic Doctrine* (Chicago, 1896), p. 9.

78. As quoted in *ibid.*, p. 14.

79. Zahm to Albert Zahm, March 21, 1896. John Zahm Collection, UNDA.

80. "Dr. Zahm," *The Review*, April 23, 1896. A week later, this journal accepted the Kansas City *Catholic's* unfounded report that Zahm was sent to Rome by his superiors to prevent him from lecturing at the next Madison Summer School. *The Review*, April 30, 1896.

81. *Catholic Citizen*, April 25, 1896.

82. Provincial Report. PA.

83. Français to Zahm, February 21, 1896. PA.

84. Burns Collection. PA.

85. *Ibid.*

86. *Catholic Citizen*, April 25, 1896.

87. Cf. John L. Morrison, *A History of American Catholic Opinion on the Theory of Evolution, 1859-1950*. (Unpublished Doctoral Dissertation, University of Missouri), 6.

V

An American in Europe
and at Notre Dame

"I Submit Unreservedly to the Decree"

During the twenty months after April 1, 1896, Zahm was involved in fascinating religious and political maneuvers on the European scene. His new position, in essence that of diplomat for his Congregation, brought him into contact with leading Catholic churchmen and face-to-face with the interesting liberal American approach to Church policy as exemplified by Archbishop Ireland. Intellectual compatibility with these ideas and a close friendship with their exponents brought him into the camp of the so-called Americanists and to the field of ecclesiastical power-politics. Conservatives under various banners sought to restrict these ideas. With great faith in the separation of Church and State as practiced in the United States and eager for progressive Church policies, he, together with Archbishop Ireland, Bishop Keane and Monsignor O'Connell, fought to forward the liberal pattern. Thus, his labors took on a significance which was international during this era. His mission of educating Catholics, though abbreviated, continued. Strong objections resulted, in some instances more because of his membership in the American group than because of his specific stand on evolution. Despite the setback regarding his stand on evolution, these years were filled with important tactical victories for the future of his Congregation and his ideals concerning Catholic University and the separation of Church and State.

In spite of his forty-six years, Zahm's reception in Europe amazed and delighted him. The fascinating swirl of French society provided only a foretaste of his reception shortly afterwards in Rome where he was cordially received by Pope Leo XIII and many Cardinals. Shortly after his arrival, he asked the Holy Father for a brief, commending the new Holy Cross College in Washington, D. C. With rare promptness it was sent to him the following day. This happy event brought Zahm to promise that "this will be more than an 'eye-opener' to those who have opposed establishing the college. Is not this a *coup* of the first order? Some people will ask themselves, what next!" [1] Without question, he took pleasure in doing the spectacular and in confounding his opponents.

The official commendation by the Holy Father deeply pleased Zahm, for the establishment of the Holy Cross College in Washington, D. C., had been initiated by him in the face of almost overwhelming odds. Because of an inadequate teaching staff, the problem of ecclesiastical studies, especially Philosophy and Moral and Dogmatic Theology for seminarians at Notre Dame, had been characterized in 1881 as "an absolute disgrace to the Community, to the University and to the Congregation at large." [2]

In 1886, the Cardinal-Prefect of the Sacred College of Propaganda praised the Congregation for its intention to establish a House of Studies on Congregation property, called the House of St. Bridget in Rome, to which two students from each Province would be sent. Unfortunately, because of the shortage of teachers, another decision gave the Provincial authority to authorize students in theology and philosophy to teach an hour or two each day. With the sale of the House of St. Bridget to the Carmelite Nuns in Rome in that same year, a committee of three was appointed to locate a new residence in Rome for the Procurator-General and a House of Studies for all the Provinces.

Shortly after the death of Father Edward Sorin, Superior-General of the Congregation on October 21, 1893, and the elevation of Father Gilbert Français to that office, Zahm urged the new Superior-General to accept a definite plan of studies with emphasis upon intellectual growth in an atmosphere conducive to study. As a result of this discussion, Français announced active measures in his Circular Letter, April 24, 1895. He wrote that upon the termination of the novitiate, all young religious, Seminarians and Brothers, would complete their studies. The Brothers would have a House of Studies formed at Notre Dame; however, since

> I consider it difficult and even impossible at present to form, from our own resources alone, an effective organization for the complete series of philosophical and theological studies, a house will be established at Washington, near the Catholic University.

In addition, he assigned Zahm as Superior, along with Fathers Linneborn and Guertin as the faculty: regular courses were to be divided among those three men. The young seminarians, both American and Canadian, would attend the University courses. The United States Province would finance the house.

This Circular Letter caused a minor revolution at the University of Notre Dame. Father Daniel Hudson, editor of the *Ave Maria* found it displeasing; the Provincial, Father William Corby, famous Civil War chaplain, refused to read it after a council of priests disapproved it. However, Linneborn "let the cat out of the bag" by reading the letter to his class.[3] Father Andrew Morrissey, who became President of Notre Dame at the express wish of Father Thomas Walsh (who died on July 17, 1893) likewise opposed the plan in the beginning, because he did not believe a man could *teach* better for having specialized in a subject. A few days later prudence prevailed and a majority of thirteen overrode the objections of eight members and approved the plan. Finally, at the express command of Français, the Circular was read in church in mid-June although Hudson, Kirsch, Stoffel and Morrissey still opposed it and, most likely, Corby also disapproved. Father Daniel Spillard suggested an alternative plan whereby the University professors would come to Notre Dame and instruct the seminarians. This was rejected.

A month later, in another Circular Letter, July 12, Français appointed Zahm Prefect of Studies for the Congregation. By this appointment, Français recognized that a well-developed course of studies would attract intelligent young men to the religious vocation, give stability to the novitiate and promise of good works for the future. He wrote that the question of studies was of decisive importance for the future of the Congregation. As Prefect of Studies, Zahm was to determine the direction of all studies in the Congregation and establish a uniform program based upon the needs of various countries. Without question, it was Zahm's scholarship, reputation and influence, which led Français to choose him.

Français' encouragement gave Zahm confidence, especially when the former called him a man designated by Providence to build the House of Studies. Reluctantly, Corby went to Washington the first week of August and with Zahm searched for houses located conveniently to the University. Zahm was given permission to use the money from his books and lectures for the new House of Studies.

By the end of August, 1895, ten seminarians left Notre Dame for study—two with Français for Paris and eight others with Zahm for Washington. Both Zahm and Français were praised by young Father Burns because, as he observed, thanks to their foresight and courage it was the first instance in Notre Dame's history that a comprehensive plan for the seminarian's education had been given a try.[4]

The new foundation exhibited little glamour. Two houses were rented in Brookland, just east of Catholic University and here the students, both American and Canadian, studied theology while continuing other courses at the University. Long years after classes had begun, opponents at Notre Dame continued to complain. Morrissey refused to believe that the students were obtaining a practical education. Thus it was with pleasure that Français reported in the May 29,

1896, Circular Letter, the special benediction requested by Zahm and granted by Pope Leo XIII for the infant foundation. After reading the benediction, Zahm could well exclaim that it was a *coup* of the first order and he even believed that with the letter, Pope Leo XIII virtually made himself the patron and protector of Holy Cross College. Zahm was so encouraged by the interest in the Catholic University and the reception given his report on Holy Cross College by the Pope and the Propaganda that he hoped to improve the studies for the seminarians to such a degree as to merit even greater praise from the Holy See. Surely, he wrote, "The days of 'brick & mortar' are over. We must now form men, otherwise we have no reason for existence as a Community." [5]

The Pope's message brought strength to the weak foundation. The request by the newly arrived Procurator-General was important, for although it did not halt the objections of his Notre Dame colleagues, it weakened their cause and it quickened the spirit of the growing institution, conceived for forming well-educated Holy Cross priests.

A second victory was soon Zahm's at the Vatican when he received confirmation of the Rules and Constitution of the Holy Cross Sisters in a brief dated May 12, 1896, and signed by Cardinal Ledochowski, Cardinal-Prefect of the Congregation of Propaganda. This final approval by Rome has been considered "the crowning event of the nineteenth century in the life of the Sisters of the Holy Cross." [6] Even more important, however, this final approbation ended a sharp controversy between priests and Sisters of the Holy Cross Congregations. The Sisters at St. Mary's achieved their recognition as a distinct Congregation when they were placed directly under the Propaganda in 1896. Although some Sisters remained as working nuns at Notre Dame, they were placed under the authority and administrative jurisdiction of St. Mary's. In the last analysis, the determined attempts by Sorin, Corby, and Walsh to keep the Sisters at Notre Dame under their jurisdiction, failed when the Propaganda gave final approval to the Rules and Constitution of the

Holy Cross Sisters. Zahm and Français could be pleased with this approbation because Moreau's original plan for the Congregation, a holy family composed of priests, Sisters and Brothers, while ideally acceptable, in practice repeatedly presented awkward administrative relationships.

The two papal approvals—of Holy Cross College and a separate jurisdiction for the Sisters of the Holy Cross—were justifiable claims for rejoicing by Zahm as he began his stay in Rome. His new occupation proved to be much different from that of a physics professor. His time was quickly absorbed by attending receptions, returning calls, attending celebrations, receiving invitations to membership in famous scientific and literary societies. His literary pursuits suffered as he failed to write a line or read a page during his first month. He told of his plans to avoid any more contacts since "I do not wish to become a slave to society. I have never cared for it, & have no desire to get into its whirl now." [7] This promise involved, as he later wrote his brother Albert, refusals to several receptions and teas given by duchesses and princesses, although he might accept them later.

Only two harbingers of future difficulties appeared during these gay months of a new European life. He wrote on July 22, 1896, that the Italian and French translations of *Evolution and Dogma* were already on the press and would soon be issued—"Then look out for squalls." [8] He would not have called them squalls if he, instead of Archbishop Corrigan, had read the weather forecast by Father Salvatore Brandi, S.J. The latter wrote a month after Zahm's arrival in Rome that although he had done some extraordinary favors for Zahm two years ago, the new Procurator-General had failed to visit him yet—"I am afraid that his recent utterances on transformism, and his relations with the liberal party, well known in the Vatican and Propaganda, will interfere somewhat with his work of Procurator of the Fathers of the Holy Cross." [9]

After his return from Greece, a five-week trip through that kingdom, Zahm resumed somewhat the habits of scholarly life and managed to read some of Dante and other

Italian authors. He planned to publish an annotated edition of the *Divine Comedy* which would appeal to English-speaking Catholics more than any edition that had yet appeared.

His energies were also absorbed by diplomatic measures; his successes brought him to confide proudly to Albert, "Why was I not made a diplomat instead of a professor of physics? I am really surprised at some things I have recently done & that in the face of untold numbers & old & experienced hands." [10] Also he wrote a short time later that he had saved the head of Maurice Francis Egan, who transferred from Notre Dame to the faculty of Catholic University in the fall of 1896; he was to have been "guillotined." Thrilled, he wished Albert could see "how long my right arm has grown since you last saw it." [11] Pleased with his early triumphs, he became increasingly involved in the whirl of Roman society. His friendship with Monsignor Denis O'Connell brought Zahm to delight in the fascinating culture of Rome and Europe.

As noted above, Brandi had forecast possible difficulties for the Procurator-General because of his relations with the liberal party. This party was involved in what has been judged by a leading historian of American Catholic history as "the most notable controversy in American Catholic history." Major problems within the controversy in the United States, widely publicized in newspapers and magazines,[12] revolved around the status of the Catholic Church in America. The liberals' policies were concerned in the 1880's and 1890's with the formation of the Catholic University of America; [13] approval of the Knights of Labor; acceptance of Archbishop Ireland's Faribault School plan; condemnation of Cahenslyism; attendance at the Parliament of Religions in Chicago, 1893; and generally, the efforts of Archbishop Ireland and Cardinal Gibbons to Americanize the Church in America. Conservative leaders were Archbishop Michael A. Corrigan of New York, Bishop Bernard J. McQuaid of Rochester, Bishop Richard Gilmour and his successor, Ignatius Horstman in Cleveland, Bishop Frederick

Katzer of Milwaukee, Bishop Sebastian Messmer of Green
Bay and Bishop Winand M. Wigger of Newark. Leading
European opponents included Father Salvatore Brandi, S.J.,
editor of *Civilta Cattolica,* and Cardinal Francesco Satolli,
former Apostolic Delegate and former friend of the liberal
group.

The German element in the laity and hierarchy was
largely opposed to the progressives. As an Irish editor noted
in the *Catholic Citizen,* January 11, 1896, the German Catholic newspapers had a regular litany of liberalism and it
consisted of Archbishop Ireland, Cardinal Gibbons, Archbishop Williams, Bishop Keane, Catholic University, the
Catholic Total Abstinence Union, the Paulists, the Western
Jesuits, all Catholic papers published in English except de-
votional periodicals, the Catholic Summer Schools, the Catholic Order of Foresters, the Ancient Order of Hibernians,
all Catholics who belonged to the Republican party and
Cardinal Satolli.

Before 1896 Zahm's most important relationship with the
liberals was a personal and intellectual friendship with certain apostles of the American idea, especially Ireland, Keane
and Gibbons. However, as noted in the previous chapter,
Zahm was most welcome as a guest of Corrigan in the late
summer of 1893. Although Zahm had envisioned his own
Notre Dame University as a future Heidelberg or Bologna
or Oxford, he pleased many liberal American ecclesiastical
hearts with his plan to establish Holy Cross College adjacent to Catholic University in 1895, and also with his statements in support of Catholic University.

Zahm's assignment to Rome and his subsequent friendship (perhaps the closest friendship formed during his life)
with Monsignor Denis O'Connell increased his participation in the progressives' struggle for leadership, and as they
wrote, "making the future the present." O'Connell had been
made rector of the North American College in 1886, and
gradually became a disciple of Ireland and Keane. Because
of protests by conservative American Bishops he was asked
to resign in 1895 by Miecislaus Cardinal Ledochowski. After

the resignation, however, Gibbons had him continue on in Rome as vicar of his Titular Church, Sante Maria in Trastevere, even though he was somewhat out of favor with Pope Leo XIII and Cardinal Ledochowski. O'Connell's friendship with the two Cardinals, Serafino and Vincenzo Vannutelli, gave the American liberals influence within the liberal group in the Roman hierarchy. O'Connell occupied a position of diplomat *par excellence* in Rome; his well-furnished apartment was the setting for many gatherings of American and British visitors. Shortly after Zahm arrived in Rome, he received an invitation from O'Connell to breakfast with him and the two Cardinals Vannutelli.

The conflict took on more vicious proportions when Ireland spoke at O'Gorman's consecration on April 19, 1896, in terms highly unfavorable to religious orders. He emphasized the role of the diocesan clergy while explicitly under-evaluating the role and work of the religious orders. The speech irritated the religious orders, especially the Jesuits, Redemptorists and Dominicans, who objected to the inference that they were responsible for the loss of many Catholics in England during penal times.

Upon their return from a vacation in Greece, Zahm and O'Connell were surprised to learn of the papal request for Keane's resignation as Rector of the Catholic University which had occurred during their absence. Zahm lost no time in learning the circumstances and he assured his brother Albert a few weeks later that "it was settled nearly a year ago that he should be guillotined. But don't lose courage. The whirling of time rights all things." [14] He also told his brother that he would not take the position of Rector even if it meant a mitre, for it was much too difficult and responsible a position.

Rumors and inaccurate newspaper reports about the University, Gibbons, and Ireland spread rapidly during the fall. For example, the New York *Journal*, November 12, 1896, and November 13, 1896, carried "reports" of Satolli's harsh criticisms of Keane, Ireland, Bouquillon and Pace. It noted that Pope Leo XIII was again favoring Archbishop Corrigan's group—"The diplomacy of Leo XIII, led for a moment astray by imprudent advisers, is finding again its habitual qualities of tact, circumspection and sagacity." Zahm wrote that the Pope and Cardinal Rampolla were incensed at such reports. Furthermore, he said, when Keane reported to Rome, he was well received:

The Holy Father has discovered that Msgr. Keane has been the victim of misrepresentation & persecution, & takes every occasion of showing him special marks of esteem & affection. Msgr. Kean's [sic] enemies stand enraged & declare that the late rector of the Catholic University has captured the Pope. The silence of the opposition press in America is quite significant to say the least.[15]

Zahm also prematurely assured Gibbons in March, 1897, that victory belonged to their bloc—"All reports to the contrary, the future is ours. I know positively that Leo XIII & Cardinal Rompolla are still with us & that their policy is unchanged." [16]

Meanwhile, Zahm finished his paper for the Fourth International Catholic Scientific Congress to be held in Fribourg during the latter part of August, 1897.

He had high hopes that this paper, as it turned out, his last on the subject of science, "Evolution and Teleology," would provoke much discussion. This final chapter on the problems of evolution and religion pleased Zahm's Fribourg audience and, as he had hoped, it was a splendid success. Besides being elected President of the American group, he was elected international Vice-President, President of the anthropology section, succeeding the famous anthropologist, the Marquis de Nadaillac, and a member of the permanent commission on organization.

In the ninth session of the Congress, Monsignor O'Connell added fuel to the flames of the American controversy with his speech, "A New Idea in the Life of Father Hecker," in which he described the values of the American Declaration of Independence and Constitution in contrast to Roman law. He found Father Hecker's liberal ideas on political and ecclesiastical concepts highly acceptable and worthy of the utmost theological imitation. America, more than a land of economic opportunity was, as well, one of religious freedom for Catholicism and as such deserved high praise. Decidedly, the Church had as much freedom in the United States as it had where Church and State were united. In vain did Monsignor Charles Turninaz, Bishop of Nancy, object, for the majority in the Congress praised these ideas. American newspaper reports of the Congress, such as that of the New York *Sun,* September 12, 1897, found the Church and the United States holding the front rank in the movements of history. Archbishop Ireland thanked Zahm for the great work he and his friends were doing in Europe for America and the Church. "We in America are profoundly grateful." [17]

Unfortunately, O'Connell's ideas regarding American values were taken as a direct criticism of the Church in western Europe and were carried beyond the limits of Fribourg. Arch-conservatives, fearful of the liberal Catholic Republicans in Europe, were led by European Jesuits and Dominicans and especially by Abbé Charles Maignen of the Congregation of the Brothers of St. Vincent de Paul, whose dislike for democracy knew no bounds. Three Parisian churches, St. Sulpice, St. Clotilde, and the newly constructed Sacre Coeur, resounded in November, 1897, with the preachings of Father Coubé, S.J. and Father Gaudeau, S.J., aimed at denouncing the evils of the progressive ideas, especially Americanism. Abbé Maignen collected a series of his articles, begun in *La Verité Française* during the Spring of 1898, and published them in a book entitled, *Le Père Hecker—Est-il un Saint* which the Cardinal Archbishop of Paris refused to approve; however, Reverend Albert Lepidi, O.P., Master of the Sacred Palace, gave it an imprimatur.

One other skirmish on the battlefield of Americanism took place shortly after Zahm's return from Fribourg when the removal of the Catholic theologian Msgr. Joseph Schroeder from the Catholic University was reluctantly approved by Rome. The American liberals found conservative Schroeder a thorn in their sides because of his conservatism, Cahens-lyism, friendship with Corrigan, and his animus against many American bishops. The liberals' attack began in the early months of 1897 following the strategy mapped out by O'Connell, Zahm and of Shahan, Bouquillon, Pace and Grannan of Catholic University. Thus, they maneuvered to have the Catholic University trustees, by a vote of ten to four, ask for his resignation. This was later approved, despite Schroeder's friends in Rome. Sadly, as Zahm would learn, and as Brandi pointedly wrote, "Msgr. Shroeder [sic] has powerful friends in Rome."[18]

As the year 1897 drew to a close in Rome, Zahm, preparing for a trip to India in order to write newspaper articles and a report on the Holy Cross Congregation's Bengalese Missions at Dacca, regretted leaving. Although he had not enjoyed the environment when he first arrived, he soon found the vibrant intellectual atmosphere enjoyably different from America, for in Rome he met and entertained many world leaders. Because of his ideals, Zahm was very critical of the educational deficiencies in the United States. He confessed no desire to return to Notre Dame and regretted the absence of intellectual stimulation on its campus.

> It would indeed be a trial for me to return to the dull, humdrum, unintellectual, dwarfing environment where I spent, or rather, wasted, the best years of my life. What a pity it is that our people do not realize the necessity of a higher culture for their members, especially those who are to devote their lives to the enobling work of education. With possibly one or two exceptions among the younger priests, not one at N.D., has the faintest conceptions of the wants of a university, & the demands of the age in which we live. I look forward to the young men now being educated at the Catholic University in the hope that they will effect eventually the much deserved change, but this will require time, & patience. The old generation must die out before any real progress can be made. N.D. ought to be one of the first educational institutions of the land, whereas it is in reality nothing more than a large boarding house for elementary students.[19]

It was with great surprise that he learned of Father Corby's death, December 28, 1897. At Français' request he cancelled the trip to India and booked passage for the United States, uncertain but suspicious that he might be made the new Provincial. His suspicions were justified. By appointment of Français, Zahm became Provincial upon his arrival at Notre Dame on January 22, 1898. Many members at Notre Dame doubted he would win the election to this post which would be held the following August.

After taking up the unfinished work of Corby and despite his many duties as Provincial, Zahm often reminisced over the happy twenty months spent in Europe. Soon after his return, in a very rare show of sentiment, he wrote to O'Connell that he was terribly homesick for Rome and "the Clubs," that it was best he had not received a letter from him at this time for it would have brought tears and made him unfit for the day's duty.[20]

Believing it necessary that their "cause" required code names to keep their friends' identities secret, Zahm wrote to O'Connell to make out a good code and send him a copy.[21] The thrilling progress for the future kept Zahm planning for the continual growth to greatness of the Catholic Church in America. After a visit with him in mid-March, 1898, Ireland wrote to O'Connell that "You have surely fixed him in the movement. He is 'the movement' and will drive the Holy Cross, the *Ave Maria* & C. onward with great force." [22] Without doubt, he was, as Ireland estimated, one of the great leaders in the cause of progressive Catholicism.

As mentioned above, Zahm expected that the Italian and French translations of *Evolution and Dogma* would cause "squalls." He supplied visitors to his apartment in Rome with English copies and was pleased that the European press had praised him. The publicity, while delighting the younger members of the clergy, had "stirred up old fogies in France." [23] He was aware in August, 1896, that the Italian translation which would appear in a few days would build up a storm and enrage many in Rome but *"n'importe. The die is cast & I care not what the results may be."* [24] He was encouraged by the favorable critique in the *Dublin Review* by Father David Fleming, O.F.M. It had great impact because of Fleming's office as the Pope's special adviser on the Anglican Orders.

Before Christmas, Zahm revealed that the controversy over *Evolution and Dogma* had commenced in England and was about to begin in Rome—"The Jesuits are already training their biggest guns on me & you will see the result in a series of articles in the *Civilta Cattolica,* their greatest magazine." [25] Still confident, he watched as the controversy spread to France and Belgium.

His optimism continued after his return to America and in a lengthy letter to O'Connell he wrote that things were in excellent condition because among other events, his Fribourg address would soon appear in the *Revue des Questions Scientifiques* and *Popular Science Monthly.* Surely the liberal advances must continue through constant watchfulness. "Great, isn't it!" he remarked to O'Connell.[26]

The next move in this struggle, and a sobering one, was O'Connell's communique to Zahm (July 10, 1898) that the war was on—the Papacy had reserved the question of Americanism to itself and, among other items, the second edition of Maignen's book would get an imprimatur. The following edict dated Rome, September 10, 1898, left no doubt that the shooting had begun in earnest and at least one target was Zahm.

Office of the Secretary of the Sacred Congregation of the Index Rome, September 10, 1898

Since the published work, 'Evolution and Dogma,' written by the Reverend James [sic] Zahm, a member of the Congregation of Holy Cross has been sent to the Sacred Congregation, the most reverend Cardinals in a general meeting on September 1, 1898, having heard the exposition and vote of the consultors, after mature deliberation have decreed: 'The work of the Reverend Zahm is prohibited; the decree, however, is not to be published until such a time that the author will be heard out by his Father General whether he is willing to submit to this decree and reprove his work; he is to be advised also by the Father General that he is to make known to Don Alphonso Maria Galea, who published the Italian translation of this work, of the prohibition of the book, which prohibition, according to the Decreta Generalia (n. 45) of the Constitution, "Officorum ac munerum" extends also to all translations made in any language. Besides the Father General is not to omit to recall to the mind of the author his obligation to subject books which refer to theological matters and those related to them, to previous censorship, both of his Superior Regular and of the Ordinary (Decreta Generalia n.36 and 41). It is your duty to make known to this Sacred Congregation at an opportune time the fulfillment of this decree.'

In the meantime, while I communicate these things to your Reverence by reason of my office, I pray that all good things be given you by the Lord.

To your Reverence,[27]

Reverend Father Superior General
Congregation of Holy Cross

Only weeks earlier, Zahm had won the election for Provincial, and too, he had inaugurated plans for the construction of a large new Holy Cross College adjacent to the Catholic University. The decree precipitated a struggle immersed in tensions and frantic appeals, attempted manipulations, and finally public submission—as revealed almost exclusively in personal letters.

Français, upon receiving the document, immediately and worriedly wrote to Zahm of the possible disastrous consequences of this blow to him and to the U.S. province. He urged only one course—quickly submit in the spirit of faith and humility to the Index and promise to answer all its requests.[28] Zahm reacted quickly and powerfully in a message marked "sacredly confidential," to O'Connell. He urged him, Fleming and Cardinal Serafino Vannutelli to get busy and prevent the publication of the decree which would hurt the "cause" and seriously embarrass himself: [29] furthermore, "If there are any propositions in the book which are *contre fidem* I shall of course eliminate them when they are pointed out." His first reaction was that Bishop Bonomelli's publication,[30] and the Italian translation provoked the decree: those who resented this "bearding the lion in his den" took a characteristic manner of manifesting their resentment.

> I am not worried by the matter, although it may embarrass me in some things for a while, & that for a short while. The decree will prove to be a boomerang, & a very ugly one at that.

Sympathy came quickly from Keane who regretted that such "machinations" succeeded against Zahm: it was unfortunate for the Church that She was led by ill-advised servants into compromising situations such as that. Like Français, he advised that the only action must be to submit and show respectful acceptance of the Church's authority—this would prevent harm to Zahm and the Congregation of Holy Cross.[31]

Zahm took the sensible advice of Français as seconded by Ireland and Keane and sent a letter to the Superior-General on October 3 which read:

> Your letter with a copy of the decree announcing the prohibition by the Sacred Congregation of the Index of my book "Evolution & Dogma" is received and I hasten to assure you & through you the Sacred Congregation, that I submit unreservedly to the decree and promise to comply at once with all its injunctions. I regret that I have written anything that should be considered deserving of censure & shall be more guarded in the future. In writing the book I had in view only the good of souls & the glory of the Church. I gave the theories discussed for what they were worth & never dreamed that they were more than theories, to be passed on by the Church, should she see fit to do so. Now that she has spoken I am the first to hearken to her voice, & to yield willing obedience to her authority. Please make known my submission to the Sacred Congregation of the Index . . .
>
> Very Sincerely—J. A. Zahm [32]

Two informative reports, from O'Connell and Fleming, gave further hints of the causes for prohibition. O'Connell believed it was the desire to punish Bonomelli, who had quoted two chapters from *Evolution and Dogma,* that caused the stir.[33] Fleming's reply, though unconsoling, revealed much when he attributed the decree to the Italian translation since it brought on strong feeling in Rome and, along with various other circumstances, brought certain authorities against Zahm.[34] Also, O'Connell's work in Rome had harmed the common cause and it was to be hoped that he would soon return to America. Unfortunately, Fleming continued, it was most likely too late to be of help. Moreover, he questioned certain evolutionary problems, for example, whether the immediate formation of Adam's body by the Creator had been revealed. Remember, he emphasized, there did not have to be in evolution anything against faith and morals: if the thesis was inopportune or premature, it could be condemned. He concluded that it was very unwise to have forced the book on the authorities in Rome by virtue of the Italian translation.[35] Probably the letters were little consolation. The net result, as Ireland wrote, was that thorough discouragement enveloped Zahm. The Archbishop wrote a strong letter to Cardinal Rampolla, and asked him to read it to the Pope.[36]

By mid-October, Zahm had formulated a tactical plan regarding the decree. Personally, he wanted to correct *Evolution and Dogma* if it was at all possible. If impossible, he urged that publication of the decree be prevented—"Leave no stone unturned to prevent the publication of the decree. This would give the *réfractaires* entirely too much satisfaction, & would prejudice the cause." [37] He hoped that Keane, Fleming, O'Connell, the two Cardinals Vannutelli, Rampolla, and Français would carry sufficient weight to tip the scales in his favor.

A few days later, Zahm wrote another letter to O'Connell in which he warned that the *réfractaires* had better be cautious for if they "wish to have a repetition of the Galileo case let them condemn evolution." [38] To his mind, he judged,

If Parnassus [Father Zahm] goes on the Index, Hedley & Dave not to speak of others, ought to go on with him. But they are not sufficiently tainted with Americanism—the heresy to which Sparta [Archbishop Ireland] gave such vogue. How much trouble he has given some people! But 'All the work is not done yet.' [39]

His last instructions were for O'Connell to keep the General in Rome until it was promised that the decree would not be published. He asked O'Connell to do all he could to prevent the enemy from having anything "to crow over."

Temporary though happy news was within the envelope eagerly opened by Zahm early in November; O'Connell assured him that Cardinal Serafino Vannutelli had promised to prevent the publication of the decree. Actually the latter had confided to O'Connell that the decree had not been published up to now because there was a friendly voice for Zahm.[40] The next meeting of the Index Committee would most probably not occur before March and certainly no decree would be published before that meeting, continued the Cardinal. O'Connell also discussed the problem with Français and on the basis of his experience with Roman custom, he urged the French priest to act slowly, carefully, and prudently for many others were involved in this problem; also, to play a diplomatic game regarding Cardinal Serafino's statement that it would not be difficult to prevent the decree's publication if Zahm submitted and stated that deeper study had resulted in new viewpoints. O'Connell emphasized to the Superior-General that all negotiations revolved on this point, for an open retraction would be equivalent to the decree's publication—his Provincial's reputation would be ruined, for retractions were not the vogue in America.

A letter by Keane written November 9, repeated this assurance: Cardinal Serafino had asked the Pope that the decree remain unpublished and he had agreed. As extra insurance, however, the Bishop wanted other protests added to make doubly sure the decree would remain unpublished. Even more important, thought Keane, the Pope's eyes had been opened to the mistaken measure towards which the enemies of Americanism were pushing him and he had stopped these measures.[41]

Français, though timid, helped Zahm's cause during a visit to Rome. The wise Superior-General feared O'Connell's advice, which was to wait for the help of Bishop Keane and Father David Fleming. Français believed this meant pleading for Zahm behind a group of men who had been attacking the Congregation of the Index.[42] Rather, Français visited the conservative Cardinal Ledochowski to enlist his support even though, as he soon learned, the Cardinal was neither displeased nor surprised about the book's condemnation. Furthermore, the Cardinal found fault with Zahm as a Procurator because he took care of the general affairs of the Church rather than the Congregation of Holy Cross, that he fell into intrigue and was carried away by it. Despite these criticisms, Français defended his Provincial and told of Zahm's great administrative ability and good influence in America. In reply, the Cardinal asked him to warn Zahm about rash and excessive doctrines, that he must be more careful and prudent in the future. Français next visited Cardinal Serafino, who promised to use his influence to prevent the decree's publication. Next stop was the home of Cardinal Andreas Steinhüber, S.J., Prefect of the Congregation of the Index. Français did not mention that he had Zahm's letter but he did say that Zahm was ready to submit. Father Français explained publication of the decree would be harmful in America. When the Cardinal answered that he alone was not the sole master of the situation, that a chairman was named and each one voted, Français urged him to do all he could to help Zahm. Before leaving Rome, Father Français sent Zahm's letter of submission to Cardinal Steinhüber. A second visit to Cardinal Ledochowski brought further hope that an enemy had at least been neutralized if not enlisted. With good sense, Français warned Keane against bringing pressure upon the Index for it would further imperil the situation.

In summing up his impressions, Français noted: first, it

would be useless to think of having the decree recalled; second, the decree probably would not be published; third, displeasure over the book resulted from Zahm's interpretation of St. Thomas and St. Augustine in a manner which made them evolutionists; also, that he placed too much credence in evolution; fourth, the authorities did not oppose evolution in general but only when the Bible was endangered. Thus, they believed that the doctrine of the evolution of man's body could not be safely taught for that would make many say that the explanation for the body of woman was a myth. Although there was much consideration for Zahm, Français continued, O'Connell was considered by the court of Rome as extremely imprudent in speech. Lastly, the weary administrator implored Zahm to employ prudence and especially to remain silent in speech and writing regarding the Index, for if he were condemned publicly, many who seemed to be helping him would abandon aid and form a strong party against him and the Congregation.

All these energetic efforts in behalf of Zahm appeared successful when O'Connell cabled on November 11, 1898, *"Jubente Papa decretum supprimitur."* [43] He also wrote that it appeared now that the "Hecker and American business" were "in a way of arrangement," and he expected that evolution would enjoy an armistice.[44] Father Joseph Legrand, C.S.C., confidently wrote that, according to O'Connell, the affair was finished. O'Connell also related that Cardinal Serafino Vannutelli had had a conference with Pope Leo XIII regarding the decree and he came away with the answer, "I withdraw it with great pleasure," [45] also, that Cardinal Steinhüber had already been informed of this decision. Not the least condition had been stipulated for the withdrawal of the decree; however, the Cardinal-Prefect might yet complain to the Pope. At least, he concluded, you are safe for the time being. And that was all that could be said because, despite these optimistic predictions, the impasse had not yet ended. The tension continued. Needless to say, Zahm did not know what to believe, yet he kept hoping for victory and believed it entirely possible.

A few weeks later, Rampolla wrote to Ireland that the Holy Father had in consideration of the Archbishop's request, suspended the publication of the decree.[46] Another O'Connell letter repeated that the decree would not be published because of Cardinal Serafino's request and Ireland's letter. O'Connell offered one further suggestion—that Zahm publish a brief letter in the press in which he would explain that after further profound study, he realized that his evolution theory might be erroneous. Actually, he continued, the whole problem had arisen because of Zahm's part in Americanism, and that although the official attitude towards it was much milder now, the enemies were greatly embittered and would continue their offensive campaign.[47]

Keane gave the same reasons for non-publication of the decree—Ireland's letter and Serafino's visit. He admitted that the latter's suggestion of some sort of retraction was finally vetoed by himself and O'Connell; however, it appeared that the Holy Office would ask for a withdrawal of the book from public sale.[48] Keane advised Zahm to do nothing until he heard more because "the non publication is final." Yet, as events proved, it was not.

The publication question was definitely unanswered despite the optimistic assurances of O'Connell and Keane, as indicated by a letter from Ireland, which related that Rampolla had written and promised in the name of the Pope that the decree would not be published until Ireland could talk the problems over with him. Ireland promised Zahm that he would talk effectively.[49] Hence, Zahm, and the Americanists generally, attached great importance to the projected Rome visit, and were hopeful that "St. Paul," who left for Europe in the highest of spirits, would convince the Vatican to forget completely the whole affair.[50]

Other forces, however, continued working against Zahm and his friends. The Italian journal, *Civilta Cattolica*, published in Rome and edited by Salvatore Brandi, S.J., had favored the conservative clergy and ideals in the United States and Europe as well. The editor, Professor of Dogmatic Theology at Woodstock, Maryland, until 1892, had fought the establishment of the Catholic University. The Jesuits had looked with general disfavor upon the foundation of Catholic University in Washington because of its proximity to long-established Georgetown University. Characteristically, Ireland considered the *Civilta Cattolica* narrow and intolerant in political and theological matters and methods; consequently, he believed that it always had been the enemy of democratic institutions, of America, and of all that she represented.

Earlier, Brandi had given *Evolution and Dogma* a bad review because he believed that evolution had not yet been adequately explained by science; until it could be so explained, it was useless for Catholics to talk about it. While praising the author's zeal, he added that Zahm's good will led him to concede the enemy peace rather than justice and truth. Finally, "It is not necessary to say that we consider this book as inopportune and harmful to anyone who has the will, the means, and the time to make his own judgment of it." [51]

A concerted attack was launched by the *Civilta* on December 29, 1898, with a long article by Brandi on *Evolution and Dogma,* instituted because of an article in the *Rassegna Nazionale* of Florence on November 5, 1898, which emphasized that Bishop John Hedley in a *Dublin Review* article agreed with Zahm. Brandi posed arguments against evolution and declared Catholic authors who favored it to be illogical and incoherent. Zahm, moreover, he thought unduly sentimental. Furthermore, he leveled the charge that Zahm had used St. Thomas to prove the secondary creation of man when actually, St. Thomas held the immediate creation of man. He thought that Zahm, with typically American ingenuousness, had failed to understand Thomistic philosophy. Brandi conceded that Zahm said there had been no factual proof for man's origin from the ape; and concluded by saying that any person who insisted upon the theory of the derived origin of the human body from the ape or any other animal ran the risk of rashness, very possibly what had happened in the case of Père Le Roy. [52]

Brandi confided to Corrigan that he believed the article was a prelude to a decree against Zahm's work.[53]

January began and no answer was given as to whether the decree would be published. Wisely, Français beseeched Zahm to have his American friends do nothing and say nothing which might resemble defiance of the authorities.[54] On January 22, the Holy Father wrote the apostolic letter, *Testem Benevolentiae,* which was deemed by conservatives such as Abbé Charles Maignen as a rebuke to the Americanism typified by Archbishop Ireland, Keane, O'Connell, the Paulists and other progressives. This was not the case, however, for the letter exempted from reprobation American political and social ideas and institutions. It was, rather, a condemnation of certain dangerous opinions which some European opponents termed "Americanism" or perhaps as Ireland wrote, "The Americanism condemned is Maignen's Nightmare." [55]

The doctrines condemned by the Pope were: that the Church should relax its discipline and doctrine in order to adapt itself to modern civilization; that modification of Catholic discipline should be determined by private individuals rather than by the Church; that a liberty similar to that in civil institutions should be introduced into the Church; external guidance is not necessary in modern times since the Holy Ghost gives greater gifts than previously; that natural virtues are to be placed above supernatural virtues and active virtues are better suited to modern times; that religious vows and orders are less useful in the present age; and finally, that Catholics should abandon former methods for seeking converts. It is important to note that the Pope said that if these doctrines were held, they were to be condemned.

Upon receipt of the letter, the Americanists without exception also condemned these propositions. Others, however, such as Archbishops Corrigan of New York and Katzer of Milwaukee indicated in correspondence that the heresy did exist in the United States. In the final analysis, however, American Catholicism was and continued to be essentially the same as French or Irish or Asiatic Catholicism. The attempts by Archbishop Ireland and others to unify the different Catholic nationalities in the United States and to educate them in the ways and institutions of American democracy were not condemned and American Catholicism continued to make itself distinctive through political and social reform efforts in a society unhampered by government intervention.

By early March Zahm had become exceedingly irritable. He had been appointed Provincial by Français shortly after the death of Corby and had assumed that position immediately upon his return from Rome. He was elected unanimously in the summer of 1898. However, the election had not yet been confirmed by the Propaganda. This uncertainty resulted in a long letter to his friend Ireland stating that he had learned, apparently from Father Lambert, that he was to be summoned to Rome because of his views on the descent of man, and that he would experience difficulty in having his position at Notre Dame confirmed because of strong opposition to him from a large number of his Community. Zahm wrote:

The Index decree must be permanently suppressed & the present incumbent must be confirmed in the provincialship. Then in the words of our leader "post Orleans fortius pugnandum" —semper pugnandum. We shall win in the long war, for truth & justice are on our side; the intelligence of the world, & the increasing might of America are with us. If this were a personal fight, I should not bother you with it. But, since it is, as you know, a fight for principles in which we are both equally interested, a fight for progress, for true Americanism, for the Catholic University, a fight against Jesuitical tyranny, against obscurantism & mediaevalism, I need make no suggestions to you as to what is best to be done. You will know better than I. I hope, however, you will see our Fr. General when you are in France. He lives at 30 Ave. du Roule, Neuilly sur Seine, just outside the Porte des Ternes, Paris. If the Propaganda wishes to be satisfied that there is no opposition to me as Provincial, all it needs to do is to communicate through Martinelli with the Superiors of my province, or with

the superiors of the entire Congregation, & will find that all
are with me. It would, no doubt, be a great victory for the
enemy to get me out of my present position, but it would
cripple Notre Dame, ruin Holy Cross College, & give a terrible set back to our Community. All would be discouraged
& the important work we have in hand would never see completion. Use all your influence, therefore, I beg of you, to
prevent what, if realized, would be a real calamity for Holy
Cross, & beg for the Catholic University as well.

As you may well understand, I shall be in great suspense
until I hear from you, & should consider it a special favor
to have some reassuring words from you by cable.[56]

However, during this hectic time, Zahm found pleasure
in awarding the Laetare Medal, the University of Notre
Dame's annual recognition of an outstanding American
Catholic lay person, to Miss Mary Gwendoline Caldwell,
who had given $300,000 for the formation of Catholic Uni-
versity of America. Grimly, he wrote to O'Connell that she
deserved it due to her excellent work in "breaking the
power of the *réfractaires.*" [57]

Hopefulness too, still prevailed in his letters to O'Connell and Ireland; especially because of Ireland's *Osservatore*
letter to Pope Leo XIII following the publication of *Testem
Benevolentiae*—

Americanism, thanks to your letter, remains untouched, and
we can now go on more bravely than ever before. Nobody
in this country is interested in the vagaries of Hecker, and
Heckerism will not be more than a nine-day wonder at most.
To me the future is more promising than ever. The enemy has
done its best to crush progress and has failed most signally.
A German editor declared a short time ago that 'Ireland has
already been condemned three times, but, the trouble is, he
won't stay condemned.' [58]

Zahm concluded with his personal hope that he could have
the decree suppressed forever for the sake of the cause. He
still had reason for concern: Brandi wrote to Corrigan on
March 28 and said there was no doubt about the decree—
Zahm would be asked to submit as had Le Roy.[59]

During this time of hopes and fears for "the cause," Zahm feared that his enemies might have him called to Rome and deposed from the Provincialship on the charge that his subjects did not want him. Français, too, was fearful, and for the first time he realized the broader implications of the decree—that Zahm was one of the leaders of Americanism.[60] Zahm believed that the worst thing that could happen would be if the Pope became seriously ill, for then the Congregation would have free scope—and his own head would be the first to fall.[61] Thus it was, he believed, that Pope Leo XIII was the protector of the Americanists generally, and for Zahm especially because of Ireland's and Cardinal Serafino Vannutelli's intercession.

Zahm's hopes soared when, during the second week in April, 1899, Ireland cabled *"Papa certe prohiberit* [sic] *decretum publicari . . . omnia incerta scribo marathon."* O'Connell wrote a very pessimistic letter to him, however, a few days later. In it he revealed that the Pope had ordered at two different times that the decree remain unpublished; however, others fought this move. The danger had not passed, he wrote, and Zahm's enemies were working like demoniacs against him.[62] The Pope told Ireland that Zahm ought to come to Rome and explain but the Archbishop pleaded that he was too busy with his many duties to take a trip of such distance. Rampolla also told Ireland that the author should appear in Rome. Thus, O'Connell judged, it seemed that the object of the enemy was to bring Zahm to Rome and obtain a personal retraction which they would publish later. In which event there would be no favor in withholding the decree and it would be more prudent to reject the favor and submit to the decree when it appeared. As others before him had suggested, O'Connell too wrote that part of the reluctance to publish the decree stemmed from the fear of seeming to be in conflict with the theory of evolution, especially in England and Germany. The enemies had no desire to be drawn into a nineteenth-century Galileo case. Their purpose, wrote O'Connell, was to publish a personal retraction from Zahm in which he would state that his thesis, upon further consideration and study, was false. The tide had turned against the Americans, he wrote, "A perfect spirit of madness prevails here at present and we can do nothing." Unfortunately, their friend Fleming became a "most hurtful enemy": Serafino and Vincenzo Vannutelli were kept in the dark and Ireland could do nothing. Hope, he concluded, was absent.

During May Zahm received another urgent letter from Français explaining that the Secretary of the Sacred Congregation of the Index had written with astonishment that the French translation of *Evolution and Dogma* was still being circulated; he repeated that the decree of condemnation had included all translations. The Secretary wrote:

Office of the
Secretary of the Sacred Congregation of the Index

Rome   April 25, 1899

Most Reverend Father

According to my office and in the name of this Sacred Congregation I must call to the attention of your Reverence an article in the *Annales de Philosophie Chrétienne* of March 1899. Among "les variétés critiques" is a review of the French translation of Father Zahm's book, *Evolution and Dogma* done by A. Flageollet.

Such a review all in praise of the book and intended to advertise it has caused great surprise after Father Zahm's book in all its translations was prohibited in conformity with No. 45, tit II, Chap. IV of the Decreti Generali. You will recall that when the decree of condemnation was communicated to your Reverence only the Italian translation is mentioned because the French translation was not known to the Sacred Congregation, otherwise Father Zahm would have been ordered to prevent the circulation of this translation also, which certainly could not have been made without his consent.

Neither must I hide from your Reverence the rumor which makes us believe that the French translation is given the greatest possible circulation, even among students in seminaries.

All this is brought to the attention of your Reverence that you might order Father Zahm to stop the circulation of the French translation of his above mentioned work as he has done with the Italian.

On this occasion I renew my expression of esteem, I remain

Fr. Marcolino Cicognani, O.P.
Secretary [63]

Fr. Gilbert Français
Superior General of the Institute of the Holy Cross
Via dei Cappuccini 19

Alarmed, Français urged his Provincial to have the sale of the French edition terminated quickly or Rome might publish the decree.[64] Also, he confessed that he had incurred the blame in Rome for not having examined Zahm's books before publication.

At Notre Dame, news of the decree began seeping out in the latter part of May and early June. Zahm's successor in Rome as Procurator-General, Father Linneborn, wrote to Brother Boniface at Notre Dame, told of the decree, and explained that the decrees of the General Chapter of 1898 were delayed because the Propaganda did not want to ratify Zahm's election.[65] He also revealed that Cardinal Ledochowski had asked him why the Holy Cross members had Father Zahm in such a high office. The Cardinal also said that before the Propaganda would ratify the election, Français had to guarantee in person the book's withdrawal from circulation. Burns, who revealed the above information, concluded with the note that "Dr. Linneborn himself was warned to hold aloof from 'Americanism.' "

On May 10, 1899, Archbishop Sebastian Martinelli, Apostolic Delegate from the Holy See, arrived at Notre Dame University for a week's visit, and thus began the final stages of the decree problem. At a banquet in the Bishop's honor on Monday, May 15, Zahm arose and proposed a toast to the Archbishop, a toast filled with words of respect for Papal authority. The next day, possibly at the suggestion of Martinelli, he composed and mailed a letter to Alphonsus Galea, the Italian translator of his *Evolution and Dogma*. To Zahm's embarrassment, this confidential note was published without authorization in the *Gazette di Malta* in early June. The letter was reprinted by U.S. newspapers. It was the Rome correspondent of the *Freeman's Journal* who furnished a copy of the Zahm letter to the New York *Daily Tribune:*

My dear Alfonsos:

I have learned from unquestionable authority that the Holy See is adverse to the further distribution of "Evolution and Dogma" and I therefore beg of you to use all your influence to have the book withdrawn from sale. You have probably foreseen this result, and it will therefore, cause you no surprise.

However, we can both thank God that we labored only for His honor and glory in giving the work to the public. As for myself, it will cause me no pain to see the fruit of so much toil consigned to oblivion. God rewards the intention, and our intentions were good.

This July 2 edition of the New York *Daily Tribune* began its story, "Fr. Zahm Submits to Rome." It thought that Zahm's withdrawal of the book had averted a most bitter controversy in the Catholic Church. It also reported that a commission of Cardinals had been examining the book and a decision was expected soon. Now, however, its author had stepped forward and had the book withdrawn from sale! Sympathetic to Zahm, the *Tribune* reporter stated that since the publication of *Evolution and Dogma*, Zahm had been the target for some of the most bitter attacks ever made in any American Catholic controversy. The enemies of Gibbons, Ireland and Keane had united in assailing him, calling him not only a liberal, but some, even a heretic. The reporter failed to mention those who objected to Zahm's liberal interpretations of evolution purely on philosophical or theological grounds and completely aside from any Church politics. Concluding the report, the friendly reporter emphasized that during the visit of Martinelli to Notre Dame in May, Zahm had declared his loyalty to the Pope. The printing of this confidential explanation in newspapers at first embarrassed its author, but soon it pleased him and he confided that "should they now publish the decree, they would only stultify themselves, & do no injury to me." [66] Thus the fears of publication that had concerned Zahm and his friends over the past year had ended with the newspaper accounts. Though Zahm had not written the letter for this purpose, its subsequent publication was a fortunate solution to the complex problem. Thus, the release of the "disfavor" came with a whisper rather than the devastating explosion feared by the liberals.

Zahm remained in high spirits regarding Americanism during the summer and fall of 1899. He wrote O'Connell that they would make the enemy sicker at the Munich Scientific Congress than even at Fribourg. He hoped his friend had a nice infernal machine and would use it as well as last time: personally, "I purpose marshalling the braves of the U.S. & we shall go to Munich as a solid phalanx . . . the future is ours, & if we do our duty we can soon convert the future into the present." [67]

Français too was pleased with the situation regarding Rome and *Evolution and Dogma;* he thanked Zahm for expressing himself so graciously in his toast to the Holy See at the Martinelli dinner and added that in so doing, he had manifested great courage. Now, in Italy, all satisfaction had been given and soon, he hoped, the black storm cloud would disappear from the French edition. [68]

And for "the cause," wrote Zahm, Archbishop Ireland too believed it was stronger than ever and "Americanismo" was on firmer ground and gaining a rapidly increasing number of followers. [69] He believed that the possibility of a decree being issued was over—and it was. Finally, Zahm reported that Cardinal Moran had asked him to prepare a paper on Science and Religion for the forthcoming Australian Congress in Sydney and he had accepted. The paper was never presented, and to this writer's knowledge, never prepared.

Most likely, Français, fearful of any further difficulties, refused permission for the project and gently urged Zahm to concentrate upon building his province in the United States.

In any event, his active concern with Americanism ended and Zahm concentrated his energies on developing the Holy Cross Congregation in the United States. Surely, he was an apostle, though largely a publicly silent one, of the ideas of Archbishops Ireland and Keane. He shared their devotion to the theory and practice of the government of the United States. He too believed that the Catholic Church in America faced a future of glory within the framework of American institutions and law. However, Zahm's major role in this period was as an apologist for the Church in its endeavor to effect reconciliation with modern science. Also his work in building up the Congregation of Holy Cross and its educational system was indeed important during this progressive era in American Catholic history.

NOTES TO CHAPTER V

1. Zahm to Albert Zahm, May 16, 1896. John Zahm Collection, UNDA.

2. University Report. PA.

3. Burns Collection. PA.

4. *Ibid.*

5. Zahm to Burns, June 5, 1896. John Zahm Collection, UNDA.

6. Sister M. Francesca, "Mother M. Annunciata," *Superior-Generals: Centenary Chronicles of the Sisters of The Holy Cross, 1841-1941* (Paterson, 1941), II, 123. Also *Historical Sketch of the Sisters of the Holy Cross* (Notre Dame, n.d.), p. 87.

7. Zahm to Burns, June 5, 1896. John Zahm Collection, UNDA.

8. Zahm to Albert Zahm, July 22, 1896. John Zahm Collection, UNDA. He also wrote that Scotch, English, French, Belgian and Italian newspapers were always talking about " 'le grand savant American' in a way that amazes me. I cannot imagine why I should create such a furore among them. Newspaper men are at my house every day & if I wished to let myself out, I could not ask for a better opportunity. But I have resolved to lie low for a while, notwithstanding the fact that many Roman papers have repeatedly asked me to give them material for an illustrated biography." *Ibid.*, July 22, 1896.

9. Brandi to Corrigan, June 13, 1896. Copy, UNDA.

10. Zahm to Albert Zahm, January 10, 1897. John Zahm Collection, UNDA.

11. *Ibid.*, March 9, 1897.

12. In viewing Americanism, it is certain that had Pope Leo's request in the mid-eighteen-eighties for peace and fraternal accord among Catholic journalists been accepted, the controversy would not have assumed such scandalous proportions. Cf. Edwardo Soderini, *The Pontificate of Leo XIII*, trans. Barbara Barclay Carter (London, 1934), I, 152-54.

13. Egan, though sympathetic to the liberals, criticized Keane's failure to model the Catholic University after the University of Louvain. It seemed, said Egan, that the Rector "was so much in love with what he called 'Americanism' that I think he imagined that the Stars and Stripes saturated with a little holy water would guide him to perfection." *Recollections of a Happy Life* (New York, 1924), p. 189.

14. Zahm to Albert Zahm, November 11, 1896. John Zahm Collection, UNDA.

15. Zahm to Burns, February 17, 1897. John Zahm Collection, UNDA.

16. Zahm to Gibbons, March 9, 1897. Copy, UNDA.

17. Ireland to Zahm, September 11, 1897. John Zahm Collection, UNDA.

18. Brandi to Corrigan, November 21, 1899. Copy, UNDA.

19. Zahm to Albert Zahm, December 12, 1897. John Zahm Collection, UNDA.

20. Zahm to O'Connell, February 5, 1898. Copy, UNDA.

21. Zahm to O'Connell, March 4, 1898. Copy, UNDA. Zahm was given the code name, "Parnassus"; O'Connell, "Marathon"; Ireland, "Sparta"; and Keane, "Damascus."

22. Ireland to O'Connell, March 15, 1898. Copy, UNDA. Also, Zahm revealed that Cardinal Martinelli was to visit him on May 25 in the interest of the "movement."

23. Zahm to Albert Zahm, August 23, 1896. John Zahm Collection, UNDA.

24. *Ibid.*, August 23, 1896.

25. *Ibid.*, December 6, 1896. UNDA.

26. Zahm to O'Connell, March 14, 1898. Copy, UNDA.

27. A copy in Latin is in the Provincial Archives. Only three weeks before, an article on "Rev. Dr. Zahm," in the *Review*, August 25, 1898, had bitterly criticized him for his views on evolution. Between 1850-1899, there were 788 books placed upon the Index; between 1900-1949, only 255 were added to the list. Reverend Redmond A. Burke, C.S.V., *What Is the Index* (Milwaukee, 1952), p. 52. In January 1897, Pope Leo XIII published his constitution, *Officiorum ac Munerum*, which was a revision of the rules laid down by Pius IV. French and

German bishops requested the revision. Reverend Raymond Corrigan, *The Church and the Nineteenth Century* (Milwaukee, 1938) pp. 270-71.

28. Français to Zahm, September 16, 1898. John Zahm Collection, UNDA.

29. Zahm to O'Connell, September 28, 1898. Copy, UNDA.

30. A year earlier, Sabina di Tarravicino di Revel wrote that Msgr. Bonomelli, Bishop of Cremona was fascinated by Zahm's book. Tarravicino to O'Connell, November 29, 1897. Copy, UNDA. As a result, the Italian Bishop wrote an appendix to his book, *Sequiano La Ragione* (Milan, 1898) in which he discussed evolution, using Zahm as an authority. Apparently, because of rumors, the Bishop withdrew his thesis regarding evolution of the human body on October 22, 1898. Reverend Ernest C. Messenger, *Evolution and Theology* (New York, 1932), p. 234. In a letter written in November, 1898, Sabina di Tarravicino recognized an important aspect in the Americanist problem when she wrote, "It is noteworthy, however, that in all the attacks waged against Americanism, Zahm is never mentioned and Ireland is not spoken of either." Tarravicino to O'Connell, November 10, 1898. Copy, UNDA.

31. Keane to Zahm, September 28, 1898. UNDA. To Archbishop Ireland, Keane wrote, "Father Zahm is a very great loss to us. The 'triple funiculus' has lost one of its cords." Keane to Ireland, October 18, 1898. AASP.

32. Zahm to Français, October 3, 1898. Rough draft. John Zahm Collection, UNDA.

33. O'Connell to Zahm, October (no date), 1898. John Zahm Collection, UNDA.

34. Many leading Italian advocates of a liberal interpretation of evolution were agnostic and undoubtedly the Italian translation of *Evolution and Dogma* was used against the Church. It should be remembered that the Church was seriously imperiled by the growth of a nationalist Italy.

35. Fleming to Zahm, October 20, 1898. John Zahm Collection, UNDA.

36. Ireland to O'Connell, October 27, 1898. Copy, UNDA. Such action was not new with Archbishop Ireland; he had fought the condemnation of Mivart's articles, and earlier, he had kept Henry George's *Progress and Poverty* off the Index in 1888.

37. Zahm to O'Connell, October 20, 1898. Copy, UNDA.

38. *Ibid.*, October 31, 1898. Copy, UNDA.

39. *Ibid.*, October 31, 1898. Copy, UNDA. Bishop John Cuthbert Hedley, ignorant of the tense situation, wrote an article, "Physical Science and Faith," *Dublin Review*, 123 (October, 1898), 241-61, which was published only four weeks after the decision to prohibit *Evolu-*

tion and Dogma. The article was a summary of Zahm's writings on evolution and it commended his ideas on theistic evolution; it also noted that one's faith would not be harmed by accepting this theory of evolution. As for Zahm, he wrote, "No one can turn over his pages without feeling how deeply he is in earnest in his endeavor to place human science and religious faith in their true position, one towards the other." *Ibid.,* 123, 259. O'Connell believed that this essay would draw out a favorable letter from Cardinal Vaughan to the Pope since Hedley was the "Pope's pet-of-the English" Bishops and also on excellent terms with Cardinal Vaughan. O'Connell to Zahm, November 2, 1898, and November 7, 1898. UNDA. Vaughan's letter had not yet arrived by the end of November and it is not known whether he did write. O'Connell to Zahm, November 27, 1898. UNDA. Bishop Hedley in a letter to the *Tablet* published January 14, 1899, stated that if the authorities said, as suggested in the *Civilta Cattolica,* January 7, 1899, that Catholics may not hold the evolution of man's body, then he would accept the principle. Messenger, *op. cit.,* pp. 234-35.

40. O'Connell to Zahm, October 31, 1898. John Zahm Collection, UNDA.

41. Keane to Zahm, November 9, 1898. John Zahm Collection, UNDA.

42. Français to Zahm, November 10, 1898. John Zahm Collection, UNDA.

43. O'Connell to Zahm, November 11, 1898. John Zahm Collection, UNDA.

44. Someone told O'Connell that Zahm was not precisely on the Index, rather, he was expected to make a submission and withdraw his books from circulation as in Bonomelli's case. O'Connell to Zahm, November 10, 1898. John Zahm Collection, UNDA.

45. Legrand to Zahm, November 11, 1898. John Zahm Collection, UNDA.

46. Rampolla to Ireland, November 27, 1898. AASP.

47. O'Connell to Zahm, November 27, 1898. John Zahm Collection, UNDA.

48. Keane to Zahm, December 10, 1898. John Zahm Collection, UNDA.

49. Ireland to Zahm, December 13, 1898. John Zahm Collection, UNDA.

50. Zahm to O'Connell, December 19, 1898. Copy, UNDA.

51. *Civilta Cattolica.* Series xvi, Vol. IX (January 4, 1897), 201-204.

52. Père LeRoy published *L'Evolution restreinte aux espèces organiques* in 1891. In 1895 he was called to Rome and he retracted his thesis because, he said, he learned from competent authorities that it was untenable with regard to man's body. Messenger, *op. cit.,* pp. 232-33. Bishop Hedley wrote later that he had learned LeRoy retracted

because of condemnation from his Dominican Superiors rather than from the Holy See. *Ibid.,* p. 235.

53. Brandi to Corrigan, January 2, 1899. Copy, UNDA.

54. Français to Zahm, January 12, 1899. John Zahm Collection, UNDA.

55. Ireland to Deshon, February 24, 1899, as cited in Thomas T. McAvoy, C.S.C. *The Great Crisis in American Catholic History* (Chicago, 1957), p. 281. Chapter Six of *ibid.* gives the most complete discussion of the Pope's letter: also cf. pp. 351-54 for further treatment.

56. Zahm to Ireland, March 5, 1899. AASP.

57. Zahm to O'Connell, March 30, 1899. Copy, UNDA.

58. Zahm to Ireland, March 31, 1899. AASP. Also Zahm to O'Connell, March 30, 1899. Copy, UNDA.

59. Brandi to Corrigan, March 28, 1899. Copy, UNDA.

60. Français to Zahm, April 3, 1899. John Zahm Collection, UNDA.

61. Burns Collection. PA.

62. O'Connell to Zahm, April 12, 1899. John Zahm Collection, UNDA.

63. A copy of this letter, written in Italian, is in the Provincial Archives.

64. Français to Zahm, May 27, 1899. UNDA. In another letter on June 3, 1899, he repeated his belief that Rome might yet decide to publish the decree. John Zahm Collection, UNDA.

65. Burns Collection. PA.

66. Zahm to O'Connell, October 6, 1899. Copy, UNDA.

67. *Ibid.,* June 21, 1899. Copy, UNDA.

68. Français to Zahm, July 22, 1899. John Zahm Collection, UNDA.

69. Zahm to O'Connell, October 6, 1899. Copy, UNDA.

VI

Provincial of Holy Cross

"A Romance in Religious Life"

The death of Father William Corby on December 28,
1897, brought Father Gilbert Français, after considerable
soul searching, to recall Zahm from Rome as the new Provincial. This momentous decision, and it was just that for
the Congregation of Holy Cross as well as for Notre Dame,
brought Zahm to the post of top administrator for the
United States Province of the Congregation. The Congregation of Holy Cross in the United States had progressed in
its "prairie" and "brick and mortar" years under the aggressive leadership of Father Edward Sorin. One of his Provincial successors, the famous and kindly Civil War chaplain,
Corby, had continued this growth—but only with hesitation
since he did not believe in higher education. Under the firm
leadership of Zahm, who as a confident builder resembled
Sorin, these hesitant steps became rapid, steady strides, directed toward the goal of acquiring a learned and saintly
body of teachers. During eight and one-half years of intensive planning Zahm led the Community further into the
field of higher education in modern America. Despite the
opposition of certain men, strong in character within his
own Congregation, he, together with Father John W. Cavanaugh and Father James Burns, carefully set the pattern for
scholars, scholarships and the future greatness of both the
Congregation and its leading University in America, Notre
Dame.

Immediately after receiving Français' cablegram directing him to return to the United States, Zahm booked passage on the *Normandie*. Writing from his stateroom desk and between rounds of his usual bouts with sea-sickness, he promised O'Connell that he would cable in the event he were named Provincial. He returned home uncertain of the future, suspicious, yet not positive that the difficult job would be assigned to him.

Actually, he was formally appointed Provincial by Français in the first days of January, and although he was ignorant of this decision, it was publicized among the members of the United States Province in a Circular Letter dated January 5, 1898. In it Français confessed that he had considered waiting for the next General Chapter to choose a new Provincial by the customary election; however, he decided it was necessary to appoint one immediately. And, since Zahm, a close friend of Sorin, had an excellent aptitude for intellectual work, for which he had won admiration in the Congregation, the United States, and Europe, Français decided that Zahm should be the new Provincial. More significantly, Français noted that Zahm had pleaded with earnestness during almost twenty years for a thorough course of studies for the Congregation.

The Superior-General's decision produced a variety of reactions. Some members of his own Community were stunned. Father James Burns, the young disciple of Zahm, called the decision a dramatic piece of news and one worthy of a Napoleon.[1] Further, he noted that the new Provincial had been exiled from Notre Dame two years earlier when he was sent off to Rome as Procurator-General. And that Father Andrew Morrissey could have kept Zahm at Notre Dame, that Zahm had requested it, and yet he had been sent to Rome. He had been passed by when Morrissey became President of Notre Dame at the death of Father Walsh in 1893. According to Burns, every Superior in the Province who had any influence was against Zahm; Father Patrick Condon, future Assistant General predicted that the most difficult problem facing the next Provincial would be what to do with Zahm. "And now," wrote Burns, "he is on his way back. Coriolanus-like, clothed with almost supreme authority over all the Superiors—the leader of the Province. It is a romance in religious life."

Shortly after appointing Zahm, Français related to Father John W. Cavanaugh that it was the greatest decision he had ever made. Actually, even before the death of Corby, Français, a former Rector of the College of St. Croix at Neuilly for fourteen years, had considered replacing Morrissey as President of Notre Dame by Zahm because he was growing to respect Zahm's opinions more and more: the Superior-General was displeased with the intellectual narrowness and frequent battling against higher things as conducted by Corby and Morrissey. At least a few feared that if Zahm were named, Morrissey might resign. In addition to Burns and Cavanaugh, Father Alexander M. Kirsch, Zahm's former assistant in the Science Department, and Father Scheier, former Vice-President of St. Edward's College in Austin, Texas, were among those especially pleased by the Superior-General's choice.

Archbishop Ireland congratulated Zahm and wondered what the enemies would say because Zahm had gone to Rome, was honored and esteemed there, and now had won a crucial position—"Verily, iniquity has been made to lie to itself." [2] Bishop Keane had sensed the appointment and found it providential; further he hoped that the new Provincial could, together with the Superior-General, bring the Congregation to exemplify the best in what was known as "Americanism." [3] O'Connell accurately recognized the decision as a revolution in the Holy Cross Congregation and predicted rather optimistically that within two years Zahm would reform the Congregation according to his own ideas.[4] Like Zahm, he was an impatient man. He also believed, and correctly so, that the appointment would bring educational reforms in all the Holy Cross Colleges; in Americanist fashion, he related that the Jesuits had best be careful or they would be left in the rear.

Zahm received official confirmation of his selection upon his arrival at Notre Dame on January 23, 1898. He confided to O'Connell that his fears had been well-founded: this also meant a great change in his life and plans; however, he could do more for the cause of Americanism at Notre Dame than anywhere else.[5] Homesick for Rome, he confessed to O'Connell that the "burden of responsibility & the sacrifice of personal liberty are things which often carry me back to the sciences which for me shall ever be sacred as long as memory retains its power." However, he assumed the job in the hope he would do great work for the Church, Notre Dame and the Congregation of Holy Cross.

As Provincial, Zahm was responsible for the management of the following churches, schools and orphanages within the States of Indiana, Wisconsin, Illinois, Louisiana, Ohio, Texas and within Washington, D. C.:

INDIANA

University of Notre Dame—Notre Dame
Cathedral School—Fort Wayne
St. Mary's Parochial School—Lafayette
St. Joseph's Manual Labor School—Notre Dame
Professed House—Notre Dame
Holy Cross Seminary—Notre Dame
Holy Cross Novitiate—Notre Dame
Church of St. John the Baptist—Earl Park
St. Vincent de Paul's Church—St. Vincent
St. Mary's Church—South Bend
St. Joseph's Church—South Bend
St. Patrick's Church—South Bend
St. Hedwig's Church—South Bend
St. Joseph's Farm—Notre Dame
St. Joseph's Orphan Asylum—Lafayette

WISCONSIN

Sacred Heart College—Watertown
St. John's Cathedral School—Milwaukee

St. Joseph's Church—Richwood
St. Bernard's Church—Watertown

ILLINOIS

St. Columbkille's School—Chicago
St. Columbia's School—Ottawa
Holy Trinity Church—Chicago

LOUISIANA

St. Isidore's College—New Orleans
Sacred Heart Church—New Orleans

OHIO

Holy Trinity Parochial School—Cincinnati
St. Joseph's College—Cincinnati

TEXAS

St. Edward's College—Austin
Church of the Immaculate Conception—Austin

WASHINGTON, D. C.

House of Studies

Within the American Province there were approximately 50 priests, 175 Brothers, 70 novices and 45 postulants for an estimated approximate total of 339. The Province was large and complex; especially for a conscientious administrator who demanded sacrifice in order to begin the costly formation of scholars and new schools. It was a position which could break the health and heart of an impatient man.

In addition to the many duties, it was evident that the new administrator could not presume the full cooperation of his associates. It was a tense atmosphere in which certain persons allowed their personal bias to work against the common goal. The unfortunate conflict, marked oftentimes by an uneasy armistice, involved Morrissey on one hand and Zahm on the other—between the conservative and older priests and Brothers of the Community and the younger, aggressive priests who were eager to make Notre Dame a genuine University and the Congregation, a community of scholars.

A true Irishman, Morrissey was born in Ireland *circa* 1859 and was received as a postulant at Notre Dame on December 3, 1875, a few months after Zahm's ordination. On July 23, 1882, he presented himself for his religious profession and was accepted. After teaching at Sacred Heart College, Watertown, Wisconsin, he was ordained at St. Francis Seminary in Milwaukee by Archbishop Heiss in 1884. He became Director of Studies at Notre Dame in 1885 and Vice-President in 1892, replacing Zahm. After the death of Father Thomas Walsh in July, 1893, he became the eighth President of Notre Dame. As President, he longed for the advancement of Notre Dame; however, as Burns, his Director of Studies, wrote, Morrissey unfortunately was not a "University" man. While he was broadminded, liberal, energetic, talented and had extremely winning personal qualities, he lacked faith in higher education—in a university education for college teachers.[6] Others who knew him well have remarked about his fine social grace and winning manners.

In 1895, Morrissey had agreed with Français' plan to have the new building just west of the Church, Corby Hall, become a student hall for sophomores and freshman and not, as planned earlier, a community house.[7] Zahm, too, agreed with the idea for he believed it would be a great stride forward. Father Daniel Hudson, C.S.C., editor of the *Ave Maria*, was against the plan because he feared it would increase disciplinary problems.[8] Sorin Hall was enlarged under Father Morrissey's presidency in 1897 with the addition of forty more rooms, thus making almost ninety in all.

Like most Catholic colleges and universities in the United States during the nineteenth century, Notre Dame was not essentially a University. A sampling of student enrollment reveals the small percentage of even collegiate students. Primarily, it was a boarding school for high school students.

Enrollment 1887-8 [9]				Enrollment 1894-5 [10]		
Students	Number	%		Students	Number	%
Collegiate	79	15		Collegiate	130	24
Preparatory	72	13		Preparatory	97	18
Commercial	285	53		Commercial	223	41
Minims	103	19		Minims	97	18
Total Enrollment	539			Total Enrollment	547	

The eighteen-nineties showed a definite trend in the decrease of commercial students and a corresponding increase of college-minded lads, which pointed toward a new era of higher education at Notre Dame.

Enrollment 1895 (November) [11]				Enrollment 1896 (November) [12]		
Students	Number	%		Students	Number	%
Collegiate	125	26		Collegiate	124	26
Preparatory	82	17		Preparatory	160	34
Commercial	184	38		Commercial	112	24
Minims	86	18		Minims	81	17
Total Enrollment	477			Total Enrollment	477	

Enrollment 1897 (November) [13]				Enrollment 1898 (November) [14]		
Students	Number	%		Students	Number	%
Collegiate	130	24		Collegiate	108	21
Preparatory	238	45		Preparatory	243	47
Commercial	74	14		Commercial	88	17
Minims	91	17		Minims	81	16
Total Enrollment	533			Total Enrollment	520	

Enrollment 1899 (November) [15]		
Students	Number	%
Collegiate	143	23
Preparatory	288	46
Commercial	103	16
Minims	96	15
Total Enrollment	630	

The ratio of over 2 to 1 for preparatory and college students was common in American Catholic colleges for boys.
A report to the Catholic Educational Association in 1908
revealed that in 101 such schools, there were 10,798 boys in
the high school department, and 4,232 college students.[16]

Burns, a careful observer of this trend, judged that the increase of preparatory students resulted from three non-in-
tellectual factors: first, the entrance requirements had been
raised; secondly, a student was promised a private room in
Sorin Hall when he became a freshman (if he could pay for
it); and thirdly, the enlargement of the athletic program had
publicized the University. For example in the spring of
1897, Notre Dame's baseball team played in Chicago for
the first off-campus game in eight years. The football team
was scheduled for two games away from home in the fall of
1897 as well.

Hence with the enrollment of Notre Dame concentrated
at the high school level, Morrissey could hardly be blamed
for his failure to recognize future possibilities: he was a conservative who lacked vision and he was fearful that attempts
to enlarge the facilities for higher education would be finan-
cially dangerous. Nor was he alone in his beliefs, for of the
five priests who represented the United States Province in
1897, only Zahm was a man of higher education; of the six
Brothers on the Provincial Council, none had even a college
education. Catholic colleges generally were still in the process of becoming true centers of advanced study; they had
since their beginning been primarily institutions of moral
formation and their students were not prepared to engage in
serious college-level courses.[17]

Perhaps Morrissey's chief aide was Father Stanislaus Fitte,
a native of Germany who arrived in the United States in
1880 at the age of forty. He agreed with Morrissey and
stood opposed to the expansion begun by Zahm because he
believed the first necessity of the Congregation was to form
deeply religious men who would strengthen the existing
houses. He feared Zahm's criticism, however, and thus re-

mained formally quiet on such questions. At the same time, his letters reveal a strong divergence from his Provincial:

> I know him. He has the mania of founding, of expanding . . . I have very little confidence in those foundations. They will crumble to pieces by want of men capable of supporting them. They will create a spirit of division more and more profound. They will delay the true interior progress upon which we can hope to build with solidity, and which should above all stir up our activity. . . .[18]

With little faith, he concluded, "We shall soon be compelled to go back. Not one of our houses in America has the half of the staf [sic]."

Father Daniel E. Hudson, conservative editor of the weekly *Ave Maria,* did not agree with Zahm's expansion program either. Ordained with Zahm, he admired his companion's great intellect and considered himself a friend, although he had firmly opposed Zahm's foundation of the Washington House of Studies. He sincerely believed Notre Dame could and should educate its own seminarians.[19]

Zahm was considered a very formal man. As noted in earlier chapters, he could be extremely adept at influencing people, for example, on the western student-gathering tours and during the lectures before the student body at Notre Dame when he regularly entertained them with world-wide travelogues and physics experiments. In dealings with his superiors, scholars, and liberal churchmen, he often made tactful approaches; and consequently gained many of his objectives. With his associates at Notre Dame, however, he was very impatient with those who lacked vision. In all his dealings he sought to be a just man, a man of principle. Without question, he was ambitious for the growth and superiority of Holy Cross Congregation.

Also, he was a very human person, one to whom "A little mystery is wholesome now & then." On one of his daily walks as Provincial, he noted that the young lads at the seminary needed baseball bats and he promptly had a sufficient number delivered. His letters to his brother conveyed wholesome concern for Albert's plans, ranging from suggestions on laboratory equipment to purchasing a bicycle at wholesale cost. In conversation, Zahm often discussed problems of world importance; and although his father had been a fervent Democrat, he did not enter publicly into political or temperance discussions. Rather during the few evening leisure hours in his term as Provincial, he read the works of Dante and the Classics.

Naturally, he was a retiring man. He opposed a silver jubilee celebration in his honor for, as he wrote, he abominated such things.[20] With regard to publicity, he was readily accessible to reporters for he realized the great value of the press for accomplishing his aims. He had an acute awareness of the value of publicity and employed practical measures to obtain favorable coverage. For example, he urged Albert to construct an artificial geyser named "Young Faithful" and to have a photograph of it ready for the press. From the days of his science lectures at Notre Dame and the subsequent reports in the *Scholastic,* through the international tours and newspaper and magazine stories that described his lecture-writing on Science and Religion, Zahm became a world-wide figure through publicity.

Zahm took special pride in two of the young Holy Cross priests, James Burns and John W. Cavanaugh, and both became key figures in the development of the Congregation, Holy Cross College and the University of Notre Dame. These men were opposites in temperament—the former, dignified and modest; the latter, friendly, sociable and a fine orator.

Burns, born February 13, 1867, at Michigan City, Indiana, received his A.B. degree at Notre Dame in 1887, and his Master's degree in 1894, one year after his ordination. He became Rector of Sorin Hall and Chemistry Instructor at the University. Like Zahm, he urged that Notre Dame become a true university. Convinced that excellent professors are the foundation for institutions of higher education, he believed that instead of gilding the dome and covering the walls of the Main building with frescoes, the authorities should have used the money for professorships.

Cavanaugh was born at Laetonia, Ohio, on May 23, 1870, enrolled at Notre Dame in 1886, and received his Litt.B. in 1890. After ordination in 1894, he continued as assistant to Hudson on the *Ave Maria* magazine. With the appointment of Zahm as Provincial, Burns considered Cavanaugh an excellent replacement for Morrissey as President of Notre Dame. He urged Français to make the change.[21] Although the suggestion was rejected, he believed events would soon change the Superior-General's mind. Other young men such as Fathers Michael A. Quinlan, Michael F. Oswald, James A. Trahey and Julius Nieuwland joined Zahm in his projects after their graduation from Catholic University. They too wanted a true university at Notre Dame—the Bonn or Cambridge or Bologna of their leader's dreams. Proudly, he called them "his boys." [22]

As Zahm stepped off the westbound train at the South Bend depot on January 22, 1898, he was relieved at the gracious greetings extended by L'Etourneau and Morrissey. On the surface, at least, there appeared to be possibilities of friendly relationships, and this happy event eased the weariness he felt after the long voyage and railroad travel to Notre Dame. Although forty-six years old, he appeared younger, probably because of his intense energy; however, strong facial features and a slender body gave every indication of a mature, self-disciplined man. A cordial reception at the University pleased him and eased somewhat his yearning to be back in the Eternal City, though sobering thoughts of the Provincialship with its great personal sacrifice of liberty and heavy responsibility naturally worried him. For the moment, he believed that all the Community members, priests and Brothers, would give complete co-operation and that the future held great promise for Holy Cross and Notre Dame.[23] When asked to say a few words at the reception, he begged the assistance of his confreres, faculty, and students and concluded—"Let us labor for Notre Dame, for Holy Cross, for country, and for God." [24]

Even before his return, some members quietly speculated whether he could be elected at the General Chapter in August, 1898. It appeared highly probable; however, the Brothers generally were unfavorable to him since some believed he had discriminated against them when he had been Acting President during Walsh's trip to Europe in 1888.[25] Burns believed Zahm could win if he planned strategically.

A major problem facing Zahm was to reorganize and rehabilitate the teaching brotherhood which was slowly disintegrating because the Brothers' schools were closing one by one. Only about six were left. Burns believed one of the main causes for this depletion was that the Brothers were not qualified to teach since they were only one-half educated. Thus, he recommended to the new Provincial a four-year course for the Brothers and Zahm was highly pleased. A few days after his arrival, when told of the gossip regarding the coming election, Zahm replied that he would be conciliatory but *he* would be Provincial, and he would use no gifts to assure reelection—that he would "do his duty fearlessly and prudently, and leave the rest to God." [26] He also revealed that he would much rather have his former job in Rome than the heavy Provincial responsibilities. In recording this, Burns wrote, "He is full of ambition, but I believe, on the whole, with all his faults, that it is ambition for God's honor and glory." [27]

Election speculations continued during the spring of 1898. Brother Engelbert, Director of the Brothers' House of Studies and a member of the General Chapter, promised his support. Français believed he could count on the six votes from France and thought he could convince the Canadian members that their fears of Zahm were ill-founded. Zahm too helped the campaign as his prudence and broad-mindedness amazed his opponents and even surprised his friends. By the end of March the Community was moving smoothly and successfully forward. By April 19, 1898, the Superior-General wrote that the Capitulants in Canada without exception would vote for the incumbent: it looked as if the Brothers too were turning to favor him.[28]

One of the main concerns of Zahm during these first
months in office was the unsteady Washington, D. C., House
of Studies, founded in 1895 by his design and pleading. The
Holy Cross Congregation was the third religious community
to found a House of Studies at Catholic University. It began
in Brookland in 1895 under Father Peter J. Franciscus as
director and thirteen Holy Cross Seminarians from the
United States and Canada as students. The seminarians had
spent four years at Notre Dame in preparatory school, then
four years in college. Upon receiving their bachelor's degrees, they pursued graduate study at Catholic University
in addition to their theology and other sacred sciences for
four more years. Morrissey, French, and Hudson had opposed the foundation, for they believed, as noted previously,
that Notre Dame should train its own men. They discounted
Zahm's wise observation that the busy seminarians were permitted neither the time nor the professors to pursue higher
studies at Notre Dame.

During the first years, the foundation continued with uncertainty; hostile forces planned to have it abandoned in the
forthcoming Chapter of 1898.[29] When the Superior-General
notified Zahm of these circumstances, shortly before Corby's
death, he received a characteristic reply urging him to ar-
range a *coup d'état* by taking the foundation out of the
hands of the Chapter and proclaiming to all capitulants and
chapters—"*Sic volo, sic jubeo*." [30] Français was reluctant to
take this step for he believed he did not have the power.
He did consider a plan, however, whereby he would simply
remove all the young men of the Holy Cross Congregation
from the Provincial's hands and personally decide their educational future.[31]

However, Zahm tried another measure. Shortly before he
departed from Rome in 1898, he begged Keane to urge Gibbons, Ireland and a few other members of the hierarchy to
bring strong pressure upon the Superior-General and himself, if he were Provincial, for maintaining the House of
Studies, thus averting a major disaster.[32] Zahm also mentioned that Corby had declared shortly before his death that

he intended to terminate the Washington school in the next Chapter. Keane wrote to Ireland and urged him to inform the Father General and Zahm that the removal would be an injurious action because of the recent trials of the University, and moreover it would be prejudicial to the Congregation of the Holy Cross. In describing the situation, he noted that both Zahm and Français were devoted friends of the University; however, there were many other voting members in the Chapter not as enlightened.

In his letter to Zahm, Ireland related he had heard in Washington that the Congregation might abandon its foundation. If true, he urged reconsideration, because the hierarchy had been pleased over the close relations between Catholic University and the Holy Cross Congregation. Moreover, their young men were much better prepared as Americans after having lived in the capital city. Appealing to patriotism, he continued: "You are yourself so thorough an American, and you know so well the conditions of this country, that I think you will readily agree with what I am saying." [33] What was necessary in America was a fraternal spirit among all the Church's armies even though customs in other countries were different. Too often, he added, coolness between the armies of Christ had harmed religion. And cleverly he concluded, the Congregation of Holy Cross had never shown such a coolness, for their founder in the United States, Sorin, was a model of unselfish thoughts and affections.

Gibbons also related that even the suggestion of a severance caused him pain because Notre Dame was the first large institution to ally with Catholic University. If the severance did occur, it would be a calamity to Catholic University and, even more important, the hierarchy of the United States could not view it in a friendly light.[34] From the West, Archbishop Patrick Riordan, an alumnus of Notre Dame, wrote along similar lines and added that Zahm now had a fine opportunity to bring a strong desire for the intellectual life into the Congregation. A college, he said, was more than bricks and mortar, it was an island of learned men and learning students. He urged that the Congregation under Français and Zahm continue its House of Studies.[35]

These letters served to increase Zahm's confidence that the Washington establishment would be continued, even improved and enlarged. He believed only three or four Capitulants from Notre Dame would oppose it—and he did not include among these Morrissey, the head and heart of the opposition. Rather, he felt that he could win Morrissey to the cause and he counted heavily upon a few Vatican letters praising the Holy Cross establishment.

Two months before the crucial General Chapter, Zahm publicized his ideas on education in a Circular Letter; in effect, it was his election platform. He expressed the dire need for a better intellectual atmosphere within every one of the Congregation's schools. With vision, he described the goal of them all. Summer school studies would enable them to learn the latest educational methods and subject content so that they could meet the demands of their competitors. He reminded them that as Holy Cross members they were devoted in a special manner to the work of Christian education, and thus it should be their deep and holy ambition to fulfill this task as well as if not better than any one else. In fact, they must be the courageous leaders in the modern American educational movement. Good will and determination would produce these results which some called impossible—remember, he proudly promised, "We are called upon to do great things for education and religion, for God and for His Church. Let us then be up an [sic] doing. Let us cultivate a love of study, a taste for serious and profitable reading." [36] He predicted that a brilliant future awaited Holy Cross Congregation if the members would devote their best energies and qualify themselves for truly educating their students. In effect, Zahm's leadership and determination were directed toward providing scholars who in turn would form others. He more than any other member of the Congregation recognized the necessity for making the Holy Cross priests learned men.

Just eight days before the scheduled General Chapter meeting in Canada, Zahm raised the question of the House of Studies at Washington in the Provincial Council at Notre Dame: he urged unsuccessfully that the Council vote for it. After he assured them that the Chapter would pass it over their heads, they unanimously agreed to leave things as they were, and to erect a permanent building there in the course of time. Thus, as the Council Secretary wrote, "In this way the question of higher education becomes for this Province, a provincial matter." [37] This decision was exactly what Zahm desired for now he could legislate as he saw fit.

The General Chapter held in the Provincial House of Côte des Neiges, Canada, during the first days of August, 1898, brought victory to Zahm in his bid for election. It was a vote of confidence for both Zahm and Français. Election results also revealed that Father Patrick Condon, Father Lemarié, Brothers Ernest and Victorien were elected Assistants to the General; Father Frederick Linneborn, Rector of the Notre Dame Seminary, was elected Procurator-General at Rome. On another vote, the Chapter members overwhelmingly approved the House of Studies as a permanent establishment in Washington, D. C., thus climaxing with success the three years of appeals and maneuvering by Zahm and Français. The design for the formation of priest-scholars was assured. With alacrity and shrewd financial acumen, Zahm left immediately after the Chapter for Washington, D. C., and took an option on a piece of property for a building site. Thus he was able to make arrangements before news of the Chapter's decision reached real estate men in the area and prices skyrocketed. The purchase of four and one-half acres near Catholic University for $16,000 was approved by the Provincial Council on September 24, 1898.[38] Morrissey, realizing it was futile to block this relentless advance, made no objection.[39] At the same Council meeting, Zahm's two protégés moved up to important posts; Burns replaced French as secretary and Cavanaugh succeeded Linneborn as Rector of the Seminary.[40]

Zahm chose A. O. Von Herbulis, a young Vienna-trained architect, to submit plans for the new Holy Cross College building. They were approved in December, 1898, by the

Provincial Council with the building cost estimated at $30,-000. In January, 1899, ground was broken; contracts were completed by the end of that month. The cornerstone ceremonies took place on Sunday, March 19, 1899, with Zahm's summer school friend, Bishop Thomas O'Gorman of Sioux Falls, South Dakota, officiating.[41] By August 1, the center portion of the building, sixty-four apartments with accommodations for fifty-five students, was ready for occupancy: the dedication, set for October, was attended by many of the hierarchy after their annual meeting.

At the impressive dedication of the classical, Corinthian-style building, Bishop John L. Spalding spoke on "The University: The Nursery of the Higher Life." Like Zahm, he declared that modern conditions required the intensive cultivation of the mind; a well developed intellect was second only to virtue as a prerequisite for every Catholic priest. After this address, which pleased the founders of the Catholic University because of its appeal for intellectually trained priests, the guests adjourned to the College dining room for a banquet at which Gibbons was the guest of honor. Archbishops Martinelli, Williams, Ryan, Riordan, Ireland, Kain, Keane and Christie, along with Bishops Spalding, Maes, Horstmann and Msgr. Conaty were among the honored guests. Even the arch-foe of the Americanists, Corrigan, was in attendance.

Thus, one year after the General Chapter meeting, Zahm had fulfilled his desire to establish a permanent House of Studies at Catholic University. Such efficiency brought Français to comment that he had not seen such initiative and smooth administration for a long time.[42] Zahm believed that culture should be integrated into Holy Cross College. Under his personal direction, an excellent art collection was gathered from Italy to educate and inspire the young seminarians in the traditional styles of Western painting and sculpture. Forty marble and alabaster busts of great historians, poets, orators, scientists, philosophers, and statesmen lined the hallways on the first floor. Dupre's "Pietà," and copies of celebrated madonnas and frescoes, along with carbon photographs, photogravures, steel engravings of the paintings of famous Renaissance artists, for example, Raphael, Rembrandt, Ghirlandaio, Botticelli and Fra Filippo Lippi, plus several hundred color photographs of the Holy Land, world-famous abbeys, cathedrals, castles and temples covered the walls. An excellent library of over one thousand volumes, largely on philosophy and allied subjects, was also personally established by Zahm.[43]

With Holy Cross College, the pattern for providing scholars within the American Congregation had been completed.[44] By 1912, eighty-five priests completed their studies at the College: twenty-five received their Ph.D. degrees; five their Licentiates in Theology; and eight, Bachelor's degrees in Theology.[45]

Students other than Holy Cross seminarians were not enrolled in Holy Cross College, since it was conceived and operated as the last formal phase of the seminarian's education. However, blueprints for construction of Holy Cross College were barely completed before Zahm was again invited by authorities at Catholic University to establish a new college in conjunction with the University.[46] This proposed college would accept only collegiate-level students from throughout the United States: a consideration deemed urgent because many applicants who applied for entrance to Catholic University (which admitted only graduate students) were not sufficiently prepared and therefore registered at other eastern schools, such as Harvard or Yale, to complete their college courses. Unfortunately, the authorities said, these students remained at these other schools for graduate training.[47]

Although lacking money and faculty, Zahm with characteristic vigor decided to accept the opportunity and establish a college unique among Catholic colleges since only collegiate students would be allowed admission. In 1900, a five-acre plot, the Thayer Estate, valued at $18,000, which adjoined Holy Cross College in Brookland, was considered for purchase by the Provincial Council as a future site for the college,[48] and it was agreed to try to exchange some other Holy Cross property for it. Morrissey had not been told of the plan but likely he suspected it for even the Brothers were discussing the probability.[49] Surprisingly, despite all the recent debts, and the memory of the battle waged over the House of Studies, discussion on the proposal was not too highly emotional in the beginning. But it soon became charged with anger due to the Provincial's extraordinary manner of purchase.

Zahm went to Chicago to learn more about this property, and while there a Chicago banker suggested that Thayer be offered $15,000 cash. The banker even offered Zahm a low interest loan for an indefinite time when he learned of the hard-pressed financial condition of the Congregation. Thayer accepted the offer, and Zahm had the contract signed. Naturally, Morrissey, among others, objected to this unorthodox procedure.[50]

The college plan lay dormant for the next three years. However, one month after O'Connell's arrival in 1903 as the new Rector of Catholic University, it came to life.[51] Zahm warned O'Connell, "Perhaps you would serve the interests of 'Caserta' by not extending premature invitation to 'our Fathers' to do what they will eventually be bound to do—*nolens volens.*" [52]

A harbinger of failure for the grand design appeared in a strongly worded report by Dr. Albert Zahm, a member of the faculty at Catholic University, to his brother. He wrote that a new ruling by the Academic Senate of Catholic University was announced on November 18, 1903, which required professors to prepare schedules for complete undergraduate courses in Philosophy, Law and Technology so that they might soon be offered to high school graduates and others who lacked a bachelor's degree. Thus, wrote Albert, the Senate, in order to attract more students began a plan to become a rival of Notre Dame and Georgetown. Only six months earlier, Albert continued bitterly, the faculty had been told that it was not numbers that made a university.

The announcement by the Senate came as a great surprise and disappointment to many of the faculty, he revealed, and they believed that should the ruling be carried out, it would be the largest downward step taken by the University—"It will put a premium on mediocrity by giving professors who have neither the ability nor inclination to do creative work the excuse of excessive routine, and those who have high ideas may be hampered by large classes of mere boys."[53] Antagonistic to the plan, he thought that if the steps were taken, Notre Dame should also offer the doctorate and thus become the equal or superior to the University in a couple of years. Well aware that this proposal meant the end of his brother's project, he complained that after years of boasting of being the only graduate school in the country, the Senate, in order to win more students was willing to establish a half-equipped college. Realizing the dire condition of the University's finances, he thought a few score scholarships would be a better solution to the problems. He hoped that the Board of Trustees would nullify the Senate's action and save them from this "disastrous departure." Truly, he wrote, the University was badly in need of a "salvadore."

Some faculty members of Catholic University, and especially the Board of Trustees, were ignorant of the previous planning by Zahm, Keane and O'Connell; when they learned of it, they resented the recommendations. The Provincial Council at Notre Dame which met January 26, 1904, to consider O'Connell's informal proposal for establishing a college, could not agree and therefore it adopted a "wait-and-see" attitude. Unofficially, however, Morrissey wrote or spoke to every Board member at Catholic University and told them Notre Dame opposed this venture.[54]

At the Catholic University Board of Trustees meeting on January 28, 1904, O'Connell submitted the proposed contract for the first time. If approved, it would go into effect on July 1, 1904. The major provisions of the plan were:

1. Catholic University will lease Keane Hall free of rent for five years and the lease can be renewed to Holy Cross Congregation.

2. Students of Keane Hall will be permitted free use of athletic grounds and the gymnasium by Catholic University.

3. Holy Cross Congregation will maintain Keane Hall in good condition and repair.

4. Keane Hall will be considered as an affiliated college and thus enjoy the rights and privileges of that status.

5. The Rector of the University and the Rector of Holy Cross College will decide the courses studied at Keane Hall and, in any case, they will lead up to the University courses.

6. If a student splits his course work between Keane Hall and McMahon Hall, Holy Cross College will pay the University one-half the tuition fee.

7. The Holy Cross Congregation will, while in Keane Hall, teach all the collegiate courses of ancient and modern languages and introductory philosophy: for all other classes the students will be taught in the University.

8. When the Congregation has its own building, it will teach all undergraduate courses leading to the bachelor's degree. Post-graduate and professional studies will always be carried on in the University.

9. Holy Cross College shall always remain affiliated with the University.[55]

As feared by Albert Zahm, however, some members within the University demanded that the proposed undergraduate school remain under the University's administration. Thus, at the trustees' meeting, the Committees on Organization and on Studies suggested and agreed to establish their own undergraduate courses; however, the final decision regarding the Holy Cross proposal was postponed until the next meeting.

During the interim, there was little cause for optimism by Zahm. O'Connell and his predecessors should have realized that no religious society could become a part of the University Administration under the terms of the University Charter.[56] Furthermore, O'Connell did not have great faith in the proposal, as revealed in his letter to Ireland in March, 1904: "I am not wedded to that Zahm plan. In-

tellectually I believe in it, but if it is not found feasible it
would not cost me an effort to drop it." [57] It was a diplomatic way of withdrawing support. Although Bishop Maes
wrote to Français in France urging that the Congregation
approve the project, all signs pointed to defeat.[58] The Board
decision made on April 13 favored the establishment of the
long-needed college; however, Zahm's venture was abandoned, and instead, the University began its own college as
recommended by the Committees on Organization and
Studies.

Although Zahm was disappointed by the decision, it is
likely that Français breathed a sigh of relief for he had
approved the projected foundation only reluctantly. Also
he reminded his Provincial that the last General Chapter
had decided to put off the question of a new college until
the next Chapter. Recalling the drain the Portland University project had been, Français wrote that after adequately
staffing the colleges at Notre Dame, Portland, New Orleans,
Austin, Watertown, Cincinnati and the House of Studies,
there would be insufficient personnel for such a new venture.[59]

Discussion of the college plan did not end with the
Board's decision, however. As late as a year and one-half
later, Ireland wrote to Zahm and explained his position on
this delicate question. He agreed that he had been one of
the first to approve of the undergraduate project as established by the Holy Cross Fathers; however, he had changed
his mind when he found the Catholic University faculty
members unanimous in their opposition. Because of this
and also because he believed such a college would be a constant source of bitterness within the University, he opposed
the venture. He suggested that the original mistake, for
which, he quickly added, no one was responsible, was that
the faculty members were permitted to believe the new
college would be under their direction rather than that of
an independent community.[60]

Keane wrote from Dubuque one week later. In reply to
Zahm's letter of protest concerning the negotiations on

Keane Hall, he wrote that surely no one could have so misunderstood plain, simple facts as to believe that either Zahm or O'Connell had the idea of transferring Keane Hall and the organization of the undergraduate departments to the Holy Cross Congregation without the mutual understanding and agreement of the faculty and directors. Such a notion had not even a shadow of plausibility and if the question should ever come before the directors, the Archbishop promised to state this.[61] This was the last piece of correspondence in Zahm's files regarding the ill-fated venture. It was a disappointment to the Provincial who had prayed and planned for a day when Holy Cross priests would prepare, on the University's grounds, college students for graduate school at Catholic University.

Other building projects, particularly at Notre Dame, were begun soon after the death of Corby. Zahm, whose aggressive temperament was similar to Sorin's, reviewed Notre Dame's needs and began improvements at such a rapid rate as to frighten conservative co-workers and, as well, seriously endanger his personal health. In these actions, Zahm resembled the captains of industry, men of action, who were so famous in the business community at the turn of the century, and it was perhaps no accident that Charles Schwab came to consider the Holy Cross Provincial as a close friend and companion. During the first months after his appointment, Zahm initiated the second phase of the development of Notre Dame's physical plant.

The need of a gymnasium became acute because of the larger student enrollment and the growing popularity of athletic contests. Zahm sought to obtain the Mechanics Building from the World's Fair of 1893 for a gymnasium at Notre Dame, but when his bid was turned down, the Provincial Council approved a new gymnasium on February 26, 1898, only one month after Zahm took office. Construction costs were estimated at $10,000 in the request for approval sent to the Superior-General.[62] Permission was granted later, and in less than a year the gymnasium was dedicated in Zahm style. Mr. A. C. Yates, American Consul at Patras, Greece, following Zahm's request, mailed four parcels of wild olive and laurel branches from the groves surrounding Olympus. As in the days when the ancient Greeks crowned the Pythian game victors, this material was fashioned into crowns and awarded to the winners of the indoor games at the dedication ceremonies.

Plans for a new library developed during these same months. The General Chapter in August, 1898, authorized Notre Dame authorities to construct a new library building and the Holy Cross College architect, A. O. Von Herbulis, drew up plans for the fireproof structure during the next year. However, the library was never constructed during Zahm's administration, probably because of other more pressing problems such as those created by the destructive fire in the new gymnasium in the fall of 1900. Shortly before the fire, Français gave encouragement to Zahm and told him to go ahead with the construction of the fireproof building to house his beautiful library and museum if he had the financial means.[63] When, five years later, Zahm sought to build it, he was refused permission by Français —likely because of the large debt within the Province.[64] It was not until 1917 that this building was finally constructed at Notre Dame.

Shortly after the completion of the gymnasium, the Community House designed by Von Herbulis was begun on Mount St. Vincent.[65] The swamp area bordering Mount St. Vincent had been previously dredged at a cost of $10,000. Partially as a fund-raising project, Corby Hall, the residence of the priests and Brothers, was partitioned in the summer of 1899 and over forty private rooms were given to students, thus following the system set in Sorin Hall. The rooms in Corby, however, were given to preparatory students for $50 a year whereas in Sorin Hall, the rooms were for college students only.

By midsummer, 1900, the conservative element at Notre Dame was extremely fearful that the expenses of the new improvements and buildings would "swamp the Community."[66] According to the *Scholastic* November 17, 1900,

$300,000 had been spent over the previous four years for buildings and improvements. Improvements by Zahm after his return were, in addition to those already mentioned, a new steam heating plant, a new office building in the back of the college, an extension of the steam heating system to the church and various halls, the conversion of the old steam-house into a bathing department, replacement of all existing pumps by newly-designed ones and also a new water line from the new steam house directly to St. Joseph's lake and, finally, the installation of baths in the seminary. Also over two hundred acres on the north and east of Notre Dame's campus were acquired. In vain did Burns attempt to have Zahm postpone some of the improvements because the Provincial's health was at the point of breaking. Anxiously, Burns wrote:

> He is like Napoleon. His plans are so great and expansive, and his energy so intense, that each improvement only opens up a prospect for another and a greater one. At the same time, he says that he has given careful consideration to the financial conditions, and although all the improvements are being put up on borrowed money, he claims to see his way through without danger.[67]

With almost uncanny accuracy, he judged:

> But Father Zahm will never be understood, nor his work appreciated by this generation. He is too far in advance of the men among whom he is living. He is a man of the 20th century, and we are still I believe, living in the 19th.[68]

In the midst of the building boom, a disastrous fire, reminiscent of 1879 swept through the new gymnasium on November 9, 1900. Despite the fact that $298,616 had been spent in the previous four years for buildings and improvements, Zahm and Morrissey immediately called a meeting and with Sorin-like determination, they approved construction of a larger and better field house. Tardily, they also completed a plan, begun three months earlier, for a student volunteer fire department of two companies and a water pumping system whereby, within five minutes, two thousand gallons of water per minute might be directed on any building.

A second serious problem at the University absorbed Zahm during this time, that of scholarships. In 1899, after a great deal of planning, he suggested a program whereby wealthy donors could give their fortunes to Notre Dame on the condition that the interest be made absolutely secure to them for the duration of their lives. At their death, the principal would go to Notre Dame. To Zahm, it appeared that a quarter of a million dollars might be raised for a scholarship fund by using St. Joseph's farm and other property to secure the interest.[69] This plan was hurriedly developed when he learned of an elderly couple with $100,-000 who might be interested in such a program; however, much to Zahm's chagrin, the old gentleman died before Zahm's friend was able to use his influence and arrange a meeting.

Scholarships did come in though. One for $5,000 was established by a doctor in Watertown, Wisconsin; another of similar size was promised. True to style, Zahm optimistically predicted that he would obtain two hundred scholarships for Notre Dame.[70] The following story exhibits Zahm's characteristic manner of achieving results. On a Wednesday he received a letter from a priest in Chicago who revealed that a lady desired to leave her possessions to some educational institution. Zahm took the first train to Chicago, persuaded her to give the money to Notre Dame, and immediately had a lawyer draw up the deed of transfer. The Provincial returned to Notre Dame on Friday night (after leaving his suitcase in a Chicago hotel rather than miss the train), had the deed signed and sealed that same evening, and had it returned by a steward on Saturday morning to be recorded. The property thus won was worth $50,000, the yearly income $2,500: ten student scholarships known as "The Catherine Ford Scholarships" were formed.[71]

Despite the costly building program under way at Notre Dame and the expense of Holy Cross College at Catholic University, the Provincial, his Council, and the Superior-

General accepted Archbishop Christie's urgent request to take over the impoverished Columbia University in Portland, Oregon, in the spring of 1902. The Archbishop of Portland, anxious for a Catholic college, had taken over a defunct Methodist Episcopal School in that city on July 20, 1901. Fifty-two students met during the school year, 1901-1902, in the one small building on the limited campus. The faculty consisted of a few priests, a layman-graduate of Notre Dame, and a former Chinese missionary. At the very beginning the Archbishop found the new venture too imposing for his limited resources; thus, he turned to Notre Dame for assistance in the fall of 1901. At Notre Dame, the Archbishop was successful in "inoculating everybody with Portland fever." [72] The Provincial Council was so interested in the Archbishop's generous offer that it agreed to abolish the classical courses at the colleges in Cincinnati and Watertown, Wisconsin, if necessary in order to have enough men to staff the Portland project; subject, of course, to the approval of the Superior-General.[73] With Français' permission, the Council approved the purchase of forty-three acres fronting the Willamette River, near Columbia University, at $500 an acre.[74] This purchase, added to the twenty-eight acres previously given by Christie, formed the college campus.

Aware of the future, Zahm envisioned a "Notre Dame and St. Mary's of the Northwest." [75] Columbia University, the fifth college in the United States Province, began in the fall of 1902 with Father Michael A. Quinlan, President; Father William Marr as Vice-President, and Father John Thillman, Director of Studies. Quinlan had been graduated from Notre Dame in 1893, and had spent three years at Catholic University in historical and economic studies. Following ordination, he remained at Notre Dame as an Instructor of Rhetoric and proved himself very successful in the administration of athletics as secretary of the Faculty Board of Control of Athletics.

In the spring of 1903 Zahm, in his attempt to make Columbia University the Notre Dame of the West, won authorization to erect a new, large frame building valued between six and seven thousand dollars.[76] The building was planned to house the Sisters who would do the domestic work and care for a future Minim department. Interestingly, this authorization was granted just a few weeks after Christie wrote saying he had started a school for young boys in Portland. In reply, Zahm complained that the Holy Cross Congregation was attempting to make Columbia a great school but that it would take four ingredients to do so—money, hard work, prudent management and especially the harmonious active co-operation of all. The harmonious co-operation did not result and although the University continued to expand physically[77] and scholastically, disagreements between Christie and Quinlan became more frequent.

In the midst of the extensive projects for developing Notre Dame and the Congregation in America generally, there arose a serious problem of morale within the ranks of the Brothers. On August 12, 1901, a letter of grievance, signed by eleven of the Brothers at Notre Dame, was addressed to Zahm. The practical problems of the Brothers, their complaints over injustice and, especially, Zahm's role in the question, can be fully understood only in the light of the educational and religious difficulties which surrounded the Brotherhood. The Brothers' objections began long before Zahm's term as Provincial. While it is true that some of the problems were accentuated during his administration, it is equally important to emphasize that this was largely because of conditions over which he had no control. These same problems continued after his Provincialship and were solved finally by the development of new high schools.

The history of the Brothers' society began in 1820, when Father James Dujarie, pastor of Ruille-sur-Loire in France formed a society known as the Brothers of St. Joseph. In 1835, he relinquished control to Father Basil Moreau who was also at that time superior of the Auxiliary Priests of Le Mans. Moreau united the two societies as the Congregation of Holy Cross and remained its superior until 1857 when the Holy See formally endorsed the Congregation; he then became the first Superior-General of the Congregation.

Pope Pius IX convoked the General Chapter of 1868 to seek methods for maintaining harmony between priests and Brothers after the latter had complained about the mismanagement of the Congregation and, also, the tendency to advance the Brothers with the most ability to the priesthood. Other complaints centered about alleged unnecessary distinctions between the priests and Brothers. After the Chapter, it was decreed that the Superior-General, the Procurator-General and the Provincial could only be chosen from the priests. Also, local superiors could be priests or Brothers; however, in mixed houses only priests could be superiors.

Although one of the original purposes of the Brothers' society in France was to teach Catholic doctrine to the young children in the small French villages, a majority of the Brothers attached to Notre Dame was engaged in manual labor by 1888. While some worked on University farms, others were shoemakers, tailors, carpenters, tinsmiths, painters, gardeners, electricians, blacksmiths, undertakers, butchers, and plumbers. In addition, the Brothers operated the *Ave Maria* printing press; and eight Brothers solicited subscriptions. A few others were in charge of the bakery and the post office.

The teaching Brothers, a few decades after their arrival with Sorin in 1841, took charge of parish grammar schools in certain larger cities throughout the Midwest such as Chicago, Milwaukee, Cincinnati, Fort Wayne and Philadelphia, as well as in Trenton and Camden in the East. After the Third Plenary Council in 1884 and during the 1890's, however, the teaching Brothers began losing their schools. A variety of reasons accounted for these losses. For example, nearly all the eastern high schools were conducted by religious groups that had their own elementary departments. These grammar schools were considered rivals of the parish schools by many pastors who wanted the children to attend parish schools through the eighth grade; hence, the rivalry served to alienate the pastors.[78] This problem affected the eastern schools more than the midwestern ones since a large majority of Holy Cross schools in the Middle West were elementary or grammar schools. An even more important consideration was that the teaching Sisters replaced the Brothers because of the great savings involved. One estimate is that one Brother taught for one-half the cost of a male public school teacher and that a Sister taught for one-half the Brother's salary.[79] An increase in vocations to the Sisterhood together with permission for the Sisters to teach boys up to the age of thirteen also began the decline of the teaching Brothers' power.[80]

The Provincial Chapter under Corby which met at Notre Dame in 1895 discussed, among other matters, the possibility of the Brothers being replaced at the Cathedral School in Fort Wayne. Father Spillard was sent to find out the status and with relief he brought news that they would be retained again.[81] The Chapter which met the succeeding year was faced with this new trend in Catholic education when they received word that St. Joseph's Parochial School in Hamilton, Ohio, was no longer under the control of the Brothers; however, two high schools were offered to the teaching Brothers, Cathedral High School in Minneapolis and the Polish High School in Milwaukee.[82] Here were definite indications for the future trend of Catholic school education —the Brothers were being asked to move upward. However, and here was the dilemma, the teaching Brothers were not sufficiently trained for secondary school teaching. In 1897, Brother Engelbert, Superior of the Brothers' House of Studies, Mount St. Vincent, wrote to Zahm, who was then Director of Studies for the Congregation, and stated that the Brothers' program of studies roughly corresponded to the University preparatory department. He added quickly that they had indeed studied; however, it was a difficult process since they were exceedingly deficient when they entered the institute; hence only one Brother, who had studied two years and finished the commercial course, was qualified for mission work that year. Obviously interested in thorough preparation, Engelbert reported that many of the younger Brothers then teaching in the elementary schools were eager for another year of study. Since the Brothers' House of Studies had been established, it should be developed and utilized to its fullest possibilities. "There should be a course of studies, globes, maps, and other teachers' aids of which there is no vestige on the premises." [83] In fact, Engelbert urged, no Brother should be sent on the mission before he had completed as a minimum, the commercial course—the Father General should prohibit it.

Doubtless, and with justice, ill feeling existed among the Brothers because of the large expenditures for the new House of Studies for the seminarians in Washington; while the Brothers lacked even globes and maps. Burns, when he assessed the decline of the Brothers' schools, believed it was happening because of ill-educated teachers, men who were sent out to teach when only half-educated or not at all. Also the scarcity of vocations together with the college expansion at Notre Dame stunted the teaching Brothers' growth. He suggested to Zahm a plan involving a four-year pedagogy course in college for the training of Catholic school teachers and the additional requirement that every Brother must graduate from the program before being permitted to teach.[84] Zahm liked the plan and even suggested that the more talented Brothers be sent to Catholic University for advanced work.[85] As a partial solution, Zahm secured two experienced men from the East to conduct "Institute Work" for the teaching Brothers during the summer of 1898.[86]

The Brothers themselves were divided on the issue. Some such as Engelbert favored the four-year plan of Burns; others thought four years too long, while a few thought one year would be sufficient. The General Chapter which met in August, 1898, settled the problem by assigning the Brothers to a three-year course—equal to the college preparatory course except that commercial subjects were substituted for Latin and Greek.[87]

Even before the return of Zahm as Provincial, an uneasy peace existed between the priests and Brothers. Shortly before the death of Corby, Français, on his visit to Notre Dame, recognized the problem of morale and pleased the

Brothers very much by moving from the Presbytery to the
Community House; he, in addition, urged better care for
the older Brothers.[88] During his stay, he found some justifi-
cation for the complaints of the Brothers. The Provincial
Council, less than a year after Zahm's appointment as Provincial, discussed a recruiting program for obtaining talented candidates for the Brotherhood. Father O'Keefe was
finally chosen to go to Ireland and Brother Engelbert sought
postulants in Germany.[89] Bright hopes for the Brotherhood
took root when the Irish priest returned with seven men
who had paid their own transportation costs. The Council
also agreed to send for twenty-five other capable applicants
who applied but did not have funds for the voyage. These
men were all teachers in the National Schools.[90]

A sobering situation soon dimmed this optimism. In August, 1899, after the Brothers had received their obediences
for the next year, Zahm received a letter from the pastor
announcing that the Brothers were no longer needed in St.
Columbkille's School in Chicago.[91] An emergency Provincial
Council meeting was held to decide the new obediences for
the ten Brothers who were withdrawn from the parish
school. In the light of future events, it is well to note that
only one was assigned a strictly manual job; two, to other
non-teaching duties; and seven to teaching positions in other
schools.

As noted previously, some Brothers did not like Zahm's
personality, preferring the amiability of Morrissey and Fitte.
It is probable that the Provincial's absorbing interest in
higher education met silent opposition from these Brothers
who were teaching in grammar schools. This attitude was
compounded by the fact their grammar schools were being taken from them and at the same time they were inadequately trained in many instances to move into high
school teaching. It was also apparent that this frustration,
together with Zahm's brusque manner, increased the resentment which existed between priests and Brothers. The grievances of the Brothers were summarized in a letter of petition to Father-General Français, dated August 12, 1901, and

signed by eleven teaching Brothers. They complained that their group was rapidly becoming extinct, that ten years ago they numbered ninety but now there were only about fifty left. Nine teachers had left last year, sixty-five within the last ten years. In addition to this decline, very few candidates came from this country and of those who did, most persevered only a short time. Their list of six major grievances concerned: (1) the better food and living quarters accorded to the priests; (2) the Brothers' inadequate authority in community decisions, e.g., there were five priests and two Brothers on the Provincial Council; (3) the transfer of teaching Brothers from grammar school to college teaching; (4) immaturity of the Brothers' superiors; (5) especially that many teaching Brothers were assigned manual work instead of the opportunity to teach—"That we are prevented from following our vocation as teachers, is perhaps the chief source of our anxiety." [92]

In conclusion, these eleven Brothers promised to await the reply of their Superior-General. If none came, then a document of complaint dated December 1 would be sent to the Propaganda in Rome. Français received the letter and replied to his Provincial that the same thing had happened one time in Canada. Français also added that judging from his own observations during his stay at Notre Dame during the latter months of 1897 (before Zahm was Provincial), he believed there were several very real sides to their complaints. [93]

One month later, one of the chief agitators retracted most of his complaints in a letter to Français. He revealed that he was mainly disturbed because the schools were closing but that Zahm had told him the Community was responsible for closing only one school—the others were closed by persons outside the Community.

Following Français' recommendation, an investigating committee composed of Zahm, Morrissey, L'Etourneau and Cavanaugh interviewed each signer. The committee found every complaint in the document to be false, that not one of the Brother-signers had a real grievance; rather they had signed the petition without carefully reading it.[94] Zahm admitted that there were infractions of the rules at Notre Dame as at every other Community; however, each time he had been told of one, he remedied it.

Problems within the teaching Brotherhood continued. The Provincial Chapter of 1904 discussed with concern the several vacancies at New Orleans and Fort Wayne. Zahm told how difficult it was to get vocations for the Brotherhood and his hope that it was only a passing phase in Holy Cross development. It was agreed that the priests would offer one Mass per month for the intention of increasing the size of the teaching Brotherhood; the Brothers would offer Holy Communion, the Rosary, and the Way of the Cross monthly for the same intention.[95] In the secular order, suggestions were made for placing advertisements in Catholic newspapers and magazines for candidates; also Father Spillard's motion that a letter be sent to pastors who were friends of Holy Cross, asking their aid in recruiting Brothers and offering to send a speaker on religious vocations, was passed.

Brother Kievan was sent to Ireland a few months later on another recruiting venture in quest of candidates for the Brotherhood and also candidates for St. Mary's. Zahm wrote to Kievan in Ireland and explained that some members were saying Zahm had told him not to obtain any new subjects for the teaching Brotherhood. Actually, what the Provincial had said, and Kievan agreed, was that no young boys who were in doubt as to their vocation should be brought. In addition, Zahm instructed him to enlist as many candidates as possible for the teaching and working Brotherhood.[96] Loyal Kievan replied that the vicious rumors were not true but that he was not surprised by anything heard from Notre Dame—rather "Dear Father do not let that report trouble you. May God forgive those foolish people that don't mind their own business." [97] He added that he had about fifty applications, although many drew back when they were told they must pay their own fare or at least most of it. After extensive searching, only eight postulants for the teaching Brotherhood returned with Brother Kievan in July, 1905.[98]

A form of "peace offering" for the Brothers was erected under Zahm's direction on the campus of Notre Dame in the fall of 1905 and dedicated on the Feast of St. Joseph, March 19, 1906. This statue, honoring the first Brothers to come with Sorin to Notre Dame, was located near the new home of the Brothers, Dujarie Hall, which was formally opened that same day. The first college building, the "Little White House" erected in 1843, was remodeled to become the new Hall. Young candidates for the Brotherhood pursued their studies in it. A replica of the first log chapel completed the new project.

In reply to questions on the declining Brotherhood, Zahm wrote in 1906 to his Superior-General that the future priests of Holy Cross had excellent seminaries and if this was not true of the Brothers' House of Studies, it was not through any fault of the administration. "We have done everything that human ingenuity could suggest to increase the number of subjects for the Brotherhood, but the results achieved in no wise respond to the efforts put forth." [99] Other communities too were watching a decline in their ranks, he explained, and Holy Cross had been more fortunate than many of them.

The General Chapter of 1906 concerned itself again with the problems of the Brothers and their future.[100] Willingly, the Brothers ceded any rights which they thought they had to the offices of the Procurator-General, Provincial or General Prefect of Studies.[101] However, the compromise rewarded them well. Their rights to the control and administration of the parochial and high schools as well as the commercial colleges, orphan asylums, and industrial schools was recognized. Furthermore, it was agreed that an equal number of priests and Brothers would be members of the General Chapter and General Council; a similar ratio would also hold for the Provincial Chapters, Provincial Councils, and Boards of Trustees. However, in local Councils, equality of representation would only be strongly attempted.[102]

Also leaders among the Brothers were aware of the necessity of intellectual training; therefore, in answer to their
demand for a large House of Studies and Postulate, the
General Chapter promised immediate construction of a new
building at Notre Dame to be known as Dujarie Institute.

At the Chapter sessions, the Brothers accepted the explanation that circumstances had prevented carrying out the
decrees and regulations of former Chapters concerning the
spiritual and intellectual training of the young Brothers—
especially in Indiana; however, they stated that further de-
lay would cause serious injury to the teaching Brothers. Still
skeptical, they promised that if the prescriptions and recommendations of 1898 and 1906 were not fulfilled within
two years, an appeal for justice would be made through
the Superior General to a higher authority.

New methods for obtaining more vocations to the teaching Brotherhood were also considered because the administration had had to refuse offers of high schools because of
a real shortage in membership.[103] As a result of this increased demand, the Brothers' House of Studies was put under the control of Brother Aiden who had previously sought
postulants in Ireland.[104] The columns of the *Catholic Directory* for 1907 carried an advertisement which reported
that the Congregation of Holy Cross was in urgent need
of vocations to the Brotherhood. The advertisement promised that young men or boys of fourteen and upward would
be given every opportunity for preparing themselves as religious teachers. By 1908, the numbers of students at Dujarie Institute numbered twenty-eight.[105]

However, despite the beliefs of those who then disliked
Zahm, the General Chapter of 1906 and the election of
Morrissey as Provincial at its sessions did not solve the many
problems of the teaching Brotherhood. Although Morrissey
appealed to some of the Brothers because of his genial personality, he too was confronted by the same problems. The
Brothers petitioned for separation in 1910; unsuccessfully,
however.[106] The complaints of the Brothers were of the
same nature as those in 1901! They believed they were be-

ing unfairly employed; that the rights of procedure and honor for the Brothers were not observed; young Brothers in schools or scholasticate did not have sufficient study time; the Brothers did not have enough of their own schools, especially commercial schools for which they were especially fitted; and there was still insufficient recruiting and training.[107]

In the last analysis, Français was correct, when he wrote in 1912, that a new future was open for the Brothers—that although they had lost the parochial schools, Catholic high schools had grown and become more indispensable. "From this time forward, the High School is the outstanding vocation of our Brothers!"[108] And they would be the special work of the teaching Brothers. Thus, instead of being buried in the general work of the Congregation, a new field with ample scope for personal initiative and opportunity was open—"In a word the High School furnishes an element of durable and holy peace between the two branches of our society. Both will hereafter march unitedly forward like two distinct forces that make but one, and that aid each other mutually." With some relief then, Français could report after the 1912 General Chapter that the teaching Brothers were happy and the grievances contained in the petition laid before the Chapter of 1906 were largely dissolved. However, a great shortage in vocations to the teaching Brotherhood continued to be felt not only for Holy Cross but for other Communities as well.

The year 1912, then, and the upsurge of Catholic high schools, brought an armistice to the generations-old differences within the Congregation. Zahm was not the cause of the conflict, nor was any one person the final peacemaker. The Catholic secondary school system, and the subsequent assignment of teaching Brothers to this new field of endeavor, largely dissipated the administrative and personality problems which had hampered the Congregation, almost since its founding.

In addition to the costly projects already mentioned, a number of land purchases and an addition to St. Joseph's

College were authorized in 1902 at a cost of approximately $50,000.[109] Others at Notre Dame shared Zahm's enthusiasm, for when a fire wrought havoc at St. Edward's College in Austin, Texas, in early April, 1903, the Council, despite Zahm's absence, authorized St. Edward's President, Father Boland, to rebuild the college and, in addition, to build a dormitory sufficient to accommodate 150 students with rooms! [110]

With a view to lowering the interest on the American Congregation's debts, Zahm attempted what he had dreamed for many years—refunding the entire debt of the Province by the issue of debenture bonds. As early as 1904 he had sought to secure the loan, but unsuccessfully. Thoughout the summer of 1905 he again failed to get a loan of $100,000 for seven years to refund the debts of Texas and Portland. He refused to give the Notre Dame or the Washington, D. C., property for mortgage and preferred to use the property at New Orleans, Louisiana, Watertown, Wisconsin, Portland, Oregon, or Austin, Texas, for that purpose. Apparently, however, this wise financial consolidation was never accomplished and it, like his re-election, was doomed to failure.

When Zahm was appointed Provincial in 1898, Burns had urged Français to remove Morrissey from the presidency of Notre Dame. Little did Burns realize that this same problem would come up seven and one-half years later and the result would terminate Zahm's power. At the annual Provincial Chapter meeting Monday, July 11, 1905, Morrissey was replaced as President by the young, energetic Cavanaugh, who had been Superior of the Holy Cross Seminary since 1899.[111] This action was a strategic mistake by those men eager to continue the programs of Zahm. It began a vicious circle which is described below.

Another major change made during Notre Dame's "July Days" involved the replacement of the Vice-President, Father James French by Father Thomas A. Crumley, who had been a Philosophy and English Professor at Notre Dame after completing his graduate courses at the Brookland

House of Studies in Washington, D. C. Father Joseph Maguire, another product of Catholic University via Holy Cross College, was appointed new Superior of the Seminary, thus filling the vacancy left by Father Cavanaugh. Father William Molony became the new Director of Studies.

The new Superior of the Professed House, Fitte, reported that everyone at Notre Dame, except those self-interested in the changes, was grieved and complained not of the changes, but rather the manner, "so sudden, so radical, so heartless!" [112] Sister M. Aloysius wrote from St. Edward's Hall that Morrissey received a year's vacation—he would spend three weeks at French Lick, Indiana, and then travel on to Europe and the Holy Land. Upon his return he would go to Columbia University in Portland, Oregon, since Quinlan offered him the presidency.[113] Many of the Brothers and all the Sisters at St. Edward's Hall felt terrible about it but "Poor Father Morrissey is taking it like a man." [114]

Soon after the revolutionary Chapter meeting, the serious political maneuvering began. Recovering somewhat from the surprise move, Morrissey decided to go directly to Paris and confer with the Father-General about three major provincial problems in the United States: financial danger; the situation of the Brotherhood, whereby the priests' rights had been greatly increased; and lastly, the usurpation of authority by Zahm—"I will try to ascertain whether or not he wants him again—if so, the cause is about lost, if not I will be governed accordingly." [115] Thus the former President announced his intentions to wage war. With this confidential letter, there began almost a solid year of political campaigning, carefully systematized, planned, and executed.

Immediately after his arrival in France, Morrissey began probing to find Français' feelings regarding Zahm and the election for the Provincialship in General Chapter scheduled to meet in August, 1906. His efforts were speedily rewarded soon after arrival when Français revealed that Zahm would only briefly mention provincial affairs and would insist later that he had explained everything. Also, Français confided that he was opposed to young men winning im-

portant offices so quickly; and the seminary development
was too rapid. In his turn, Morrissey enlightened him about
the debts at Notre Dame. The strategy, thought Morrissey
after the conference with Français, was to convince the Superior-General that if Zahm remained in power the General and his friends at Notre Dame would be miserable
and that Zahm would even try to be General. It was important, wrote Morrissey, to keep the Brotherhood question
hot: Brothers Marcellanus, Paul, and Albeus should help—
and of course, Fitte.[116]

Morrissey also revealed that Father A. Jamet told him
that the Superior-General had tired of the incumbent Provincial and that the Brothers could be counted on to vote
against Zahm. After learning these encouraging facts, Morrissey decided to "lead the fight, I have nothing to fear,"
and he was understandably happy when Français invited
him to go on tour with him throughout the Canadian and
American Provinces. But as late as December 1, 1905, Morrissey was still not positive that Français would support the
move to unseat Zahm.[117]

Archbishop Christie, visiting Europe at the time, unhappy
with Quinlan's management of the University at Portland,
and Morrissey, managed to convince Jamet that a change
was necessary at Notre Dame. Christie was especially force-
ful and urged the French priest to write Français immediately to that effect. After the visit Jamet, believing the complaints, hoped "that it is not to [sic] late to save our dear
Congregation." [118]

Morrissey's strategy worked well for Français soon lost
faith and wrote critical letters to his Provincial at Notre
Dame. After receiving a number of them, Zahm wrote a
masterful review of his work, ideas, and the state of the
Province.[119] The finances, he emphasized, were in excellent
condition and every important decision had been made with
the consent and approval of local and Provincial Councils.
Notre Dame did not have a three million franc debt, rather
it was only $150,000; the assets had doubled since Français'
last visit. The Washington property was free of debt, many

Notre Dame improvements were paid for, and the net revenue from St. Joseph's College in Cincinnati was eight times greater than before the new building was constructed. Six thousand dollars per year had been saved in fuel costs. The improvements at Notre Dame had truly made it the leading Catholic institution in the United States, had given it eminence, prestige and ability to meet its aggressive competitors. Intensely aware of a dynamic United States, Zahm further predicted:

> To keep our place in the forefront of the Catholic institutions of America, we must give continual and striking indication of progress, energy, and initiative. We can not permit a stand-still for even a single year. To do so would mean loss—it might be a very great loss. Our friends look for constant growth, never ceasing evidence of vitality and development in a material as well as in an intellectual way. Such growth necessarily means expenditure of money as well as expenditure of energy. It means the erection of new buildings whenever called for; it means the equipment of new and large laboratories; it means a large and a better and more expensive staff of professors.

Recalling that success in any purely temporal enterprise was never certain, Zahm was confident of the future. He could not, he continued, eliminate all elements of danger: we depended upon God for success,

> To be over cautious is to become stagnant; to endeavor to conduct such an institution as Notre Dame so as to incur no risks is to do what no sane business man would dream of doing. How much less should this be the case in a religious, who, while fully recognizing the necessity of human prudence, and individual effort, has what the ordinary business man of the world has not, a firm belief in the efficacy of prayer, and relies, for ultimate success, on Divine Providence.

With pride he reported that the Province was filled with an enthusiasm which had eliminated the word "impossible" in the material, intellectual and spiritual spheres. The excellent seminaries produced pious, learned, and cultured priests. The religious had worked hard and loyally; the Superiors, without whom little could have been accomplished, had accomplished great things. They had been loyal, zealous, unselfish, and progressive. Because of these co-operative efforts between Superiors and subjects, an entire material and intellectual transformation had occurred and brought Holy Cross prestige throughout the United States. According to estimates of the hierarchy, he proudly asserted, it was at the head of the teaching communities in America. This had fired the young seminarians and priests who were justly eager for the day they too could actively build and develop their proud Community. All energies had been directed towards spiritual formation now that the material and intellectual foundation was secured, and soon Holy Cross would be famous for genuine piety and religious observance—"Notre Dame shall soon, like some of the great intellectual centers in the Church's past, be also a recognized home of saints and scholars."

Thus concluded Zahm's *Apologia*. It marked its author as confident of the future greatness for the Congregation— a future designed by an aggressive Provincial and begun by young men. Together they envisioned a new era in American Catholic education and willingly they sacrificed. With a few exceptions they sacrificed their offices and their personal future as well. The *Apologia* did not quiet the doubts of Français.

The Morrissey movement grew relentlessly. While accompanying the Father-General on a tour of the Province, Morrissey proceeded with care. Still uncertain of the outcome, Morrissey warned that the General had made Zahm and given him absolute power; thus he might resent undue influence.[120] However, Morrissey thought that since great efforts had and could be made to end Zahm's influence, it was necessary that the General learn of the many members who favored Morrissey: "All that can be done is to send us all off to some one house and I think there will [be] enough of us to make a lively house and be happy." And further, though the young men might threaten a schism to frighten Français, and refuse to work under any other man, the Father-General would stand by the Chapter's decision. Finally, Morrissey said Français must be shown that he had many friends because it seemed that all he looked for was help to carry out his plans.

The Holy Cross colleges in Washington, D. C., New Orleans, Louisiana, Austin, Texas, Portland, Oregon, and Watertown, Wisconsin, were all inspected and the religious interviewed before the pair continued on to Notre Dame in April, 1906. Morrissey's good fortune mounted for in late March, Français wrote to the Holy See suggesting that Morrissey deserved an honorary doctor's degree for his twelve years of educating Christian students while President of Notre Dame.[121]

At a campus celebration on May 12, as Zahm listened to Keane's sermon honoring Sorin, he must have realized deep satisfaction because another of his personal projects was completed. Father Sorin's statue, modeled by Ernesto Biondi, was unveiled that day. Mindful of the college's Christian heritage, Zahm added other monuments to the Notre Dame campus during his last days as Provincial. As mentioned above, a statue of St. Joseph, built in honor of the first Brothers who accompanied Sorin to Notre Dame in 1841, was dedicated on March 19. After negotiations with Archbishop Elder of Cincinnati, Zahm had Father Stephen Badin's body returned to the Notre Dame campus, the land on which Badin had Christianized the Indians some seventy-five years earlier. On May 3, the remains were placed in the new log cabin chapel, modeled after the original and completed a few months earlier.

Zahm's final addition to his beloved University were two marble statues, one of *Christ the Redeemer,* twenty-five feet high, of Cararra marble, placed at the head of Sorin's grave; the other, a copy of Michelangelo's *Pietà,* in the center of the graveyard.

As he conferred the habit on a number of postulants on a warm June day in 1906, the tired Provincial realized he would lose the election in August. His fears were realized when members of the General Chapter submitted their votes on August 20, 1906. Morrissey was elected Provincial: his partisans termed it the "Triumph of truth and honesty." [122]

The defeat was in reality a blessing, for Zahm's health had declined seriously. He had wanted to retire towards the end of 1904 but Burns and Cavanaugh begged him to stay on.[123] Zahm was a man broken in health and spirit as he packed his personal effects in the Provincial's office in the Presbytery. In order to recover his health two physicians prescribed a minimum of two years' rest. For more than a year, Zahm confessed, he had failed to have a single night's refreshing sleep and felt fortunate if he had two or three hours rest out of twenty-four. He had not read a book for more than twelve months, and study, which had been an integral part of his life, was impossible; he found that it took immense energy even to read a single page from a magazine.[124] In view of this, he begged Français' permission to return to the project interrupted by Corby's death and visit Bengal to write a series of articles for the American press. He needed, rather than the rest in Canada or the United States suggested by Français, to spend six months in Europe with his literary and scientific friends before going to India. The permission Zahm sought was refused.

The man who had not wished to be appointed Provincial, left Notre Dame saddened, for in designing an American congregation of "saints & scholars" he had lost the confidence of his Superior-General and a majority of the other Superiors. The Provincialship was his last experience with administration. As Burns had predicted, he was not understood by his colleagues, perhaps because he failed to use the cautious qualities which made him so competent as Procurator-General in Rome. It is certain that he understood, whereas others only saw the future. It is also certain that he was dedicated to scholarship within his Congregation and particularly, Notre Dame. He inaugurated an educational age of enterprise within them both; education which has richly rewarded his successors in terms of a learned religious life. He left Notre Dame, never again to return to his University, one he loved dearly and perhaps too deeply.

NOTES TO CHAPTER VI

1. Burns Collection. PA.

2. Ireland to Zahm, February 5, 1898. John Zahm Collection, UNDA. One newspaper regarded his appointment as a "triumph for the progressive scientific party in the Roman Catholic Church." Indianapolis *Journal,* January 16, 1898.

3. Keane to Zahm, January 20, 1898. John Zahm Collection, UNDA.

4. O'Connell to Sabina di Tarravicino di Revel, January 21, 1898. Copy, UNDA.

5. Zahm to O'Connell, February 5, 1898. Copy, UNDA.

6. Burns Collection. PA.

7. *Ibid.*

8. *Ibid.*

9. *Ibid.* Detail in the sets of figures does not necessarily add to totals of 100 per cent because of rounding.

10. *Ibid.*

11. *Ibid.* Burns, in his calculations, did not break down the total of twenty-five law students who were either in the preparatory or collegiate department.

12. *Ibid.* There were thirty-two additional students in law whom he did not classify as collegiate or preparatory students.

13. *Ibid.* Burns hopefully added that the time had come to drop commercial students, but very, very cautiously.

14. *Ibid.*

15. *Ibid.* The number of students at Notre Dame continued an overall increase during the following years: 1900—725 students; 1901—825; 1902—850; 1903—835; 1904—800; 1905—800; 1906—800. Cf. *Catholic Directory* (Milwaukee 1900-1906), 15, 293; *ibid.,* 16, 297; *ibid.,* 17, 307; *ibid.,* 17, 312; *ibid.,* 19, 320; *ibid.,* 20, 334; and *ibid.,* 21, 334.

16. James A. Burns, *The Growth and Development of the Catholic School System in the United States* (New York, 1912), p. 361.

17. Edward J. Power, *A History of Catholic Higher Education in the United States* (Milwaukee, 1958), pp. 90-94.

18. Fitte to (no name), (no date, although probably written in late 1901). PA.

19. The differences between Zahm and Hudson caused certain administrative problems. For example, Hudson was elected President of the Board of Trustees soon after the death of Corby and he refused to resign from his office in favor of Zahm. It had been customary for the Provincial to hold that office since the two previous ones, Sorin

and Corby, had held it. Zahm had a plan for foundation-type scholarships, and thus he believed it necessary that he hold the position of President of the Board. After a year of unsuccessful attempts to unseat Hudson, Zahm asked the members of the Board of Trustees to remain after the local Council meeting (Hudson, not a member of the Council, was of course absent). Brother Edward then moved that Zahm be elected President and the motion was seconded and passed by the members, Burns, Morrissey, French, and Brothers Edward and Engelbert. It is likely that Hudson learned of the election only when he saw Zahm's name in the *Catalogue*. Cf. Burns Collection. PA.

20. Zahm to Albert Zahm, June 1, 1900. John Zahm Collection, UNDA. Nevertheless, the silver jubilee celebration was held on June 4, 1900: Father Cavanaugh preached the sermon; Pope Leo XIII sent his blessing.

21. Burns Collection. PA.

22. Father Julius Nieuwland, Notre Dame's most famous scientist, was a special friend. Zahm admired his ability and searched for the best chemistry books, the rarest too, in second-hand stores in America and Europe. Interview with Father Eugene Burke, July 20, 1954.

23. Zahm to Albert Zahm, February 5, 1898. John Zahm Collection, UNDA.

24. *Catholic Citizen*, January 29, 1898.

25. Burns Collection. PA.

26. *Ibid.*

27. *Ibid.*

28. *Ibid.*

29. *Ibid.*

30. *Ibid.*

31. Burns agreed with this plan and urged the Father-General to follow it. *Ibid.*

32. Keane to Ireland, January 24, 1898. AASP.

33. Ireland to Zahm, February 9, 1898. John Zahm Collection, UNDA.

34. Gibbons to Zahm, February 12, 1898. John Zahm Collection, UNDA.

35. Riordan to Zahm, February 13, 1898. John Zahm Collection, UNDA.

36. Circular Letter of Provincial J. A. Zahm, June 6, 1898. John Zahm Collection, UNDA.

37. Province Report. PA.

38. *Ibid.*

39. Burns Collection. PA.

40. Father Cavanaugh fell heir to the position of council secretary shortly after Burns became President and Superior of Holy Cross College in 1900.

41. "The New Holy Cross College," *Catholic University Bulletin,* V (April, 1899), 287.

42. Français to Zahm, September 28 and October 31, 1899. John Zahm Collection, UNDA.

43. Shortly after Father Morrissey became Provincial in 1906, the art collection was removed because he believed that the seminarians' environment should be more austere. Interview with Father Eugene Burke, July 20, 1954.

44. The Canadian Province used the Washington House of Studies from its inception in 1895. In 1900, however, the Canadian seminarians were transferred to Laval University, Quebec.

45. "Circular Letter of the Members of the General Chapter—August 8, 1912," *Circular Letters of the Very Reverend Gilbert Français* (Notre Dame, 1913), p. 450.

46. Rector Keane believed a model college was an urgent necessity and he thought it appeared as if the Holy Father gave Zahm a "passport" for its foundation in the Papal Brief of May 13, 1896. These conclusions may be wrong, he wrote, but we can indeed hope and pray for the day when there is a preparatory college at the University with its professors trained by Catholic University and the courses, actual University preparation. Keane to Zahm, June 16, 1896. John Zahm Collection, UNDA.

47. In 1888, Notre Dame was considered an auxiliary to Catholic University by Father Edward Sorin and Father Thomas Walsh since it would send its best graduates to the University. Notre Dame *Scholastic,* August 25, 1888. Professor James Edwards of Notre Dame also told Cardinal Manning a few years later that since Notre Dame lacked endowments, Catholic University would take up the education where Notre Dame left off. *Ibid.,* January 23, 1892.

48. Burns Collection. PA. Also Province Report. PA.

49. Burns Collection. PA.

50. *Ibid.* The property became the Congregation's by May 1, 1900. Purchase of the acreage for $15,000 increased the Holy Cross holdings to twelve acres, purchased at the cost of $31,000. Cf. "University Chronicle," *Catholic University Bulletin,* VI (July, 1900), 444. Still more property adjoining Holy Cross College was purchased by the Congregation in the spring of 1902.

51. Reverend Colman J. Barry, *The Catholic University of America 1903-1909: The Rectorship of Denis J. O'Connell* (Washington, 1950), p. 66.

52. Zahm to O'Connell, June 28, 1903. ACUA.

53. Albert Zahm to Father Zahm, November 18, 1903. John Zahm Collection, UNDA.

54. Province Report. PA. Reverend Patrick Carroll, "Mind in Action," *Ave Maria,* 63 (April, 1946).

55. These provisions are summarized from a copy of the contract which is in the Provincial Archives. Cf. also Barry, *op. cit.,* p. 67.

56. Barry, *op. cit.,* p. 68.

57. O'Connell to Ireland, March 16, 1904. AASP.

58. Maes to Français, February 29, 1904. Copy, CA.

59. Français to Zahm, April 24, 1904. PA.

60. Ireland to Zahm, October 23, 1905. PA.

61. Keane to Zahm, October 30, 1905. PA.

62. Province Report. PA.

63. Français to Zahm, July 29, 1900. PA.

64. Morrissey to Edwards, October 21, 1905. PA.

65. Burns Collection. PA.

66. *Ibid.*

67. *Ibid.*

68. *Ibid.*

69. *Ibid.*

70. Burns believed that even one hundred would be the making of Notre Dame.

71. Burns Collection. PA.

72. Zahm to Christie, March 4, 1902, as found in a Sketch of Holy Cross Parish in Portland, Oregon, PA.

73. Province Report. PA.

74. *Ibid.*

75. Reverend Raymond J. Clancey, "The Founding of Columbia University," *Columbia University 1901-1935 and University of Portland, 1935-1952* (Portland, 1951), p. 15. Zahm planned to reserve part of the property for the Sisters of Holy Cross in the event they would build a college for girls.

76. Province Report. PA. Cost of both the buildings erected in 1903 was $20,000. Zahm to Messrs. Squire and Annis, September 27, 1905. Copy, PA.

77. Father Quinlan, in 1905, estimated the value of Columbia University at $210,000. Quinlan to Zahm, June 6, 1905. PA. He valued the land within the city limits at $2,000 an acre or four times its purchase price in 1902.

78. Reverend James A. Burns, *Catholic Education: A Study of Conditions* (New York, 1917), pp. 52-53.

79. Burns, *Growth and Development of Catholic School System,* p. 100.

80. Interview with Father Thomas Crumley, June 11, 1953.

81. Province Report. PA.

82. *Ibid.*

83. Engelbert to Zahm, July 13, 1897. PA. Formally, the Brothers' studies embraced a commercial course, English classical course, general science course, drawing, and music. There were three professors and ten students in 1898. *Catholic Directory* (Milwaukee, 1898), 13, 275.

84. Burns Collection. PA.

85. *Ibid.*

86. Province Report. PA.

87. Burns Collection. PA. Cf. "Circular Letter of Father Français, April 23, 1899," *Circular Letters of the Very Rev. Gilbert Français* (Notre Dame, 1913), p. 147. The House of Studies for the teaching Brothers who had finished their novitiate continued to be at Mount St. Vincent. *Ibid.*, p. 146. The Postulate for Brothers destined to teach would also be there. "Decrees of the General Chapter, 1898." *Decrees of the General Chapters of the Congregation of Holy Cross* (Notre Dame, 1912), p. 35.

88. Burns Collection. PA.

89. *Ibid.*

90. *Ibid.*

91. E. M. Dunne wrote from the Rectory that he had an interview with the Archbishop who was indifferent to the return of the Brothers, "Hence it will probably be better and preferable for you to send them elsewhere." Dunne to Zahm, August 22, 1899. PA. Also interview with Father Thomas Crumley, June 11, 1953; he thought the St. Columb-kille incident depicted Father Zahm's problem of the teaching Brothers extremely well. It appears that the new pastor had some difficulties with the Brothers and desired to replace them with Sisters. Interview with Brother Peter Hozinski, July 21, 1954.

92. This grievance letter to Français, dated August 12, 1901, is in the Provincial Archives.

93. Français to Zahm, September 1, 1901. PA.

94. Zahm and Morrissey to Français, December 2, 1901. Copy, PA.

95. Province Report. PA.

96. Zahm to Kievan, January 3, 1905. Copy, PA.

97. Kievan to Zahm, January 19, 1905. PA. He also had one or two applicants for St. Mary's.

98. Fitte to Edwards, July 23, 1905. UNDA.

99. Zahm to Français, January 12, 1906. Copy, PA.

100. The Sacred Congregation of the Propaganda suggested that the prerogatives, obligations, and offices of the two societies be discussed. "Circular Letter of Father Français, September 14, 1906," *Circular Letters of the Very Rev. Gilbert Français* (Notre Dame, 1913), p. 235.

101. "Circular Letter of Father Français, May 13, 1909," *ibid.*, p. 323. The great fear in this problem was that the Brothers might form their own independent society unless their requests were accepted. Cf. "Decrees of the General Chapter, 1906," *Decrees of the General Chapters of the Congregation of Holy Cross* (Notre Dame, 1912), pp. 51-63.

102. "Circular Letter of Father Français, May 13, 1909," *op. cit.*, p. 324. The General Chapter of 1898 had already decreed that general or provincial councils must have an equal number of Brothers

and priests, "Decrees of the General Chapter, 1898," *op. cit.*, p. 46.

103. "Circular Letter of Father Français, September 14, 1906," *op. cit.*, p. 235.

104. *Catholic Directory* (Milwaukee, 1907), 22, 352. Almost traditionally, the *Directory* had listed "three professors and ten students" at Mount St. Vincent between 1898-1907. In 1907, the number of students is listed as fourteen. Brother Aiden brought one or two postulants from Ireland who did not stay. Interview with Brother Peter Hozinski, July 21, 1954.

105. *Ibid.*, 23, 355. This was approximately eighteen more than during Zahm's provincialship.

106. French to Morrissey (no date), PA. Français to Morrissey, January 27, 1911. PA. In the latter letter, the Superior-General told of his hopes for peace and counseled courage.

107. Cf. "Decree of the Sacred Congregation of Religious, February 3, 1911," *Decrees of the General Chapter*, Appendix G., pp. 116-18.

108. "Circular Letter of Father Français, January 2, 1912," *Circular Letters*, p. 368. Also, see Burns, *Growth and Development of the Catholic School System in the United States* (New York, 1912), pp. 365-66, where he noted the opening of Catholic high school in Philadelphia; this was a central high school and for the use of all the parishes: by 1901, there were fifty-three such schools and by 1911, it was estimated that there were over three hundred. Sisters outnumbered Brothers by over three to one, due to the shortage of vocations within the Brotherhood. Reverend James Burns, *Catholic Education* (New York, 1917), p. 58.

109. Province Report. PA.

110. *Ibid.*

111. *Ibid.*

112. Fitte to Edwards, July 13, 1905. UNDA. Also, see Brother Albeus to Edwards, July 16, 1905. UNDA.

113. Sister M. Aloysius to Edwards, July 16, 1905. UNDA.

114. *Ibid.*, Morrissey believed the plan was to make him President of troubled Columbia University because of his friendship with Archbishop Christie. Since Zahm urged him to accept the new post, Morrissey believed Zahm had originated the proposal. Cf. Morrissey to Edwards, December 1, 1905. UNDA.

115. Morrissey to Edwards, September 11, 1905. UNDA. Part of his strategy was to have Edwards, some Bishops and lawyers and other influential people write to Français and complain, because, as Corby had once said, this opened the eyes of the French. *Ibid.*, September 11, 1905. The General Chapter had been scheduled for 1903 but was postponed to 1906 because of the difficulties with the Laic Laws in France. Cf. "Circular Letter of Father Français, May 27, 1903," *Circular Letters* (Notre Dame, 1913), p. 212.

116. Morrissey to Edwards, October 21, 1905. UNDA. Too, he hoped the Chapter would stand by him so that "peace and happiness may come to us all again at Notre Dame." *Ibid.,* October 21, 1905.

117. Morrissey to Edwards, December 1, 1905. UNDA. Also, see Notre Dame *Scholastic,* November 18, 1905.

118. Jamet to Edwards, December 8, 1905. UNDA.

119. Zahm to Français, January 12, 1906. Copy, PA.

120. Morrissey to Edwards, March 1, 1906. UNDA.

121. Français to Holy See, March 23, 1906. Copy, PA. Fitte prepared the various testimonials which were sent later. The degree was finally conferred by Pope Pius X and formally presented by Bishop Herman J. Alerding in Fort Wayne on January 3, 1907. South Bend *Tribune,* January 3, 1907.

122. Fitte to Edwards, August 20, 1906. PA.

123. Zahm to Burns, December 11, 1907. UNDA.

124. Zahm to Français, August 25, 1906. "Confidential" Copy, PA. The diagnosis was nervous exhaustion complicated by high vascular pressure and the prescription made by the doctor was a "long vacation." Harold N. Mayer, M.D. "To Whom it May Concern," June 2, 1908. UNDA.

VII

Explorer, Author and Critic, 1906-1921

"For the Benefit of Religion and Education"

Eight and one-half years of incessant activity coupled with heavy responsibilities took their toll. Zahm left Notre Dame in serious need of a complete rest: freedom from responsibility and foreign travel were prescribed. In his quest for health, Zahm returned again to an activity he enjoyed— travel to new and foreign lands and writing of their citizens, history, and culture. Again came the freedom and full desire for apologetical authorship. Seven books were written during these fifteen years as he became a leading American Catholic apologist and essayist. As his writings and explorations indicate, he aspired to be a clerical Churchill and DeSoto. Without a doubt, he possessed fine literary talents.

Zahm left Notre Dame for the east coast in August, 1906, after failing to obtain the Superior-General's permission for European travels. No evidence remains of the first few months following his departure. Probably, he went to Holy Cross College in Washington, D. C., which was under the rectorship of Burns. Shortly before Christmas he wrote Albert Zahm from New York City that he would return home to Washington, that he had been detained longer than expected.[1]

As he wrote some years later, toward the close of January he had decided to leave the winter lands and go southward to another hemisphere in search of rest and relaxation. A few days later, he left for Florida. The last letter he wrote from the States was to his brother from Savannah, Georgia, on February 1, 1907, saying that he was going to the mountains or the woods and enjoy the natural surroundings: he would make his way by slow stages to the Pacific coast and spend six or eight months there if the climate agreed with him. Since he would avoid civilization, telegraphs, and post offices, he warned Albert against being alarmed if he failed to write. His few letters for the next eleven months were addressed from "Goldfields, Nevada"; "Yosemite Valley" and "Mount Shasta, California"; and "Illicitiwart Glacier, Northwest Territory, Canada"; but postmarked, San Francisco, New Haven, Connecticut, Venezuela and Costa Rica. It seems that the Superior-General gave him permission to travel in Canada or the United States, and later extended it to South America. However, Français apparently said nothing for even Father S. Fitte and Professor James Edwards who were close to the administration did not know the whereabouts of Zahm. Albert Zahm and the Superior-General were probably the only ones who knew his tentative travel schedule.

Zahm's journey of twelve months, shrouded in mystery, actually took him through the Caribbean, Venezuela, Colombia, Panama, Ecuador, Peru, Bolivia, and finally down the Amazon River. By steamboat, motor launch, saddle horse, and mule, Zahm made his way through these lands, retracing when possible the trails of the Conquistadors, and recording observations of the people, their traditions, and the rich resources awaiting "Yankee" investments. The journal of this expedition is contained in two volumes, *Up the Orinoco and Down the Magdalena* and *Along the Andes and Down the Amazon,* written under the pen name, H. J. Mozans, and published a few years after his return to Washington, D. C. The latter book won Colonel Roosevelt's praise as the best book of its kind on South America. As sympathetic appraisals of South America rather than simple travel ledgers, both volumes told the past and present his-

tory of these lands, for as Roosevelt wrote, Zahm, like Secretary Elihu Root

> acted as much an Ambassador and his sympathy with and
> appreciation of, the people whom he met . . . earned for him
> thoughtful and unwearied kindness in return, and admirably
> fitted him, while on his journey to interpret our nation to
> those among whom he traveled.[2]

As in his earlier pre-evolution writings, Zahm lauded the
Jesuit, Dominican, and Franciscan missionary work of the
past while describing the patient industrious Indians under
oppression:

> Ah, if they could only have the advantages of that govern-
> ment which the saintly Las Casas had planned for them, how
> different would be their condition to-day! Instead of being so
> often but virtual serfs and the victims of untold wrongs, they
> would be the happy prosperous citizens of a great and flour-
> ishing commonwealth.[3]

These comprehensive studies continued the era of Hispanic-
American historical studies begun by Bernard Moses at the
University of California as they publicized the Spanish Cath-
olic bases throughout the southern continent.

The state of Zahm's health when he returned from the
Amazon to New York City is somewhat of a mystery. According to his published account he found both health and
relaxation in the southern continent and returned "with
health restored and with a greater capacity for work than
I had known for years." [4] In fact, however, during the last
stage of the journey he wrote to Albert that he had suffered pleurisy for four months and a slight lung hemor-
rhage which seemed serious at first; therefore, he sought the
Kneipp cure at a Denville, New Jersey, sanatorium. A medical fad at the turn of the century, the cure was initiated
by Father Kneipp, a Catholic priest in the Bavarian village
of Woershofen, who experimented with the regenerative effects of water for returning the body to health. Attributing
most diseases to the debilitating effects of modern luxuries,
Kneipp prescribed fresh air, exercise, and a special diet. A

principal treatment involved tramping barefoot on dew-moistened grass, and for a time, the New York City Park Board was flooded with requests for permission to take early morning walks on the park lawns! Very popular with the clergy, the cure almost resulted in Pope Leo XIII's death. Apparently, Zahm met with small success.

From New Jersey, Zahm returned to Holy Cross College and began the research and writing for the two volumes describing the recent South American journey. During the next few years his assignment was rest and recreation for, although his health had improved since leaving the provincialship, he still was bothered with nervous exhaustion.[5] Despite uneven health, he found these years most productive in writing. The two South American books were finished and published by 1911. They were his first published works since 1898. As a critic he wrote a number of unsigned book reviews for the *Bulletin of the Pan American Union,* which were, in fact, essays. In one, he found no fault with Sir Clements Markham's book, *The Incas of Peru* and, while commending the scholarly qualities of the volume, he added observations from his own travels along the Incas' Andean home.[6] His critical review of C. H. Haring's book, *The Buccaneers in the West Indies in The XVIII Century,* suggested that the author should have used Spanish government records along with the English and Dutch accounts for an objective presentation.[7] A subsequent review, almost Rousseauan in viewpoint, described the Indian in the wilds of South America. In this review of Dr. Theodor-Koch-Grünberg's book, *Zwei Jahre Unter den Indianern,* Zahm also emphasized the kindness and friendliness of the natives. The Indians were, he found, neither cannibals nor deceitful: instead they lived on a high moral level. As a harmless child of nature, the noble savage proved himself a friend to the white man, especially one who believed in the fatherhood of God and the brotherhood of man. Quite cleverly, he suggested in conclusion that Dr. Koch-Grünberg's views were the same as Dr. Mozans' ideas in his two recently published volumes *Up the Orinoco and Down the Magdalena* and *Along the Andes and Down the Amazon!* [8]

Meanwhile, Zahm's series of articles on El Dorado, published during 1912 in the *Bulletin of the Pan American Union,* under the pen name, "J. A. Manso" (apparently borrowed from the first bishop to set foot on American soil), were later modified and printed in a book entitled, *The Quest of El Dorado.* This volume is still a standard reference for South American history and geography. [9] Zahm did not claim it to be an exhaustive study, rather he urged someone to undertake such a project for he presented only the more important chronicles regarding the search for the "gilded king." In the chapters on El Dorado's Conquistadors he wrote that though these fruitless explorations for a fabulous city ended in disheartening failures, they were portrayals of a glorious era characterized by an intense desire for gold and glory.

After an interim of nearly twenty years, Zahm again contributed an essay to the *Ecclesiastical Review* in 1913, this time a lead article tracing the first bishops and archbishops in the new world. Rather than employ his recent pen-name, "Manso," he chose a third one "Solis." The essay described the establishment of the metropolitan see of Yaguata near the city of Santo Domingo and its two dependent sees, Magua and Baynúa, established by Pope Julius II in 1504. [10]

A tour which was known as the Colonel Roosevelt Scientific Expedition to South America was for Zahm a culmination of many years of secret ambition and, in a sense, salesmanship. Zahm's excursion into South America during 1907 had increased his yearning to explore South America's deepest interior; in fact, for a trip directly through South America's middle from north to south. He sought to interest President Theodore Roosevelt shortly before the latter's second presidential term ended in 1908; however, since Roosevelt's African expedition had been arranged, his offer was refused. [11] Sporadic correspondence between the two continued and Zahm hoped that the former president would make such an expedition in order to direct scientific and diplomatic attention to the area. The mutual interest in Dante promoted their friendship. Zahm had supplied Roosevelt with Dante material the day before President Taft entered the White House.[12] President Roosevelt's decision to send Secretary Root on tour in South America, thought Zahm, did more to establish friendly relations between the United States and the southern republics than could have been done by fifty years of formal diplomacy. Likewise, Zahm interpreted the resolution to send the fleet around the world as a striking demonstration that the United States was prepared and able to defend the Monroe Doctrine.

The presidential campaign of 1912 prevented a trip that year. In a letter to Roosevelt, Zahm reported the direction of the political wind among Catholic voters as early as June 3, 1912, and included clippings from several Catholic newspapers. He urged Roosevelt, *"Prospere procede et regna."* [13] Roosevelt welcomed Zahm's opinion for he had feared that his failure to visit Pope Pius X in Rome in 1911 might cost him many Catholic votes. He replied with gratitude that certain friendships had been tested in the campaign and that he was grateful for Zahm's loyalty—"Yes, your prophesy is being proved true." [14] Even in Roosevelt's defeat, Zahm wrote encouragingly to him that millions of friends would be with him in the great campaign for social justice and progress.[15]

During the spring of 1913, Roosevelt was offered speaking engagements in Argentina, Brazil and Chile; he then considered the plan whereby a return through the interior of South America might be made. Despite his intention to write Zahm of this proposal, he did not do so before inquiring at the American Museum of Natural History in New York City about some first-rate naturalists to accompany him. At a luncheon given by the distinguished curator of the New York Museum of Natural History, Frank Chapman, in mid-June, plans for the trip were discussed, and Zahm was present. He had come at the invitation of Chapman. Tentative suggestions were made for a trip up the Paraguay and then down the Amazon or Orinoco River

Valleys. They discussed this plan again at Oyster Bay a few days later, but Roosevelt was as yet uncertain about going. Recalling the Panama incident, the Colonel was certain about one phase of the trip—"Of course, I could not under the circumstances touch on Colombian territory." [16]

The expedition grew in interest as Colonel Roosevelt wrote:

> I have a funny little Catholic priest, who is a friend of mine, a great Dante scholar, and with a thirst for wandering in the wilderness coming with me. He has for years been anxious to have me go north through the middle of South America. I should like to do this because it enables me to avoid the more Bryce-Bryan route sea trip around South America . . .[17]

They would start up the Plata and Paraguay Rivers, portage to the headwaters of the Amazon, then cross the Amazon basin, voyage down the Orinoco River into Venezuela and return to the United States in April or May, 1914. Roosevelt wanted little publicity because it seemed that it was an ambitious trip for a "stout, elderly, retired politician, who is no longer in good condition, and I may not be able to make it." Mr. Frank Harper, Colonel Roosevelt's secretary; George K. Cherrie, an ornithologist; Leo E. Miller, a mammalogist; and the noted Arctic explorer, Anthony Fiala, were also invited to take part in the expedition.

During the summer months, Zahm was busy arranging the journey. Roosevelt accepted Zahm's advice to prepare a major address for Buenos Aires, and to have it translated into Spanish beforehand.[18] By mid-August, Zahm had signed a contract with the Rift Climbing Boat Company for two power boats, named "Edith" and "Notre Dame." Only then did he feel at ease about the most difficult part of the journey—through the Matto Grosso. As it happened, these boats were abandoned in South America when Brazilian guides said it would be impossible to transport them through the jungle.

The Roosevelt-Zahm expedition finally began when the

S.S. Van Dyck left New York harbor on October 4, 1913. Brief visits in the Caribbean Islands, Rio de Janeiro, São Paulo, and Montevideo preceded their arrival in Buenos Aires on November 5.

Even before their arrival, the plans for the journey through the interior were changed. Brazilian authorities including Senor Lauro Müller, Brazil's Minister of Foreign Affairs, promised to have Colonel Candido Mariano da Silva Rondon at Colonel Roosevelt's disposal from the time the expedition left Paraguay headwaters until it reached Manaos or Santarem.[19] Rondon, a former Professor of Mathematics and Astronomy at the Brazilian Military Academy, had explored this area in 1907, 1908, and 1909 in preparation for building a telegraph line through it. The minister also offered a dangerous alternate route to the projected voyage down the Tapajos. This suggestion appealed to the adventuresome and imaginative Roosevelt. A large unexplored river which Rondon had discovered and named Rio da Dúvida was this alternate route. It was believed that the river's headwaters lay between the Tapajos and the Madeira Rivers. It was suggested that the expedition follow it to where it might open into the Tapajos, then the Madeira and finally the Amazon River. Delighted with the prospects of such a thrilling adventure, Roosevelt asked Zahm and the others if they wanted to go, warning that it was a more hazardous plan and offering instead to take them as far as the headwaters of the Rio da Dúvida where he, his son Kermit, and Rondon would embark on the dangerous descent. The others could take the museum collections to the Paraguay and then home. However, all were eager to go. Thus, the original route planned by Zahm was radically changed and, as Roosevelt wrote:

> Father Zahm is a perfect trump, but he knows nothing of any of the country which we have planned to go through, and in practice can give us no help or advice as to methods of traveling and what we will or will not be actually able to accomplish.[20]

The expedition became known as the Roosevelt-Rondon South American Expedition and became geographical in character rather than zoological.

The stay in Buenos Aires proved pleasant. South Americans were pleased, though surprised to see Roosevelt, a Protestant, accompanied by a Catholic priest. They found the pair a good illustration of tolerance in practice. During these ten days, Zahm and Roosevelt weathered a whirlwind of luncheons, formal receptions, and speeches. According to the Buenos Aires *Southern Cross,* November 14, Roosevelt not only adequately defended the Monroe Doctrine and his unselfish presidential action in Panama, Cuba and Santo Domingo, but he also urged the United States and Argentina to recognize social justice in dealing with their citizens. At the same time he emphasized in his Monroe Doctrine speech, given in Buenos Aires as suggested by Zahm, that the Monroe Doctrine in the sense of a "special guardianship by the United States" no longer applied. Rather, reported the Buenos Aires *Herald* of November 14, Argentina was well prepared to be the champion of its own Monroe Doctrine!

Feeling the best he had for years, Zahm spoke at a banquet in his honor. Recalling the spirited days of Archbishop Ireland, of Keane and O'Connell, he said the United States had a loyal laity and clergy. "They, of a truth, in the words of our illustrious Archbishop Ireland, are going forward with the Gospel of Christ in one hand and the Constitution of the United States in the other." [21] Aware that his audience recalled his former writings in science, he assured them again that no conflict between science and religion could exist, and that the apparent differences between men of science and religion were only temporary. The Bible's comprehensive statement, "In the beginning God created heaven and earth," could never be controverted by any legitimate induction from any scientific facts despite the imaginations of biologists, palaeontologists and anthropologists to the contrary.

After leaving Buenos Aires, the entourage took a two

week "good will" tour through the Argentine interior and Chile. Stopping briefly at Asuncion, Paraguay, they then sailed up the Paraguay River to Corumba.

Thus far their entire journey through South America had been, Zahm remarked, a triumphal march filled with continuous ovations. The royal receptions, accommodations in exclusive hotels, city-wide celebrations, and formal inspection tours had made the "march" unique and memorable. No other group had ever seen more of South America in such a short time. Nor had the governments permitted even the slightest discomfort.[22]

The point of departure for the wilderness expedition along an uncharted river drew closer. Zahm, in particular, was eager to explore the uncharted world along the river avenue and hoped the exploration would yield material for him to write ten to fifteen volumes. Movies of native dances and religious rites, recordings of native life, collecting of flora and fauna, specimens, scientific note-taking: these and many other daily projects continued as the yacht slowly made its way up the Paraguay River. The Americans were in high spirits as they moved northward in relative comfort.

From time to time the yacht docked at various small hamlets to take on fuel wood and provisions. At one tiny settlement, according to Roosevelt, Zahm visited a native family with many children including two little ones, ages one and two, whom he was asked to baptize since no priest had visited the area for three years. Under questioning, both parents said they were not Roman Catholics—rather the father called himself a "free-thinking Catholic" and the mother termed herself a "Protestant Catholic" which, she revealed, meant her mother had been a Protestant. Since apparently the Bishop of Asuncion had baptized the older children, Zahm, at the plea of the parents, baptized the little ones.[23]

Continuing upstream, the troup met Rondon and the other Brazilian members who had come overland from Rio de Janeiro. On Christmas Eve, it was decided that the group, which had grown to 40 persons and 200 saddle and pack animals, would divide in two at Utiarity. In the days that followed this decision it was agreed that Roosevelt, his son Kermit, and Rondon would follow the River of Doubt while Zahm would lead the second group to the Madeira River and then down to Manaos. Furthermore, if his health held up, he would continue from Manaos to Caracas, thus making such a journey for the first time in history. He hoped for success for it would make South America better known and

> I shall then be able to feel that I can take an honored place among the great missionary explorers who, in colonial times, shed such honor on the Church & on Catholic Spain. I shall also have been instrumental in making North & South America better known to each other and this will redound to the benefit of religion & education as well as to that of social and commercial relations.[24]

By the time the expedition reached Utiarity where it was planned to divide into two groups Zahm had decided, probably because of poor food, heavy rains, and poor preparation by the Brazilian group (over one-half of the pack animals were wild oxen which made lassoing, blindfolding, and packing a daily ritual), to abandon the expedition and instead he returned to Buenos Aires. The decision was a prudent one, for at sixty-two years of age he did not have the stamina required to go into Caracas. Roosevelt's six weeks' descent of the River of Doubt (now named Rio Teodoro), 1,500 kilometers long, was a treacherous journey: five of the seven canoes were sunk, one native peddler was murdered by a berserk companion, another drowned, and Roosevelt himself almost died from an infected leg wound. Leo Miller, who had replaced Zahm as leader of the second group, had to wait thirteen days at Magosso, a wretched place laden with malaria and dysentery, for a boat which arrived only by accident. Chagrined over leaving the well-publicized expedition, Zahm wrote Albert that he was returning home by way of Europe and if anyone asked merely to say that he would be home in April.

Zahm therefore, the designer of the original South American expedition, returned to the United States unheralded
and alone. Admittedly he had failed to take an honored
place among the great missionary explorers; however, his
original purpose was achieved in that subsequent publicity,
and his book on the journey, *Through South America's
Southland,* did benefit religion and education and improved
the friendly relations between the two continents.

His friendship with Roosevelt continued through visits
and correspondence. Again Zahm sent him clippings from
the Catholic press regarding Roosevelt's "splendid pronun-
ciamento" on the Mexican question.[25] In acknowledgment,
Roosevelt thanked him and observed that he could not imagine how any people could be so unpatriotic and fatuous
as Wilson and Bryan. "Do you remember when you told
me that you knew they were planning to give Colombia
twenty-five million dollars and I could not believe it?"[26]
Later, Roosevelt's insistent demand that America join the
Allies in World War I caused a rift in their friendship since
Zahm was not convinced of Germany's guilt.

Zahm's three travel books on South America, with their
well synthesized references to literature and to foreign
countries from classical times to the twentieth century, rank
as his best writings. The volumes contained an immense
amount of historical material carefully selected and fused
into one story. Within the pages there was an overt tendency to favor South Americans, their traditions, and most
especially, their Catholicism. Undeniably he emphasized the
best aspects of South America. In the last analysis the volumes were a presentation in depth of South America and
surely the work of a scholarly apologist intent upon bal-
ancing the historical accounts of South America. It was to
his honor that he was the first English-speaking American
Catholic author to write a more accurate appraisal of South
America's history and culture.[27]

Although Zahm never returned to Notre Dame after his
departure in 1906, his heart and scholarly interests were still
there. On August 30, 1913, in reply to a letter of inquiry

from Reverend Matthew Schumacher, Director of Studies
and one of the few original Holy Cross graduates still at
the University, Zahm wrote that he believed the next buildings needed for the University were: one for seminarians
who had finished their novitiate but were not yet ready for
Holy Cross College in Washington, D. C.; a library, pref-
erably located near the Father Badin Chapel, which was a
safe area in the event of fire; a series of residence halls
south of Walsh Hall and the Chemistry Building, thus forming a beautiful college quadrangle; [28] lastly, a spacious dining hall. Zahm's blueprint for expansion and emphasis upon
fireproofing the buildings were followed in the years 1917-
1927 although the order of priority was modified. Zahm
ended his reply with characteristic principle:

> But more important by far than buildings is the proper prep-
> aration of our young subjects for their work as teachers. What
> every university needs and what every community needs above
> everything else is scholars and specialists, as well as devoted
> religious. Large and imposing buildings have little value un-
> less those in charge of them and teaching in them be thor-
> oughly educated and properly trained to teach the special
> classes which may be assigned them. It must be evident to
> everyone who knows anything at all about modern university
> work that this is an age of specialists, and that it is hopeless
> for us to compete with sectarian or government institutions
> unless we have the corps of trained specialists for every de-
> partment in each of our own colleges.[29]

Zahm had not changed his views since leaving the Provincialship.

When the new library was finished in 1917, a special
room, at Zahm's request, was set aside for his Dante collection. Like Pope Leo XIII, he had become interested in
Dante, especially during his stay in Rome, 1896-1898, and
he began the collection shortly after his return as Provincial. Much of the Dante library, collected by the famous
Dantofilo of Italy, Giulio Acquaticci, was purchased by
Father Zahm in 1902-1903. The chief translations of the
poet's work in over thirty languages and dialects, together

with etchings, paintings, marble busts, and medallions of the Italian poet were acquired. He hoped there would be a Dante Chair established at Notre Dame and that his gift would precipitate this action. His enthusiastic quest for Dante material continued to the time of his death and made this Dante collection of over five thousand books the third best in the United States.

During the last years of his life and even during the South American writing period, he wrote other historical books. These included two volumes calculated to interest all women, suffragettes and anti-suffragettes, as well as scholars and general readers interested in the growth of education and science. The first volume, *Women in Science* was decidedly apologetical as it described the long struggle of women for educational opportunities from earliest times in ancient Greece to the days of 1913. He related how they had been the colleagues, if not the peers, of the famous men-educators and scientists, and emphasized that their minds were as capable and receptive as any great men. Enthusiastically, he agreed in essence with Peter Lombard, that "Woman was not taken from the head of man, for she was not intended to be his ruler, nor from his foot, for she was not intended to be his slave, but from his side, for she was intended to be his companion and comfort." At long last, he exclaimed, over all the Western World, a new era of acceptance had begun.

> Woman's long struggle for intellectual freedom is almost ended, and certain victory is already in sight . . . so effective and so concentrated has been their work during recent years that they have accomplished more toward securing complete intellectual enfranchisement than during the previous thirty centuries.[30]

A good judge of the past, he realized that leisure time enabled woman in the modern generation to achieve intellectual advancement.

This study proved to be a popular seller. Reviewers called it a wonderful book, having the romantic interest of a novel and the inspiration of a battle hymn:[31] it was declared a "must" for every woman's suffrage club.[32] Within five years, a reading audience concerned with the second-class status of women purchased over a thousand copies of this volume.

A second volume, hybrid in character and less universal in appeal, appeared in 1917, and was entitled *Great Inspirers*. It contained excerpts from the lives of four women who inspired St. Jerome and Dante. In a sense the book was an antidote to the excesses within the suffragette movement, for it was a sensitive study of the role women had played as gentle guides and sources of encouragement to great men —"of the power which they are secretly, but not less effectively wielding from the family hearth to the homes of science and the halls of legislation."[33] This book led the reviewer of the New York *Freeman's Journal* to predict on March 10, 1917, that "It will be a long time before Catholics in this country form a true appreciation of the work of Fr. Zahm as apologist . . . the form of his apologetics is valuable because it is primarily constructive."

While Emeritus Professor of Apologetics at Holy Cross College, Zahm began a new book, *From Berlin to Bagdad and Babylon*. His plan for the book crystallized sometime before September, 1917, as noted by his request for permission from Français to visit the Holy Land after the war ended. He related that when he visited this area in 1887 with Sorin, he had had little time for research. Now he had the time and especially the desire to incorporate the latest results of archaeological research on the Bible and Higher Criticism —"No sane investigator can deny that these results have all been in favor of the Sacred Text & that many of them have corroborated it in the most surprising manner."[34] And since English-writing Catholic authors had not treated this topic, there was little scientific refutation of the enemy. In order that a large reading public might be reached, he believed it important to insert local color as in the South American volumes, and therefore to visit these lands. Characteristically, Zahm asked that the projected journey be kept an absolute secret.

The manuscript was partially completed by the summer of 1921. It contained a wealth of information on the social, economic, religious and intellectual history of the people living along the direct route between Germany and the Middle East, especially, the Bible lands. Fully one-third of his manuscript was a plea for a sympathetic understanding of the Turks and of their deep Moslem faith. Writing on the theory of evolution for the first time since 1898, he briefly explained that new excavations and geological studies had made no changes in the Bible story.[35]

This travelogue, like the South American trilogy, though somewhat lyrical gave a good insight into these lands. With the manuscript almost completed, he desired to travel through these countries and embellish his research with atmosphere and local color. On October 4, 1921, exactly eight years to the morning after leaving New York with the Roosevelt expedition, Zahm, now seventy years old, white-haired and physically trim, left New York on the S.S. *George Washington*. This trip, paid for by his dear friend, Charles Schwab, as probably were his South American expeditions, was to the Middle East—and was calculated to take four or five months. The voyage was pleasant and Zahm felt exceedingly well.[36] He made brief stops in London, Paris, Berlin, and Dresden. In the latter city he caught a cold which became more severe in his unheated hotel room. In spite of the illness, he went on to Munich and arrived on Wednesday, October 26. He sayed in the Bayerischen Hof Hotel in a suite near the A. Benziger family, publishers and close friends of the Schwabs. When cough medicine did not ease the condition, Benziger took him to Dr. May of the University who prescribed medicine for bronchitis and high temperature and ordered immediate hospitalization. Reluctant to leave the hotel, Zahm stayed in his rooms and the Benziger family nursed him over the weekend. His condition grew steadily worse. When, a short time later, he complained of a severe pain in his right lung, a Red Cross Sister was assigned as his private nurse. Though very ill, he told the doctor not to be too concerned about his weak heart for he had had one for years.

After showing slight improvement during the next few days, he again hemorrhaged, his temperature increased and continuous pain shot through his chest. Bronchial pneumonia was taking its course. Though moved to the hospital, and despite oxygen and camphor treatments, he continued to become weaker. He received the last sacraments. Still hopeful that he would recover, he told Marie Benziger that he wanted ten more years to live—to finish his present book, which would only mean adding a few pages here and there, and then to write his great work, a life of Dante. He said if he had to die, it was a blessing to die away from home because it was too painful to see his family in sorrow. Weakened and restless, he received general absolution and a few hours later died on the morning of November 10, 1921, in room 400 of the Roten Kreuz Hospital.[37]

A short time later his body was returned to the land and the University he loved. Following funeral services in Sacred Heart Church on January 7, 1922, he was buried in the Community graveyard at Notre Dame alongside his friend Sorin and the other great builders of a Catholic religious congregation and University. At long last the weary traveler was home among the saints and scholars he had envisioned.

NOTES TO CHAPTER VII

1. Zahm to Albert Zahm, December 19, 1906. John Zahm Collection, UNDA.

2. Zahm, *Along the Andes and Down the Amazon* (New York, 1911), p. x.

3. *Ibid.,* p. 95.

4. *Ibid.,* p. 526.

5. Harold N. Mayer—"To Whom it May Concern," June 2, 1908; also Mayer to Zahm, June 23, 1908. John Zahm Collection, UNDA.

6. Zahm, "Review of Sir Clements Markham's *The Incas of Peru,*" *Bulletin of the Pan American Union,* XXXII (February, 1911), 300-309.

7. Cf. Reverend John A. Zahm, "Review of C. H. Haring's *The*

Buccaneers in the West Indies in the XVII Century," ibid., XXXII (March, 1911), 517-21.

8. (M.L.K.) "Idyllic Homes and Lives of Indians in South American Wilds," *ibid.,* XXXII (October, 1911), 730-47.

9. Reverend John A. Zahm, *The Quest of El Dorado* (New York, 1917).

10. A. H. Solis, "Who Were the First Bishops and Archbishops in the New World, and Where Were the First Sees Established?" *Ecclesiastical Review,* 48 (April, 1913), 385-92.

11. Around 1904, Zahm became acquainted with President Roosevelt through Maurice Francis Egan, former professor at Notre Dame, who was appointed Minister to Denmark by Roosevelt.

12. Zahm to Roosevelt, March 6, 1911. "Confidential." Copy, UNDA. Roosevelt's articles, "Dante and the Bowery," appeared in the *Outlook,* XCVIII (1911), 927-30; it gave praise to this Italian poet who judged contemporary political figures as well as those ancient ones.

13. Zahm to Roosevelt, June 3, 1912. LC.

14. Roosevelt to Zahm, June 6, 1912. John Zahm Collection, UNDA.

15. Zahm to Roosevelt, December 31, 1912. LC.

16. Roosevelt to Zahm, June 17, 1913. John Zahm Collection, UNDA.

17. Roosevelt to Arthur Hamilton Lee, July 7, 1913, in Elting E. Morison, ed., *The Letters of Theodore Roosevelt* (Cambridge, 1954), VII, 741.

18. Roosevelt to Zahm, July 7, 1910. John Zahm Collection, UNDA.

19. Roosevelt to Chapman, November 4, 1913, in Morison, ed., *op. cit.,* VII, 754.

20. *Ibid.,* VII, 755.

21. *Southern Cross,* November 14, 1913. O'Connell expressed the same idea in his address at Fribourg in 1897.

22. Zahm to Albert Zahm, December 12, 1913. John Zahm Collection, UNDA.

23. Roosevelt, *Through the Brazilian Wilderness* (New York, 1920), pp. 57-58.

24. Zahm to Albert Zahm, January 18, 1914. John Zahm Collection, UNDA.

25. Zahm to Roosevelt, December 23, 1914. LC.

26. Roosevelt to Zahm, December 29, 1914. John Zahm Collection, UNDA.

27. Thomas F. O'Connor, "John A. Zahm, C.S.C.: Scientist and Americanist," *The Americas,* 7 (April, 1951), 462. Zahm gave his South American library of over one thousand volumes to Notre Dame in 1917.

28. Zahm had planned this before leaving office, and had obtained permission from the County Commissioners to have the road running

near the post office moved south of the cemetery; however, for some reason it was not carried out. Zahm to Schumacher, August 30, 1913. Copy, PA.

29. *Ibid.*

30. Zahm (H. J. Mozans), *Women in Science* (New York, 1913), p. 101.

31. Madison *Journal* (Wisconsin), December 10, 1913.

32. *Women's Journal* (Boston, Mass.), December 20, 1913.

33. Reverend John A. Zahm, *Great Inspirers* (New York, 1917), p. viii. Chapter One of this book had been published earlier as "Woman's Work in Bible Study and Translation," *Catholic World*, 95 (April, 1912), 463-77 under still another pseudonym, A. H. Johns!

34. Zahm to Français (no date). John Zahm Collection, UNDA.

35. Zahm, *From Berlin to Bagdad and Babylon* (New York, 1922), pp. 367-68.

36. Zahm to Albert Zahm, October 10, 1921. John Zahm Collection, UNDA.

37. His last days were fully recorded by Gertrude Benziger to Mrs. C. Schwab, November 10, 1921. Copy, UNDA. Also, see Marie Benziger to Father Robinson, November 10, 1921. Copy, UNDA. A. Benziger to Albert Zahm, November 12, 1921, UNDA; and Albert Zahm to Sister Angeline, November 14, 1921, copy, UNDA. Reverend Patrick Carroll reprinted part of these letters in an essay "Mind in Action," *Ave Maria*, 64 (July, 1946), 45-49. Cf. obituary printed in the New York *Times*, November 12, 1921, and the *Catholic Citizen*, November 19, 1921.

Appendix

A LIST OF ONE HUNDRED BEST BOOKS

Compiled by Father Zahm for Students
at Notre Dame in 1887.

As printed in the Notre Dame *Scholastic,* May 21, 1887.

THEOLOGY AND RELIGION

The Bible; A. Kempis (Challoner's translation), *The Following of Christ; Confessions of St. Augustine;* Gibbons, *Faith of Our Fathers;* Faa di Bruno, *Catholic Belief;* Stone, *The Invitation Heeded;* Faber, *Creator and Creature;* Allies, *The Throne of the Fisherman;* Lambert, *Notes on Ingersoll;* Lilly, *Ancient Religion and Modern Thought;* Lacordaire, *Conferences;* Marshall, *Christian Missions.*

SCIENCE

Mivart, *Lessons from Nature;* Mivart, *Genesis of Species;* Molloy, *Geology and Revelation;* Wiseman, *Science and Revealed Religion;* H. Miller, *Testimony of the Rocks;* Johnston, *Chemistry of Common Life;* Tissandier, *Scientific Recreation;* Newcomb, *Popular Astronomy;* De Quartrefages, *The Human Species;* Van Beneden, *Animal Parasites and Messmates;* Tyndall, *Fragments of Science;* Huxley, *Lay Sermons.*

HISTORY

Rawlinson, *Ancient Egypt, The Seven Great Monarchies;* Grote, *History of Greece;* Mommsen, *History of Rome;* Lingard, *History of England;* Janssen, *History of the German People;* Bancroft, *History of the United States;* Digby, *The Ages of Faith;* Montalembert, *Monks of the West;* Darras, *History of the Church;* J. G. Shea, *History of the Church in the United States;* Thebaud, *The Irish Race;* Bossuet, *Discourses on Universal History;* Schlegel, *Philosophy of History.*

BIOGRAPHY

O'Meara, *Life of Ozanam;* Chocorne, *Inner Life of Père Lacordaire;* Irving, *Life of Washington;* Ratisbonne, *Life of St. Bernard;* Bowden, *Life of Father Faber;* Vaughan, *Life of St. Thomas of Aquin;* Knight, *Life of Columbus;* Russel, *Life of Messofanti;* De Falloux, *Life and Letters of Madame Swetschine;* Strickland, *Queens of England;* Hurter, *Innocent III;* Roscoe, *Leo X; Louis Pasteur,* by his son-in-law.

ART AND MUSIC

Rio, *Christian Art;* E. A. Starr, *Pilgrims and Shrines;* Hanzi, *History of Italian Painting;* Sedley Taylor, *The Science of Music;* Von Seeburg (translated by Reverend J. M. Toohey, C.S.C.), *Life of Haydn.*

POETRY

Dante (Carey's translation), *The Divine Comedy;* Tasso, *Jerusalem Delivered;* Milton, *Paradise Lost;* Homer (Derby's translation), *The Iliad;* Virgil (Dryden's translation), *The Aeneid; Dramas of Shakespeare;* Wordsworth, *The Excursion;* J. Boyle O'Reilly, *In Bohemia;* Goldsmith, *The Deserted Village;* Longfellow, *Evangeline;* Newman, *Dream of Gerontius.*

TRAVEL

Ringlake, *Eothen;* Milliard, *Six Months in Italy;* Lady Herbert, *Impressions of Spain;* McGahan, *Campaigning on the Oxus;* Stanley, *The Dark Continent.*

FICTION

Wiseman, *Fabiola;* Newman, *Callista;* Miles G. Keon, *Dion and the Sybils;* Manzoni, *The Betrothed;* Lew Wallace, *Ben Hur;* Gerald Griffin, *The Collegians;* Cervantes, *Don Quixote;* Johnson, *Rasselas;* Lady Fullerton, *Too Strange Not to be True;* Christian Reid, *Heart of Steel;* Mrs. Craven, *A Sister's Story;* Farrar, *Eric or Little by Little.*

MISCELLANY AND CRITICISM

Chateaubriand, *Genius of Christianity;* Archbishop Spalding, *Miscellanea;* Balmes, *Protestantism and Catholicity Compared;* Donoso Cortes, *Catholicism, Liberalism and Socialism;* Brownson, *The American Republic;* De Toqueville [sic], *Democracy in America;* Ozanam, *Dante and Catholic Philosophy in the 13th Century;* Dr. Ward, *Essays and Reviews;* Lilly, *Characteristics of Newman;* Lilly, *Characteristics of Manning;* Macaulay, *Essays and Reviews;* Jeffrey, *Essays and Critiques;* Christopher North, *Essays;* Sydney Smith, *Essays;* De Quincey, *Confessions of an Opium Eater;* Chas. Lamb, *Essays of Elia;* Drain, *Christian Schools and Scholars.*

PUBLICATIONS OF FATHER ZAHM

Father Zahm's publications, as listed in chronological order, provide not only an indication of the exceedingly extensive range of topics which he presented to reading audiences in America and abroad, but also reveal how his interests came full circle back to travel essays and accounts of distant lands.

Colorado, Its Past, Present and Future (Notre Dame: University Press, 1883), pamphlet.
The Catholic Church and Modern Science (Notre Dame: University Press, 1883), pamphlet.
"Catholic Church and Modern Science," *Ave Maria,* 19 (1883), 241-48, 261-68.
The Great Southwest, Its Attractions, Resources and People (Notre Dame: University Press, 1883), pamphlet.
"What the Church Has Done for Science," *Ave Maria,* 21 (1885), 191-98, 212-16, 233-37, 247-52.
The Age of the Human Race According to Modern Science and Biblical Chronology (Notre Dame: Ave Maria [no date]), pamphlet.
Alaska, The Country and Its Inhabitants (Notre Dame: University Press, 1886), pamphlet.
Letters from the Hawaiian Islands (Notre Dame: University Press, 1887), pamphlet.
"Catholic Dogma and Scientific Dogmatism," *American Catholic Quarterly Review,* XV (1890), 434-67.
"The Friends and Foes of Science," *American Catholic Quarterly Review,* XV (1890), 630-57.
"The Omar of the New World," *American Ecclesiastical Review,* 7 (1892), 81-101.
Sound and Music (Chicago: A. C. McClurg & Co., 1893).
"Age of the Human Race," *Review of Reviews,* VII (1893), 605-606.
"Faith and Science," *Donahoe's Magazine,* XXX (1893), 265-74.
"Louis Pasteur and His Life-Work," *Catholic World,* 58 (1893), 445-63.

"Louis Pasteur and His Life-Work," *Review of Reviews*, VII (1893), 215-16.

What the Church Has Done for Science (Notre Dame: Ave Maria, [n.d.]), pamphlet.

The Antiquity of Man According to Astronomy and History (n.p., n. pub.), 1893, pamphlet.

Catholic Science and Catholic Scientists (Philadelphia: H. L. Kilner & Co., 1893).

"Christian Faith and Scientific Freedom," *North American Review*, 157 (1893), 315-24.

"The Age of the Human Race According to Modern Science and Biblical Chronology," *American Catholic Quarterly Review*, XVIII (1893), 225-49, 562-88, 719-34; XIX (1894), 260-75.

"The Warfare with Agnosticism," *Donahoe's Magazine*, XXXII (1894), 265-76.

"The Forerunner and Rival of Pasteur," *Rosary*, IV (1894), 433-50.

"A Galaxy of Catholic Scientists," *Donahoe's Magazine*, XXXII (1894) 595-610.

"The International Catholic Scientific Congress," *Donahoe's Magazine*, XXXII (1894), 459-67.

"Mendacity of Voltaire," *Ave Maria*, 38 (1894), 365-68.

"Moses and Sciences," "Allegorism and Literalism," "St. Gregory of Nyssa and the Nebular Hypothesis," "St. Augustine and Evolution," "Modern Theories of Cosmogony," *American Ecclesiastical Review*, 10 (1894), 161-227.

Bible, Science, and Faith (Baltimore: John Murphy & Co., 1894).

Moses and Modern Science (Philadelphia: D. J. Gallagher & Co., 1894), pamphlet.

"A Distinguished Orientalist, Monsignor Charles De Harlez," *Rosary*, V (1895), 262-71.

"Leo XIII and the Social Question," *North American Review*, CLXI (1895), 200-14.

"A New System of Writing for the Blind," *Catholic World*, 61 (1895), 32-43.

"A New System of Writing for the Blind," *Review of Reviews*, XI (1895), 590.

"Some Lights of Science and the Church," *Rosary*, V (1895), 239-350.

"Leo XIII and Science," *Catholic University Bulletin*, 2 (1896), 21-38.

Evolution and Dogma (Chicago: D. H. McBride & Co., 1896).

Science and the Church (Chicago: D. H. McBride & Co., 1896).

Scientific Theory and Catholic Doctrine (Chicago: D. H. McBride & Co., 1896).

"Evolution and Teleology," Appleton's *Popular Science Monthly*, LII (1898), 815-24.

(H. J. Mozans) *Following the Conquistadores: Up the Orinoco and Down the Magdalena* (New York: D. Appleton & Co., 1910).

(H. J. Mozans) *Following the Conquistadores: Along the Andes and Down the Amazon* (New York: D. Appleton & Co., 1911).

"Review of C. H. Haring's *The Buccaneers of the West Indies in the XVII Century,"* *Bulletin of the Pan American Union,* XXXII (1911), 517-21.

(M.L.K.) "Idyllic Homes and Lives of Indians in South American Wilds," *Bulletin of the Pan American Union,* XXXIII (1911), 730-47.

"Review of Sir Clements Markham's *The Incas of Peru,"* *Bulletin of the Pan American Union,* XXXII (1911), 300-309.

(A. H. Johns) "Woman's Work in Bible Study and Translation," *Catholic World,* 95 (1912), 463-77.

(A. H. Solis) "Who Were the First Bishops and Archbishops in the New World, and Where Were the First Sees Established?", *American Ecclesiastical Review,* 48 (1913), 385-92.

(H. J. Mozans) *Women in Science* (New York: D. Appleton & Co., 1913).

"Roosevelt's Visit to South America," *Review of Reviews,* LVIII (1914), 81-86.

Following the Conquistadores: Through South America's Southland (New York: D. Appleton & Co., 1916).

Great Inspirers (New York: D. Appleton & Co., 1917).

The Quest of El Dorado: The Most Romantic Episode in the History of South American Conquest (New York: D. Appleton & Co., 1917).

"Theodore Roosevelt as a Hunter-Naturalist," *Outlook,* CXXI (1919), 434-36.

From Berlin to Bagdad and Babylon (New York: D. Appleton & Co., 1922).

REPRESENTATIVE REVIEWS OF FATHER ZAHM'S BOOKS

Age of the Human Race, Review of Reviews, VII (1893), 605-606.
Along the Andes and Down the Amazon, Ave Maria, 73 (1911), 664-65.
Bible, Science and Faith, Catholic World, 60 (1894), 135-37.
Bible, Science and Faith, Donahoe's Magazine, XXXII (1894), 568-69.
Evolution and Dogma, Ave Maria, 42 (1896), 468-69.
Evolution and Dogma, Catholic University Bulletin, 2 (1896), 235-38.
Evolution and Dogma, Catholic World, 63 (1896), 130-33.
Evolution and Dogma, Civilta Cattolica, Series xvi, Vol. IX (January 4, 1897), 201-204.
Evolution and Dogma, Appleton's *Popular Science Monthly,* XL (1896), 414-15.
"Evoluzione & Dogma," *Civilta Cattolica,* Series xvii, Vol. 5 (December 29, 1898), 34-50.

Fleming, David, O.F.M. "Review of Evolution and Dogma," *Dublin Review*, 119 (1896).
From Berlin to Bagdad and Babylon, Ave Maria, 17 n.s. (1923), 152.
From Berlin to Bagdad and Babylon, Review of Reviews, LXVII (1923), 109.
Great Inspirers, Ave Maria, 5 n.s. (1917), 342.
Heuser, Herman, "Review of Evolution and Dogma," *American Ecclesiastical Review*, 14 (1896), 568-70.
O'Hagen, Thomas, "Following the Conquistadores," *Catholic Historical Review*, 2 (1916), 258-68.
The Quest of El Dorado, Ave Maria, 6 n.s. (1917), 343.
Sound and Music, Atlantic Monthly, 72 (1893), 560-61.
Through South America's Southland, American Ecclesiastical Review, 54 (1916), 622-29.
Up the Orinoco and Down the Magdalena, Ave Maria, 70 (1910), 696.
Women in Science, Ave Maria, 77 (1911), 505-506.

INTERVIEWS

Interviews with contemporaries, and in some cases, co-workers of Father Zahm, provided fascinating insights into his personality, enthusiasm, and progressive programs in education. The writer was amazed by the fine memory displayed by each of these men in their recollections of Zahm and the various major programs inaugurated by their associate and friend. Chief among the contemporary witnesses was the late Albert Zahm who reconstructed at great length his brother's enthusiastic support of a university education for qualified Catholic laymen and seminarians. Albert was in a real sense, an apprentice to his brother at Notre Dame, and later, when Albert became famous in his own right by his nationally recognized contributions to the study of aerodynamics, the two shared their plans for the future through correspondence and visits. Too, they complemented one another, for Albert's fine sense of humor provided diversion for his brother's studied seriousness; and while Father Zahm popularized the study of science, Albert advanced science in the laboratory.

Another brother, Pius, recounted at great length the dignity and poverty of the Zahm family during the early years on the frontier around Huntington, Indiana. Thus, how his strict father, Jacob, explained that at the time of his marriage, "he had but fifty cents, an axe, and a wedding suit." Also Pius described the educational and economic hardships in those years: how his father could neither read nor write; the lack of formal educational facilities in this German community. The first Zahm homestead covered but two acres and only gradually, with profits from logging, did Jacob Zahm purchase adjoining bits of land until, as Pius explained, he got "enough land to work us fellas on, we went into farming." Also he explained how John Zahm came home reluctantly during his early college years at Notre Dame for fear he would be forced to discontinue his studies and help farm the land. From these recollections of Pius, the writer realized the exceedingly difficult and personal barriers Father Zahm surmounted in order to achieve a college education. Too, these early years provide an understanding of Zahm's strong sense of responsibility and self-discipline.

Fathers Eugene Burke, C.S.C., Thomas Crumley, C.S.C., Matthew Schumacher, C.S.C., and Father Zahm's secretary during the Provincialship, Father Joseph McGuire, C.S.C., all provided perspective regarding the internal American policies of the Congregation of Holy Cross during Zahm's term as Provincial. They shared his designs and hopes for the future during that time and they too realized the absolute necessity for providing a university education for Holy Cross seminarians. Father Crumley and Brother Peter Hozinski, C.S.C., were helpful in reconstructing the situation of the Brotherhood during that time: the former in his explanation of the administrative problems involved in the Brothers' decline, and the latter, in their attitude and discouragement. Father William McNamara recalled Zahm's latter years at the Holy Cross College in Washington, D. C., and his friendly assistance to the young seminarians; also his insistence that they read widely and commit themselves to true university studies. Zahm's own habits of research, study and writing set the example.

MANUSCRIPT SOURCES

Certain manuscript collections listed below gave valuable information for reconstructing Zahm's life and contributions:

Archives of the Archdiocese of St. Paul: Ireland Papers.

Archives of the Catholic University of America: Keane Papers, O'Connell Papers.

Archives of the Diocese of Covington: Maes Papers.

Archives of the Holy Cross Priests in the U.S. Province: Burns Papers, Corby Papers, Fitte Papers, Morrissey Papers, Zahm Papers. Also located here are: "Circular Letter No. 13 of Rev. Gilbert Français, January 5, 1898"; University Report. Province Report. "Summary of Lands Owned by University of Notre Dame Du Lac and Brothers of Saint Joseph Compiled by William S. Moore"; Reverend Joseph Maguire, "Historical Sketch of Notre Dame"; "Report of the Committee on Constitution and By-Laws to the Board of Directors of the Columbian Catholic Summer School, January 16, 1896"; Reverend

William Corby, C.S.C., "Circular Letter on the Catholic Educational Exhibit at the World's Columbian Exhibition, April 1891."

Archives of the Sisters of Holy Cross, St. Mary's College, Notre Dame, Indiana: Emma Zahm Papers, Juliana Zahm Papers, Teresa Zahm Papers.

Archives of the University of Notre Dame: photostats of Brandi Letters to Corrigan, Edwards Papers, photostats of Zahm letters to O'Connell, Sabina di Tarravicino di Revel (Microfilm), Albert Zahm Papers, John A. Zahm Papers.

Library of Congress: Roosevelt Papers.

NOTE ON OTHER STUDIES OF FATHER ZAHM

Aside from those sources noted above, the best study of Zahm was found in a series published in 1946 in the *Ave Maria* magazine by Father Patrick J. Carroll, C.S.C., entitled "Mind in Action." This account, based upon historical research, contributed a broad understanding of Zahm's enthusiasm in the intellectual life. Father John W. Cavanaugh's testimonial of Zahm published in the *Catholic World* in 1922, while praising Zahm's superior contributions, understandably fails to record the serious conflict of ideas within the Congregation and, as well, the problems following publication of *Evolution and Dogma*. Father Kerndt M. Healy, C.S.C., who wrote a brief essay on Zahm in *America* in 1921 describes only the main outline of his subject's work. The best evaluation of Zahm's writings on South America may be found in *The Americas* magazine in 1951 written by Father Thomas F. O'Connor, entitled "John A. Zahm, C.S.C.: Scientist and Americanist."

Index

Abbeloos, Msgr. Jean, honorary president of Catholic Scientific Congress, 74

Academic Senate of Catholic University, undergraduate plan of, 146; opposed by Albert Zahm, 147-48

Acquaticci, Giulio, 192

Agassiz, Louis, opponent of Darwin, 22, 25

Aiden, C.S.C., Brother, 164

Albeus, C.S.C., Brother, 168

Allard, Paul, participates in Catholic Scientific Congress, 74

Along the Andes and Down the Amazon, 181, 184

Aloysius, C.S.C., Sister M., 167

American Cyclopedia, 38

Americanism, opponents of, 101 ff; rebuke to, 116; untouched, 118

Ancient Order of Hibernians, 101

Archconservatives, fears of, 101; led by, 100

Aristotle, and evolution, 62, 80

Ave Maria, 83, 157

Azarias, Brother, 55

Bacon, Lord, on evolution, 80

Badin, Rev. Stephen, 3, 171

Benziger, A., 195

Benziger, Marie, 196

Bert, Paul, 51 n

Bible, Science and Faith, 71-72

La Biblia and la Ciencia, 80

Biondi, Ernesto, 171

Boland, C.S.C., Rev., 166

Boniface, C.S.C., Brother, 121

Bonn University, 15

Bonomelli, Bishop, 109, 110, 126 n

Bouquillon, Rev. Thomas, 102, 105

Brandi, S.J., Rev. Salvatore, forecasts difficulties, 99; about Catholic University, 114-15; and *Evolution and Dogma*, 115-16

Brothers of St. Joseph, 156

Brownson, Orestes A., 11; opposes evolution, 22, 31 n

Brussels International Catholic Scientific Congress, 59

The Buccaneers in the West Indies in the XVIII Century, 183

Burns, C.S.C., Rev. James A., authority on Catholic education in the United States, 35; protégé of Zahm, 56; on Zahm, 88; praises Français and Zahm, 97; reveals information, 121; sets pattern, 129; disciple of Zahm, 130; Director of Studies, 134; observation of, on enrollment at Notre Dame, 136; early years, 138; views on Notre Dame, 138; considers Cavanaugh as replacement, 139; recommendation of, 140; writes of Zahm, 140; replaces French, 144; attempts to postpone Zahm improvements, 153; and pedagogy course, 159; urges removal of Morrissey, 166

Byrne, Major John, 55

Cahenslyism, condemnation of, 100

Caldwell, Mary Gwendoline, 118

Carrier, C.S.C., Rev. Joseph C., contributions and service at Notre Dame, 6; confides to Professor James Edwards, 10 n; appointed president of St. Mary's College, 8; on science, 7, 13

Catholic Citizen, 59, 84

Catholic Educational Union, 55

Catholic Order of Foresters, 101

Catholic Reading Circle Review, 55

Catholic Scientific Congress, scheme of, 73; first Congress, 73; second, 73; participants, 74; fourth international, 103

Catholic Summer School Movement,

54-55; inaugurators of, 55; first summer school, 55; criticized by Thorne, 58-59; Western, 59; Eastern, 59, 64-65; executive committee, 59; decisions of executive committee, 59-60; controversy between Messmer and Zahm, 68-70

Catholic Sun, defends Zahm, 64

Catholic Total Abstinence Union, 101

Catholic University of America, 100, 101, 115, 118, 139, 141, 142, 145, 146, 147-51, 175 n

Catholic University of America, Board of Trustees, on resignation of Schroeder, 105; studies undergraduate plan, 148-51

Catholic University Bulletin, 84

Catholic Winter School, 55, 70

Catholic World, 83

Cavanaugh, C.S.C., Rev. John W., helps set pattern, 129; early years, 139; succeeds Linneborn, 144; member of investigating committee, 161; replaces Morrissey as president, 166; Superior of Holy Cross Seminary, 166; council secretary, 174 n

Chapman, Frank, 185

Cherrie, George K., 186

Christie, Archbishop Alexander, 145, 155, 156, 168

La Civilta Cattolica, 107, 114, 115

Columbia University, 155, 156, 168, 171

Columbian Catholic Summer School, Committee on Studies for, 59; inauguration of, 60

Conaty, Bishop Thomas, president of summer school, 67; honored guest, 145

Condon, C.S.C., Rev. Patrick, 130, 144

Congregation of Holy Cross, controversy ends, 98; Moreau's plan, 99; ambition of Zahm for, 139; and House of Studies, 141; and O'Connell's proposal, 148-49; problem of morale, 156; letter of grievance, 156; history of Brothers' society, 156-58; endorsed by Holy See, 156; teaching Brothers lose schools, 157-

58; recruiting program for, 160, 162-63, 164; Brothers prefer Morrissey and Fitte, 160; difficulties between priests and Brothers, 160-65

Conway, S.J., Rev. J. J., 89 n

Corby Hall, 134, 152

Corby, C.S.C., Rev. William, president of Notre Dame, 13; and refusal, 97; attempts fail, 98; death of, 106; provincial and higher education, 129; intention of, 141; and Provincial Chapter, 158

Corrigan, Archbishop Michael A., 53, 54, 100, 116, 118, 145

Coubé, S.J., Rev. R. P., preachings of, 104

Cretin, Bishop Joseph, 6

Crumley, C.S.C., Rev. Thomas A., 166

Cummings, Thomas Harrison, 55

Damien, Rev. Joseph De Veuster, 41

Dana, Charles, 22

Dante, 138, 192, 194

De Harlez, Msgr. Charles, 75

de la Hailandière, Bishop Celestine, 3

de Lapparent, Albert, participates in Catholic Scientific Congress, 74

de Maistre, Count, 28

de Naddaillac, Marquis, gives assurance, 59; famous anthropologist, 103

Descartes, on evolution, 80

Descent of Man, 22, 26

De Smedt, S.J., Rev. Charles, chief of Bollandists, 59; participates in Catholic Scientific Congress, 74

Desmond, Humphrey, on summer school, 58; a liberal, 69

Dion, C.S.C., Rev., appointed Provincial of Canada, 87

Divine Comedy, annotated edition of, 100

Dominicans, 102, 104

Donahoe's Magazine, opposes evolution, 85

Doonan, S.J., Rev. James A., 55, 56

Dujarie Hall, 163

Dujarie Institute, 164

Dujarie, C.S.C., Rev. James, 156

Edbrooke, W. J., 35
Edwards, James, 10 n, 181
Egan, Maurice Francis, 36; Catholic
    Summer School Movement, 54-55,
    59; *Recollections of a Happy Life*,
    89 n; best lecturer, 89 n; saved by
    Zahm, 100
Elder, Archbishop William Henry,
    171
Engelbert, C.S.C., Brother, member of
    General Chapter, 140; Superior,
    158-59; favors Burns' plan, 159;
    seeks postulants, 160
Ernest, C.S.C., Brother, 144
Evolution, American Catholic's toler-
    ant attitude, 22; books on, 22, 24,
    26, 62, 71-72, 77-82, 99; Darwin,
    Charles, 22-23, 24, 26, 44, 46, 47, 81;
    appraisal of theory of, 22-28, 31 n,
    85; Zahm's views on, 26-29, 45-47,
    55-58, 60-67, 71-72, 77-82, 85-87,
    188; views of Mivart, 24, 25, 27,
    62, 65, 76-77, 78, 82; *Evolution and
    Dogma*, 77-82, 106-11, 115, 120-23;
    Darwin, Erasmus, popularized it,
    81
Ewing, John G., 61

Fiala, Anthony, 186
Fitte, C.S.C., Rev. Stanislaus, as chief
    aide of Morrissey, 136; divergence
    from Zahm, 136-37; preferred by
    Brothers, 160; Superior of the Pro-
    fessed House, 167
Fleming, O.F.M., Rev. David, partici-
    pates in Catholic Scientific Con-
    gress, 74; reviews Zahm's *Evolution
    and Dogma*, 83-84; Pope's special
    adviser, 107; urged by Zahm, 108;
    report from, 110; "hurtful enemy,"
    120
"The Catherine Ford Scholarships,"
    154
Français, C.S.C., Rev. Gilbert, pre-
    fers Zahm, 87; elevated to Superior-
    General, 95; and Circular Letters,
    96, 97, 130; appoints Zahm Provin-
    cial, 130; encourages Zahm, 97;
    praised by Father Burns, 97; urges
    Zahm to submit to Rome, 108; de-
    fends Zahm, 112-13; greatest deci-

sion of, 131; respects Zahm's opin-
    ions, 131; displeased with Corby
    and Morrissey, 131; and House of
    Studies, 141, 145; refuses Zahm per-
    mission, 152; and Brothers, 159-65;
    urged to remove Morrissey, 166;
    loses faith in Zahm, 168; suggests
    degree for Morrissey, 171
Franciscus, C.S.C., Rev. Peter J., Di-
    rector of House of Studies, 141
French, C.S.C., Rev. James, 141, 166
From Berlin to Bagdad and Babylon,
    194

Galea, Alphonsus, 122
Gaudeau, S.J., Père, preachings of,
    104
The Genesis of Species, 24, 62, 76
Gibbons, Cardinal James, 54; on
    science, 77; and Americanism, 100-
    103; urges continuation of House of
    Studies, 142-43
Gilmour, Bishop Richard, 100
Gmeiner, Rev. John, defends Zahm,
    63-64; American representative to
    Catholic Scientific Congress, 74
Gonzales, O.P., Cardinal, *La Biblia
    and la Ciencia*, 80; on evolution, 82
Goosens, Msgr. Pierre, president of
    Catholic Scientific Congress, 74
Grannan, Rev. Charles, and liberals'
    attack, 105
Gray, Asa, accepts evolutionary
    theories, 22, 81
Great Inspirers, 194

Haeckel, Ernst, 46, 81
Hardy, George, 55
Haring, C. H., 183
Harper, Frank, 186
Harper, T. N., 80
Hart, Thomas F., 67
Hecker, C.S.P., Rev. Isaac Thomas,
    31 n, 103-104, 113, 118
Hedley, Bishop John Cuthbert, 115,
    126-27 n
Heuser, Rev. Herman J., 64, 83
Hewit, C.S.P., Very Rev. Augustine,
    lecturer, 55; on evolution, 78-79
Hogan, S.S., Rev. John, 64

Holy Cross College, commended by Holy Father, 95; and O'Connell's proposal, 146-51; *also see* House of Studies

Holy Cross Congregation, *see* Congregation of Holy Cross

Holy Cross Sisters, 12, 98-99

Horstman, Bishop Ignatius, 100, 145

House of Studies, 95-98; founded by Zahm, 141-46

Hoynes, Colonel William, 34

Hudson, C.S.C., Rev. Daniel, opposes House of Studies, 96, 137, 141; against plan for Corby Hall, 134; difference between Zahm and, 173-74 n

Hughes, S.J., Rev. Michael, member, Committee on Studies for the Columbian Catholic Summer School, 59

Huxley, Thomas, on evolution, 23, 24, 25, 44, 46, 81

The Incas of Peru, 183

Ireland, Archbishop John, on conservatism, 32; praises Zahm, 49, 72; and Americanism, 94, 100-102, 106, 116-17; writes to Cardinal Rampolla, 110; congratulates Zahm, 131; and House of Studies, 142

Jamet, C.S.C., Rev. A., 168

Jesuits, 104, 107

Johnston, Richard Malcolm, 55, 64

Jordan, Louis, 45

Kain, Archbishop John J., 145

Kant, Immanuel, 80-81

Katzer, Bishop Frederick, 100-101, 116

Keane Hall, 148-49, 151

Keane, Archbishop John J., American representative to Catholic Scientific Congress, 74; and Americanism, 101-103, 116; request for resignation of, 102; sympathizes with Zahm, 109; advises Zahm, 114; pleased with Zahm's appointment, 131; and Keane Hall, 150-51; conclusion of, 175 n

Kelleler, Professor, 15

Kievan, C.S.C., Brother, 162-63

Kirsch, C.S.C., Rev. Alexander M., assistant to Zahm, 24; critic of evolution, 24-26; founder of Notre Dame's biology department, 44; views on subject of religion and science, 44-45; pleased with Zahm's appointment, 131

Kneipp cure, 182-83

Knights of Labor, 100

Koenig, Rudolph, 13, 15, 33

La Boule, Joseph S., 89 n

Lambert, Rev. Louis, 117

Lathrop, George F., 55

Ledochowski, Cardinal Miecislaus, Cardinal-Prefect, 98; asks resignation of O'Connell, 101; critical of Zahm, 112; questions Linneborn, 121

Lefebvre, Dr., president of Catholic Scientific Congress, 74

Legrand, C.S.C., Rev. Joseph, 113

Lemarié, C.S.C., Rev., 144

Leo XIII, Pope, approves Columbian Summer School, 60; special audience with Zahm, 73, 75; awards doctorate degree to Zahm, 75; encyclical, 75; receives Zahm, 95; grants benediction, 98; may withdraw decree, 113; apostolic letter, 116; and the Kneipp cure, 183

Lepidi, O.P., Rev. Albert, gives imprimatur, 104

Le Roy, Père, 115, 118

L'Etourneau, C.S.C., Rev. Louis, 139, 161

Linneborn, C.S.C., Rev. Frederick, and House of Studies, 96; Zahm's successor, 121; Procurator General, 144

Lombard, Peter, 193

Lyons, Joseph A., 7

McGahn, Januarius Aloysius, 2

McMahon, Rev. Joseph, 54, 55

McMillan, Thomas, 55

McQuaid, Bishop Bernard J., 100

McSweeny, Rev. Edward, attacks theory of evolution, 23

Maes, Bishop Camillus P., 60, 145, 150

Magevney, S.J., Rev., 89 n

Maguire, C.S.C., Rev. Joseph, 167
Maignen, Abbé Charles, archconservative, 104; "Maignen's Nightmare," 116
"Manso, J. A.," pen name of Zahm, 184
Marcellanus, C.S.C., Brother, 168
Markham, Clements, 183
Marr, C.S.C., Rev. William, 155
Martinelli, Archbishop Sebastian, visits Notre Dame, 121; honored guest, 145
Mediaeval and Modern Cosmology, 64
Mercier, Msgr. Désiré, participates in Catholic Scientific Congress, 74
Messenger of the Sacred Heart, opposes evolution, 85
Messmer, Bishop Sebastian, member, Committee on Studies for the Columbian Catholic Summer School, 59; objects to Zahm's arrangements, 68-70; president, Columbian Catholic Summer School, 69; takes top honors, 89 n
The Metaphysics of the School, 80
Miller, Leo E., 186, 190
Minims, 9, 18, 135
Mivart, St. George, convert and biologist, 24, 76-77; on evolution, 25, 28, 76, 82
Molony, C.S.C., Rev. William, 167
Mooney, John A., 55
Moran, Cardinal, 123
Moreau, C.S.C., Rev. Basil, Auxiliary Priests of, 3; plan of, 98-99; as superior, 156
Morrissey, C.S.C., Rev. Andrew, director of Sorin Hall, 36; replaces Zahm, 49; opposes House of Studies, 96-97, 141, 144; president of Notre Dame, 130; conflict with Zahm, 136; early years, 134; characteristics of, 136; enlarges Sorin Hall, 134; preferred by Brothers, 160; member of investigating committee, 161; replaced as president, 167-68; elected Provincial, 167-68, 170-72
Morse, Samuel F.B., 7
Moses, Bernard, 182
Mosher, Warren E., 55
Mount St. Vincent, 152

Mozans, H. J., pen name of Zahm, 181
Mullaney, Rev. John F., 55
Müller, Senor Lauro, 187
Munich Scientific Congress, 123

Nader, John, defends Zahm, 64
Neil, Professor C., 50
New York *Daily Tribune,* 57, 64, 122
New York *Herald,* 65-67
New York *Sun,* 56-57; praises Zahm and Keane, 75
Nieuwland, C.S.C., Rev. Julius, 139, 174 n
Notre Dame, University of, founding and early years, 3-5; museum, 13-14; fire of 1879, 16; electrification of, 18, 34; Science Building, 29; Mechanical Department, 37; enrollment of, 135; improvements, 151-53; dedication of gymnasium, 151; plans for new library, 152; fire of 1900, 153-54; scholarships, 154; "Little White House," 163; finances of, 168; new building plan, 191-92

O'Connell, Bishop Denis, and liberal pattern, 94; friendship with Zahm, 100, 101; named rector, 101; diplomat, 101-102; speech at Fribourg Catholic Scientific Congress, 103-104; and *Evolution and Dogma* decree, 108-14, 118, 123; new rector of Catholic University, 147; undergraduate college at Catholic University, 147-50
O'Gorman, Thomas, a liberal, 68; consecration, 102; officiates at cornerstone ceremony, 145
O'Keefe, C.S.C., Rev., 160
Oken, Lorentz, 24
O'Malley, Austin, 83
Oswald, C.S.C., Rev. Michael F., 139

Pace, Edward, subject of controversy, 68-70; criticism of, 102; and liberals' strategy, 105
Pallen, Conde B., 59
Parliament of Religious, 1893, 100
Pasquier, Professor E., 74
Pasteur, Louis, 71, 80

Paul, C.S.C., Brother, 168
Paulists, 101, 116
Le Père Hecker—Est-il un Saint, 104
Perraud, Bishop, 73
Pius IX, Pope, 157
Popular Science Monthly, 82-83, 107
Portland University Project, 155, 156, 168, 171
Praxedes, C.S.C., Sister M., 2
Preuss, Arthur, on Zahm's visit to Rome, 85, 86
Provincial Chapters, 162, 163, 164
Provincial Councils, 136, 144, 145, 146, 151, 155, 160, 162

The Quest of El Dorado, 184
Quinlan, C.S.C., Rev. Michael A., 139, 155, 167, 168

Rampolla, Cardinal Mariano, 103, 110, 114, 119
Redemptorists, 102
Reitz, Charles, 17
Renan, Ernest, 44
Rerum Novarum, 76
Revue des Questions Scientifiques, 107
Riordan, Archbishop Patrick, 142, 145
Rondon, Candido Mariano da Silva, 187, 189
Roosevelt, Kermit, 187
Roosevelt, Colonel Theodore, praises Zahm's book, 181-82; welcomes Zahm's opinion, 185; proposes South American trip, 185-86; and Monroe Doctrine speech, 188; expedition, 186-90
Root, Elihu, 182, 185
Ryan, Archbishop Patrick, 145

St. Aloysius Society, 6, 9, 12
St. Augustine, 61, 71, 80, 81, 113
St. Columbkille's School, Chicago, Illinois, 160
St. Edward's College, Austin, Texas, 166
St. Gregory of Nyssa, 61, 65, 81
St. Joseph's College, Cincinnati, Ohio, 165-66
St. Joseph's Farm, Notre Dame, Indiana, 154
St. Mary's College, 2, 12, 20

St. Thomas Aquinas, 62, 65, 80, 81, 113, 115
Satolli, Archbishop Francesco, confers degree on Zahm, 75; a liberal, 101; criticisms of, 102
Scheier, C.S.C., Rev. John B., 131
Schliiger, Professor, 15
Schroeder, Msgr. Joseph, removal of, 104-105
Schumacher, C.S.C., Rev. Matthew, 192
Schwab, Charles, 151, 195
Scientific Theory and Catholic Doctrine, 85-86
Searle, C.S.P., Rev. George, 77
Selinger, Joseph, 91
Seton, William, 77
Shahan, Bishop Thomas, 105
Sheedy, Rev. Morgan F., 55
Smith, Rev. John Talbot, 55
"Solis," third pen name of Zahm, 184
Sorin, C.S.C., Rev. Edward, golden jubilee of, 1; founder of Notre Dame, 1; accepted Zahm as student at Notre Dame, 2; birth and early years, 3; gives permission for science hall fund, 17; Sorin Hall, 34-35; pilgrimage to Holy Land, 42-43; death of, 95; founder of Congregation of Holy Cross in U.S., 142
Sorin Hall, 34-37, 134, 136, 152
Sound and Music, 48-49
Spalding, Bishop Martin John, 145
Spencer, Herbert, 81
Spillard, C.S.C., Rev. Daniel, 96-97, 158, 162
Steinhüber, S.J., Cardinal Andreas, Prefect of the Congregation of the Index, 112; informed of decision, 113
Stoddard, Charles Warren, 50-51 n
Summer School Movement, *see* Catholic Summer School Movement

Testem Benevolentiae, 116, 118
Thayer Estate, 147
Thillman, C.S.C., Rev. John, 155
Thompson, W. H., 77
Thorne, William Henry, critic of summer school movement, 58-59

Through South America's Southland, 191

Trahey, C.S.C., Rev. James A., 139

Traynor, W. J. H., 75

Turninaz, Msgr. Charles, 104

Tyndall, John, 23, 44, 46

United Scientific Association, 6, 7, 12

University of Notre Dame, *see* Notre Dame, University of

Upham, W. H., governor, 60

Up the Orinoco and Down the Magdalena, 181, 184

Vahey, Rev. J. W., 63

Van Den Gheyn, S.J., Rev., 74

Vannutelli, Cardinals Serafino and Vincenzo, 102, 108, 110, 111, 112, 113, 119, 120

J. M. Veasey Collection, 14

Victorien, C.S.C., Brother, 144

Vilas, William, 60

Walsh, C.S.C., Rev. Thomas, opposes Zahm's plan, 34-35; chooses Morrissey, 96; attempts fail, 98; death of, 130

Western Catholic Summer School Movement, 59-64

White, Andrew D., 31 n, 51 n

Wigger, Bishop Winand M., 101

Williams, Archbishop John J., 101, 145

Windhorst, Herr Ludwig, 43

Wisconsin Patriot, 68

Women in Science, 193

Yates, A. C., American consul, 151-52

Zahm, Albert J., 20, 30 n, 34, 37, 138, 147-49, 181

Zahm, Jacob, 1-2

Zahm, C.S.C., Rev. John A.:
  CATHOLIC SCIENTIFIC CONGRESS
    American representative to, 73; addresses to, 74, 103
  CHILDHOOD AND EARLY LIFE, 1-3, 5-9
  HOUSE OF STUDIES, 95-98, 141-46

Zahm, C.S.C., Rev. John A. (Cont.):
  LECTURER AND WRITER
    Articles, 16, 46, 53, 71, 75-76, 183
    Books
      Sound and Music, 48-49; *Bible, Science and Faith*, 71-72; *Evolution and Dogma*, 77-82, 106-11, 115, 120-23; *Scientific Theory and Catholic Doctrine*, 85-86; annotated edition of *Divine Comedy*, 100; *Up the Orinoco and Down the Magdalena*, 181-84; *Along the Andes and Down the Amazon*, 181-84; *The Quest of El Dorado*, 184; *Through South America's Southland*, 191; *Women in Science*, 193; *Great Inspirers*, 194; *From Berlin to Bagdad and Babylon*, 194
    Lectures, first chemistry lecture in Scientific series, 12-13; 21-22; lecture series, "What the Church Has Done for Science," 28, 45-46; *also see* Summer School lectures below
  PROVINCIAL
    appointed, 106, 117, 131; defended as, by Français, 112; responsibilities as, 132-33; conflicts as, 133-34, 140, 141-42, 156-65; characteristics of, as, 137-38; House of Studies, 141-46; gathers excellent art collection, 145-46; undergraduate college at Catholic University, 146-51; improvements at Notre Dame, 151-54; and scholarship plan, 154; and Columbia University, 154-56, 167; and problems of the Brothers, 156-65
  SOUTH AMERICAN EXPEDITIONS, 181-82, 184-91
  SUMMER SCHOOL MOVEMENT
    delivers course of lectures, 55, 61-63, 64-65; on executive committee, 59
  TEACHER AND ADMINISTRATOR
    Carrier's assistant, 8; becomes professor of chemistry and physics, 8; concern over education of

Zahm, C.S.C., Rev. John A. (Cont.):
Catholic students, 11; science education with visual aids, 12; de-
velops first-rate collection for
Notre Dame museum, 13-14, 17;
European science laboratories, 14-
16; appointed Vice-President, 33;
promotes study of science, 29, 33-
34, 38, 46-49; Sorin Hall, 34-37;
Mechanical Department, 37-38
THEODORE ROOSEVELT
seeks interest of, in South American expedition, 181, 184-85; and
Zahm expedition, 185-91; gives
advice to, 185; friendship with,
191
TRAVELS
Alaska, 39-40; Hawaiian Islands,
40-42; Holy Land, 42-43; Europe,
14-16, 73-75, 102, 195; Mexico, 20;
South America, 181-82, 186-90
VIEWS ON EDUCATION
concern over education of Catholic students, 11; science education with visual aids, 12; cultural
Pan Americanism, 21; views on
science and religion, 26-29, 45-47,
53-54, 55-58, 60-67, 71-72, 74, 78-
82, 85-86, 109, 113, 194; critical
of seminarians' education, 74
VIEWS ON EVOLUTION
enters controversy publicly, 26-
29; Theistic evolutionist, 26-28,
46-47, 56-58, 60-63, 65-67, 71-72,
78-82, 85-86, 109, 113, 194
MISCELLANEOUS
appointed fire chief, 18; electrification of Notre Dame, 18-19,
34; recruits students, 19-21, 33,
49; receives Ph.D. degree, 75;
supports Catholic University,
101; leader of progressive Catholicism, 106; awards Laetare
Medal, 118; loses confidence of
Superior-General, 168, 170;
health, 72-73, 172, 182-83; as-
sumes pen names, 181, 184; purchases Dante library, 192-93;
Emeritus Professor of Apologetics, 194
Zahm, Mary Ellen, 2
Zwei Jahre Unter den Indianern, 183